Martin H. Manser

A Dictionary of
Contemporary Idioms

Pan Books London and Sydney
in association with The Macmillan Press

First published 1983 by Pan Books Ltd,
Cavaye Place, London SW10 9PG
in association with The Macmillan Press
© Martin H. Manser 1983
ISBN 0 330 26909 7
Photoset by Parker Typesetting Service, Leicester
Printed in Great Britain by
Richard Clay (The Chaucer Press) Ltd,
Bungay, Suffolk

To my mother and father

Contents

Foreword

Everyday English conversation is bursting with the expressions and turns of phrase that are so characteristic of the spoken language. It is amazing just how many of them there are. These phrases, which trip quite unconsciously off the native speaker's tongue, make his or her speech richly idiomatic, and for that reason something of a puzzle to many users and students of the spoken word.

There already exist various dictionaries of idioms, but generally these concentrate on colourful picturesque phrases (*to take the bull by the horns*), literary expressions (*between Scylla and Charybdis*), well-worn proverbs (*out of sight, out of mind*), or grammatical oddities (*it's time we went*). Few give even partial attention to speech idioms and until now there has been no complete guide to the large number of phrases peculiar to everyday conversation. It is very much to this book's credit that its entries are so comprehensive in their selection.

Any idiom, whatever type it is, is deceptive. Its real meaning is not quite what it appears to be on the surface. Only a second's thought is enough to make us wonder why *to pull someone's leg* should mean 'to make gentle fun of'. Most speech idioms do not provide such an opaque connection between the surface sense of the words and their real meaning as in this example—but they are perhaps all the more dangerous to handle correctly through being so innocuous. Again, this book is a reliable guide. You will find in it the senses of each entry finely discriminated, clear definitions, examples illustrating typical contexts of use, and notes on particular difficulties.

All in all (you could start by looking up this idiom on page 4), you have in your hands a dependable book of reference, a guide to conversational practice, and a feast for the curious and for the browser. I know you will enjoy your reading.

Roger H. Flavell
Institute of Education,
University of London

Introduction

This dictionary explains idioms and other phrases used in typical English conversations. Modern spoken English contains many phrases that the average English speaker scarcely thinks about and foreign learners find difficult. This dictionary is an attempt to explain such phrases.

Idioms are fairly fixed phrases that consist of more than one word, with a meaning that cannot be understood from putting together the meanings of the individual words. But this dictionary of idioms is different from other dictionaries of idioms. Such dictionaries often try to give a complete list of all idioms; in this book we have concentrated on phrases that are used in certain conversational situations. Clear examples are *How do you do?* when greeting, the exclamations *Good luck!* when wishing someone well and *Well I never!* when you are surprised, and sayings such as *Great minds think alike* and *Wonders will never cease*.

This book will be found useful by all speakers of English. Those with English as their mother tongue will be surprised at the wide range of phrases used in everyday speech—think of *all right*, *I mean*, and *you know*. Students learning English as a second or foreign language will find help here that is just not included in other reference books—so this dictionary will increase the understanding of what has been heard and will also develop a proficiency in using idioms. A further application is for writers who want to catch and use what people actually say, e.g. those who write cartoons or devise titles for books or articles, or programmes on television and radio.

The index brings an additional benefit and is a unique feature among books on idioms—by consulting the list of subjects, the user is referred to appropriate phrases.

Martin H. Manser

How to use this book

The book is in two parts: the dictionary and the index. The dictionary is an alphabetical list of idioms. The index classifies idioms according to their subject or function in the language. The notes here deal with the dictionary; a note on the use of the index is placed at the beginning of the index.

Arrangement of entries

Idioms in the dictionary are listed in alphabetical order of *keywords*. A keyword in an idiom is usually its first noun, or if it has no noun, its first verb; if it has no verb, then its first adjective. For example, *Be my guest!* is listed at *guest*; *That does it!* is listed at *do*; *Not bad* is listed at *bad*. A few items are not given under their first noun or verb, etc., or do not contain a noun, verb, or adjective, but in all these cases, cross-references are included at appropriate places to help locate the entry easily. Similarly, if you happen to look up a phrase in the wrong place, you will often find a cross-reference to the right place, so you will be able to find the idiom you are looking for.

Where there is more than one idiom at a keyword, the idioms are listed at numbered entries in alphabetical order of the first word of the idiom. Note, too, that where an idiom has more than one meaning, the entry is subdivided into *a*, *b*, etc.

Each entry consists of the idiom, a definition of the idiom, and in nearly every case one or more examples. The definition is an explanation of the meaning of the idiom, and often contains notes on the situation in which the idiom is used. Examples, which are preceded by the symbol ▷, have been written to reflect usage of the idiom in natural English contexts. Dialogues between two speakers often draw out the sense. The examples are also intended to show the main grammatical patterns associated with the particular idiom.

Further information about the idiom is also given as necessary: *stress* or *pronunciation* is shown where this may prove difficult; common *variant spellings* are shown; *alternative phrases* with similar meaning are given; *etymologies* explain the origin of some idioms—where the idiom contains a proper name (e.g. *Gordon Bennett!*), in cases of Cockney rhyming slang, e.g. *head* being replaced by *loaf of bread* in the idiom *Use your loaf!*, and in other cases where the idiom has a clear origin, e.g. *Tell that to the marines!*

Certain types of phrases and idiomatic usage have been excluded from this dictionary. Proverbs have been omittted: these are dealt with in *English Proverbs Explained*, by Ronald Ridout and Clifford Witting, Pan Books. Also excluded are: single words that are common in speech, e.g. *actually*; foreign expressions used in speech, e.g. *bon appétit!*; *bon voyage!*; speech expressions with obvious meanings, e.g. the dentist's *open wide!*; and taboo and other vulgar items.

Alternative forms of the idiom

Although many of the idioms listed in the dictionary have a fixed form, some variations are often possible. These are mainly of two types:
—*alternative forms*, shown by the use of *or* or *etc.*: *How* (or *what*) *about . . .?* means that *How about . . .?* and *What about . . .?* are both used. *It's your* (*his*, etc.) *baby* means that *It's your baby*; *It's his baby*, and also *It's her baby* all may be used, depending on the object intended. (Such items are normally listed under the *you* or *I* (or *me*) form.)
—*optional forms*, shown by the use of brackets (   ): *The (very) idea!* means that *The idea!* and *The very idea!* are both used, and examples often show instances of both.

Note . . . is used in an idiom to show that a word is missing; details of what kind of word this is can be deduced from the definition, and are clear from the examples given.

Style markers

Most of the idioms listed are not given any particular style marker; this means that they are used in informal everyday conversation, e.g. that used between friends. But some idioms are limited to a particular level or register of usage. Markers such as *Formal*, and *Slang* (to indicate a very informal style heard among people of the same age group, especially the young), *Humorous*, *Nonstandard* (for phrases not regarded as correct or acceptable by native speakers), and *Literary* (used in poetry, formal creative writing, etc.) are used. A number of idioms have been marked *Old-fashioned* or *Becoming old-fashioned*. This means that they are becoming rare in modern spoken English, but are still used, mainly by older speakers or in older written works. If learners use such expressions, their language will sound rather dated. Idioms belonging to a particular country are marked accordingly, e.g. *British* and *American* are used to show distinctive national varieties, although a detailed treatment of American English has not been attempted. Note that the style marker given under a main idiom entry also applies to the alternative forms listed, unless otherwise stated.

It is important to note that many of the idioms without a style marker may not be used in formal writing. Note too that expressions containing the word *God*, *Christ*, or *Lord* are avoided by some speakers, as they are thought to show a lack of respect towards God.

Acknowledgements

Obviously it has not been possible to compile such a dictionary without some recourse to the various standard dictionaries and reference books, and I gratefully acknowledge my debt to these as they provided a useful starting-point for my own work.

In particular I would also like to record my thanks to my wife and other members of my family, friends (notably Hermann Fink), and some organisations, for their help in working out some of the definitions and examples; to Roger Flavell for his many valuable comments on the typescript, to Gloria Wren for her meticulous typing of my original manuscript, to Barry Evans and Margaret Davis of Aylesbury Keyboarding for their work in the production of the index, and to Su Ong and David Kewley of the publishers for their encouragement while writing this book.

Dictionary

a

Aboard

All aboard! An announcement to passengers to get on a train, ship, etc., that is about to leave: ▷ *'All aboard! The ship is about to sail.'*

About

1 **How** (or **what**) **about . . .?**
a An expression used to introduce a suggestion: ▷ *'How about a game of cards?'* ▷ *'What about going out for a meal?'* ▷ *'How about another piece of cake?'*
b What do you think of (something)?: ▷ *'How about the other side beating us last night by three goals?'* ▷ *'What about abortion? Is it a good or a bad thing?'*
c Have you heard about (an item of news)?; are there plans about (something)?: ▷ *'What about the weather? Is it going to get worse?'* ▷ *'How about Aunt Alice? We can't just leave her by herself, now that her husband has died.'*
d Used to ask for a decision or explanation, often as a reminder to someone: ▷ *'I've never had an accident in my car!'* *'How about that time you reversed into your neighbour's van?'* ▷ *'What about your library books? Have you returned them yet?'* Sometimes *How* (or *what*) *about* is used as a rather rude reply: ▷ *'What about that offer of taking me out to dinner?'* *'What about it?'*

2 **How** (or **what**) **about that** (**then**)! An expression of surprise or praise: ▷ *'I'm off to Africa next week.'* *'Well, how about that!'* ▷ *'How about that, then! Our school's finally beaten yours!'*

Above

1 **Above all** An expression used to introduce the most important thing: ▷ *'You should be kind to everyone, but, above all, to those who cannot look after themselves.'*
2 **Above and beyond** In addition: ▷ *Above and beyond working hard all day, he spent his evenings helping in a youth club.*

Accident

Little Jimmy's (Johnny's, etc.) had an accident! *Euphemistic* Jimmy (or another baby's name) has passed water onto the floor.

Accidental

Accidentally on purpose With the real intention of doing something, but making it seem to happen by chance: ▷ *He used to buy bottles of drink and then drop them accidentally on purpose to get another one.*

Account

There's no accounting for tastes *see* **Taste.**

Ache

My heart aches for you *see* **Heart 4.**

Act

Act your age! *see* **Age 1.**

Action

Action stations! A call to get ready and be at the point of duty: ▷ *'Action stations, everyone! The royal couple will be here an hour from now!'* ▷ *'Action stations! The programme goes on the air in one minute!'* Also, an order to soldiers, sailors, etc., to prepare themselves for fighting by getting into position.

Actual

Your actual . . . *British* The real (person or thing): used to emphasise an expression: ▷ *'So this is your actual automatic washing-machine!'* ▷ *'I'm your actual expert, you know!'* Also spelt and pronounced (*slang*) *Yer actual.*

Admit

I must admit I freely acknowledge: ▷ *'I must admit that I'm glad it's all over!'* ▷ *'I must admit, I'm not as fit as I used to be.'* ▷ *'That exam was very difficult, I must admit, even though I'd done a lot of revision.'*

Afraid

I'm afraid I'm sorry: a polite way of expressing regret

about having to refuse something, or about something bad that has happened or probably will happen: ▷ *'I'm afraid I can't help you.'* ▷ *'I've some bad news, I'm afraid—Gill's had an accident.'* ▷ *'Can you drive me into town?' 'I'm afraid not; I'm too busy.'* ▷ *'Were you beaten in the final?' 'Yes, I'm afraid so.'* In speech, *afraid* is often shortened to *'fraid*: ▷ *'Sorry, 'fraid I don't know the answer.'*

After

1 **After you** Please enter, go, etc., before me: ▷ *'After you,'* *the gentleman said, opening the door to the lady standing by.* ▷ *'After you, sir.'* The stress falls on *after*.

2 **After you with . . .** Please may I have (something) when you have finished with it: ▷ *'After you with the salt, Jo.'*

Afternoon

Good afternoon *see* **Good 3**.

Again

1 Once again *see* **Once 2**.

2 There again *see* **There 2**.

Age

1 **Act (or be) your age!** Don't be so childish!: ▷ *'Act your age, Jim, you're eighteen now!'*

2 **Age before beauty!** A humorous expression that an older person should go, enter, etc., before a younger, more good-looking person: ▷ *'Age before beauty,' the young man said to his mother as he opened the door for her.*

3 **. . . in your old age** A humorous phrase added to something to mean that a person is at last doing something: ▷ *'Have one of these apples!' 'Thanks—you're getting generous in your old age!'*

Agree

1 **I couldn't agree less** I totally disagree: ▷ *'This government's policies are really helping the country along.' 'I couldn't agree less; everything seems to have gone wrong for them.'*

2 **I couldn't agree more** I agree completely: ▷ *'Harold will just have to do better at school, if he's to pass his exams.' 'I couldn't agree more—he's about halfway down the class in most subjects at the moment.'*

Aid

What's . . . in aid of? *British* What is the purpose of (something)?: ▷ *'What are all these books in aid of? Don't tell me you've finally started your revision!'* ▷ *'What are all these wires in aid of?'* *'They connect the tape-recorder to the amplifier and the loudspeakers.'*

Aim

We aim to please A motto stating that the main purpose of a restaurant, shop, hotel, etc., is to provide a good service that satisfies its customers: often used as a response to a compliment made to those running the restaurant, etc.

Alive

You don't know you're alive *see* **Know 24.**

All

1 After all

a In spite of everything: ▷ *'It's only a game, after all.'*

b Used to introduce a reason or argument that someone has forgotten or not considered: ▷ *'Why can't I go to the party? After all, it is my birthday!'* ▷ *'I do think we should let her go to town by herself. Ater all, she is ten now.'* In this sense, the stress falls on *all*.

c Anyway: ▷ *Ron didn't think he could see the football match, because he had so much work to do, but he managed to get it done and went after all.*

2 All along All the time: ▷ *'I knew that all along.'* ▷ *'I thought all along that you two would end up getting married, and you have!'*

3 All in all Taking everything into consideration: ▷ *'All in all, this is the best party I've been to in years!'* ▷ *'All in all, we see things pretty much in the same way, although we do disagree on minor details.'*

4 All of *Informal* Used to emphasise a distance, age, etc.: ▷ *'It's all of millions of miles to the stars!'* ▷ *'She's all of eighty years old, you know!'*

5 All over *Informal* Completely: ▷ *'The man you've just described sounds like my neighbour all over!'* ▷ *'Did he say you were mean with money? That's him all over!'*

6 All right Often spelt *alright*. Also **OK**

a A conventional reply to a greeting such as 'How are you?': ▷ *'How are you keeping, Jane?'* *'All right, thanks.*

How about you?' Also used as a question to mean 'Are you well?': ▷ *'All right?' 'Yes, thanks, and you?'*

b Yes: used as reply to show agreement with a suggestion or plan: ▷ *'Shall we go to Brighton this afternoon?' 'All right, let's!'* ▷ *'All right, we'll meet at six o'clock, then!'*

c Certainly: sometimes used with *but:* ▷ *'Not much is happening on tonight's weather map. All right, there's some wind in the eastern part of the country, but that will soon die down.'* ▷ *'She's intelligent, all right, but not very good at making friends.'* ▷ *'We're agreed the country's in a mess, all right, but how are we going to get out of it?'*

d Used to express impatience or annoyance: ▷ *'All right, don't take my advice if you don't want to, but don't blame me when you fail.'* The phrase can also be used a number of times to express extreme annoyance: ▷ *'All right, all right, all right, I'm just coming!'* ▷ *'OK, OK, OK, there's no need to get so angry!'* The phrase with the words repeated a number of times is also used humorously by comedians, music-hall artists, often to introduce something.

e Used to link parts of an explanation, meaning 'Do you understand me so far?': ▷ *'You're going down the Bristol Road, then. All right, now you turn left at the bottom to get to the university.'*

7 **All the best!** *see* **Best 1.**

8 **All the same** *see* **Same 1.**

9 **All together now!** Let's say, sing, or act the words, song, etc., together: ▷ *'All together now, children, "All things bright and beautiful . . ."'*

10 **All well and good** *see* **Well 1.**

11 **And all** Pronounced *'n all.*

a Including the people or things just mentioned; and a large number of the rest: ▷ *'There were books, papers, magazines and all covering the whole of the floor.'* The phrase *Uncle Tom Cobbleigh and all* (from the ballad *Widdicombe Fair*) is becoming old-fashioned but is used humorously to mean 'and the rest': ▷ *'Bill, Tom, Joe, and Uncle Tom Cobbleigh and all were at the party!'* Often the phrase *warts and all* is used to mean 'with all its faults as well as its good points': ▷ *'Tell me what your new house is like, warts and all.'* This phrase can also function as an adjective in front of a noun: ▷ *A warts-and-all account of life in our inner cities.* This comes from the instruction by Oliver Cromwell to the painter, Sir

Peter Lely, to paint a true likeness of him with all his prominent warts.

b And all that that means: ▷ *'We never go out for meals these days, now that Bill's been made redundant and all.'*

c *Slang, British* As well; too: ▷ *'You can take that look off your face, and all, young Smith.'*

d *British* Certainly: used at the end of a statement, to give emphasis: ▷ *'It's cold today, isn't it?' 'It is, and all!'*

12 **And all that** Used to make what has been said before sound less definite and sometimes even dubious: often introducing a further limiting phrase; followed by *but:* ▷ *'The plot is very interesting and all that, but I still don't like it as a play.'* ▷ *'Sorry and all that! I didn't realise that was your toe I'd trodden on!'*

13 **As all that** As might be expected or hoped: ▷ *'He's not as clever as all that, considering what his brothers are like.'*

14 **Evening all!** Good evening, everyone!: used supposedly by policemen, and made familiar as the opening words from the policeman George Dixon in the television programme, *Dixon of Dock Green;* now usually used in a rather staged, humorous way. *Morning all!* ('Good morning, everyone!') is also common.

15 **For all . . .** So far as (something) is concerned; in spite of: ▷ *'You might as well never have gone to college, for all the good it's done you.'* ▷ *'He's been ill for two weeks, but for all that, he must be fit for next week's big match.'*

16 **For all I (you,** etc.**) know** (or **care**) As far as I (you, etc.) know (or care): sometimes used when the speaker is not really interested in the person or thing described: ▷ *'He may be very rich, for all I know.'* ▷ *'For all I care, Jim could be at the North Pole for the rest of his life—I'm never speaking to him again!'*

17 **I'm all right, Jack** *see* **Jack 2.**

18 **It's all right** *see* **Well 2.**

19 **It's all very well** *see* **Well 2.**

20 **Not at all!** *see* **Not 1.**

21 **Of all (the) . . .** Used to express annoyance or surprise: ▷ *'Of all the stupid things to do!'* ▷ *'Why choose me of all people to lead the team?'* ▷ *'Of all the cheek—he's walked off with my sweets!'* The phrase can also be used without a following noun, to show annoyance: ▷ *'Of all the . . ., someone's taken my bicycle!'*

22 That's all *see* **That 12.**

23 That's (or it's) all right   There is no need to thank me or apologise: ▷ *'Thank you for your present!' 'That's all right!'* ▷ *'I'm sorry I trod on your toe!' 'It's all right, don't worry!'* ▷ *'Thanks very much for coming to see us!' 'That's all right! Any time!'*

And

1 And all *see* **All 11.**

2 And all that *see* **All 12.**

3 And how! *see* **How 1.**

Another

1 Ask me another! *see* **Ask 3.**

2 Tell me another! *see* **Tell 15.**

3 You're another! *see* **You 4.**

Anybody

It's anybody's guess *see* **Guess 3.**

Anyone

1 It's anyone's guess *see* **Guess 3.**

2 It's anyone's game (or **race**)   The game (or race) can be won by any of the competitors: ▷ *'With only 100 metres to go, it's still anyone's race.'*

Anything

1 **Anything but**   Far from (it); just the opposite (of): ▷ *'He's anything but handsome.'* ▷ *'I don't mean she's clever—anything but!'*

2 **Anything doing?**

a What's happening?: ▷ *'Anything doing tonight?' 'Yes, would you like to come and play football with us?'*

b Will you be able to help?: ▷ *'I'd like a lift into town this morning. Anything doing?'*

3 **Anything like**   At all near; to any extent: ▷ *'She isn't anything like as nice as her sister.'* ▷ *'Winning first prize of £1000 still doesn't mean we are anything like near being able to buy a house.'* Also **Anywhere near**: ▷ *'Writing that essay shouldn't take you anywhere near two weeks.'* Also often in negative forms *Nothing like; Nowhere near*: ▷ *'It's nowhere near as cold as it was last week.'*

4 **As . . . as anything** Very: ▷ *'She's as busy as anything, with a new baby, a job, and a house to run!'*

5 **Don't do anything I wouldn't do!** A friendly humorous way of saying goodbye: sometimes with sexual overtones: ▷ *'Don't do anything I wouldn't do, Claire!' Sue said, winking at Claire. 'OK, cheerio, then!'* The catch phrase (*Be good, and*) *if you can't be good, be careful!* has a similar meaning, and is a translation of the Latin *Si non caste tamen caute.*

6 **If anything** If there is any difference: ▷ *'If anything, this glass has more in it than that one, but I can't really tell.'* ▷ *'If anything, I prefer my new car to the older one, as it's more economical.'*

7 **Like anything** Very fast; very much: ▷ *'He ran like anything down the street.'* ▷ *'I adore chocolate like anything!'*

8 **Or anything** Used to introduce other indefinite possibilities as suggestions, not for a specific purpose: ▷ *'If you want to ring me or anything, I'll be at the office all day.'*

Anywhere

1 **Anywhere near** *see* **Anything 3.**

2 **We can't take you (him, etc.) anywhere!** An expression used when someone has done or said something embarrassing, especially when visiting friends or in a restaurant: used humorously: ▷ *'That's the sixth cake you've had so far! Honestly, Peter, we can't take you anywhere, can we!'*

Apple

An apple a day keeps the doctor away A saying that if you eat an apple every day you will stay healthy and not be ill.

Arise

Arise, Sir . . . The expression supposedly used by the Queen or King of the United Kingdom when knighting a man: ▷ *'Arise, Sir Matthew!' the Queen said to Sir Matthew Smith, knighted for service to his country and fellow men.* In fact, the monarch touches the new knight on both shoulders with the flat of the sword and then invests him with the insignia. However, no form of words is used at the actual ceremony. The expression is now chiefly used in films, sketches, etc., showing this scene.

Army

You and whose army? *Becoming old-fashioned* An expression used ironically in reply to a threat, to suggest that the person is too weak by himself to carry it out: ▷ *'If you don't shut up, I'll come and hit you!' 'Yeah—you and whose army?'*

As

1   **As . . . as they make 'em** *see* **Make 1.**

2   **As if . . .**   An expression of annoyance, to show disapproval of a suggestion, statement, explanation, etc.: ▷ *'As if you expect me to believe that story!'* ▷ *'As if I cared whether you were here or not!'* Also used by itself, to show disbelief: ▷ *'I'm going to take you out for a meal on Saturday!' 'As if! You've said that so many times before, and never done it!'*

3   **As it is**   In reality; in the existing state of affairs: ▷ *'As it is, I shall probably only just finish all my work today, without taking on any more.'* ▷ *'The weather's awful today, as it is, so I've no hope of getting the washing dry.'*

4   **As it were**   If it might be expressed in this way; as if it were really like this: used with a strange way of saying something or to make a statement seem less definite: ▷ *'Language is, as it were, a mirror of what a society is like.'* ▷ *'Our house in the country is our second home, as it were.'*

5   **As you were**   An expression used to withdraw what has just been said: ▷ *'The number is 720 . . . No, it's not! As you were! It's 7202!'* Originally, a military order to return to the previous position.

Ask

1   **Ask a silly question** *see* **Question.**

2   **Ask for it** (or **trouble**)   To behave in such a way as to invite or provoke trouble, punishment, etc.: ▷ *'You were asking for it,'* Pat said as she hit her child. ▷ *'If you turn up late when you promised to be early, you're really asking for trouble!'*

3   **Ask me another!**   I do not know: ▷ *'If the government knows how to run the country, why aren't things getting any better?' 'Ask me another!—I've no idea either!'* Originally, said as a reply to someone asking an ordinary riddle. Also **Don't ask me!** The stress falls on *me*.

4   **I ask you!**   An expression showing surprise, disgust, or other strong emotion: ▷ *'Peter says he's applying for a job as a policeman! I ask you! I know he's had a lot to do with them in the past, but that's been when he's been caught* *speeding!'* ▷ *'I ask you! He came in here and demanded the keys to my car! He could have been more polite about it!'* The stress falls on *ask*.

5 **If you ask me** In my opinion: but usually used with a statement that has not in fact been asked for: ▷ *'If you ask me, Sally's a fool for going out with Alan—she's not his type at all!'* ▷ *'I don't think you're as ill as you look, if you ask me.'* *'I wasn't asking you, so shut up!'*

Assure

(You can) rest assured *see* **Rest 4.**

Attention

(Your) attention, please Please listen carefully to what is about to be said: used in official announcements but also in informal situations: ▷ *'Your attention, please. The train now standing at platform two is the fast service to London Euston.'* ▷ *'Attention please, everyone. Now's the time in the party when we're going to give Mum her present!'*

Aught

For aught I know (or **care**) *Old-fashioned or literary, becoming rare* If I know anything (or care) at all: often used when the speaker is not really interested in the person or thing described: ▷ *'I've not missed seeing her all these years. She might even have emigrated, for aught I care.'* ▷ *'For aught I know, he might be dead by now.'*

Aunt

My giddy (or **sainted**) **aunt!** *Old-fashioned* An expression showing surprise or amazement: ▷ *'My giddy aunt! It's Joe Greenway! I've not seen him for years!'* ▷ *'My sainted aunt! I've not heard that song for ages! Didn't we used to dance to it before the war?'* Also **Saints alive!**

Away

1 **Away with . . .!** A slogan used to show the speaker's disapproval of (someone or something): ▷ *'Away with the old ideas and in with the new!'* ▷ *'Away with her!'* ▷ *'Away with the universities!'*

2 **Away with you!** *see* **Get 4.**

3 **They're away!** The horses, runners, etc., have set off!: ▷

'They're away! And it's Magic Bullet *in the lead at the first fence!'*

Aye

Aye, aye

a   *Nautical* Yes: an expression indicating agreement: ▷ *'Aye, aye, sir, I'll see it's done immediately.'*

b   *British* An expression of surprise at seeing or finding someone or something, especially when this was expected: often used humorously and sometimes to indicate sexual overtones: ▷ *'Aye, aye! So Neil and Lynette are together again!'* ▷ *'Aye, aye! I suppose you gentlemen are just out for a walk at this time of night, are you? And you just happen to have jewels coming out of your pockets?'*

b

Baby

It's your (his, etc.) baby *Slang* The task belongs to you
(him, etc.) alone to deal with: ▷ *'Jack, I need your help in
working out the cost of the new centre.' 'Oh no, Freda, it's
your baby, and you can work it out for yourself.'* The stress
falls on *your (his, etc.).*

Back

1 Back to square one *see* **Square.**

2 Back to the drawing board *see* **Board.**

3 Get off my back! Leave me in peace!: ▷ *'Get off my back,
John, I've had enough of your chatter all morning; I must get
on with some work.'*

4 Mind your back(s)! Please let someone pass: ▷ *'Mind
your backs, please—Mr Jones wants to come through with the
tea trolley.'*

Bad

1 (It's) too bad It's a pity, but nothing can be done about
it: ▷ *'It's too bad that you've got to go now to catch your
bus—still, we've had a good time together.'* ▷ *'Too bad you
couldn't come to the party—you'd have enjoyed yourself
there.'* ▷ *'It's too bad of you to have eaten all the biscuits.'*
The stress falls on *too.*

2 Not bad Quite good, really: often used as an answer to a
question about someone's health or welfare: ▷ *'How are
you today, John?' 'Not bad, thanks, and you?'* Also **Not so
bad; Not too bad.**

3 Not half bad *Becoming old-fashioned* Quite good
really: ▷ *'The weather's not half bad for this time of year, is
it?'*

4 That can't be bad! An expression of approval or congratulation: ▷ *'I've just heard I've won first prize in the
competition—a trip to California!' 'Well, that can't be bad,
can it!'*

Bag

1 Bags I (or I bags) . . . *British school slang*

a Don't touch it; it's mine, I claim it: ▷ *'I bags that seat!'*

b I want (to do something): ▷ *'Bags I be goalie!'* ▷ *'Bags I go first!'*

2 **Three bags full, sir!** Yes; of course: a humorous, supposedly humble way of showing that you will do something: ▷ *'Would you come and help me?' 'Yes, sir. Three bags full, sir! Is there anything else I can do?'* From the nursery rhyme *Baa, baa, black sheep.*

Ball

The ball is in your (his, etc.) court It is your (his, etc.) turn to act now: ▷ *'You've heard what he told you about the robbery and now you've got to decide whether to go to the police or not—the ball is in your court.'*

Bang

Bang on *Slang* Exactly correct: ▷ *'Your answer's bang on and you've won yourself £100!'* The stress falls on *bang.* Originally, an exclamation by fliers in bombers in World War II.

Bargain

It's (or that's) a bargain! I agree; I accept your offer: ▷ *'You do the washing-up and I'll put the baby to bed!' 'Right, it's a bargain!'*

Bark

His bark is worse than his bite He appears rougher, more bad-tempered, or more difficult than he really is: ▷ *'Mr Pierson, our manager, isn't too bad really—his bark is worse than his bite.'*

Barn

He (she, etc.) must have been born in a barn A complaint when someone does not shut a door or window, when it is cold and windy outside: ▷ *'He must have been born in a barn—he never shuts the door.'*

Be

1 **Be a devil!** *see* **Devil 1.**

2 **Be my guest!** *see* **Guest.**

3 **Be that as it may** The facts concerning that state of affairs are of little importance: ▷ *'I know I won't be here on Monday. Be that as it may, I intend that you should do some homework, so I'm setting it today.'*

4 **Be your age!** *see* **Age 1**.

5 **Have been and gone and . . .** To have (done something amazing or something not approved of): ▷ *'After all the bother about his injury, he's been and gone and won first prize in the race!'* Also shortened to *Been and . . .; Gone and . . .:* ▷ *'Who's been and gone and bought another block of ice-cream when we've still not finished this one?'*

6 **Have been and gone and done it** *Slang* To have done something extremely bad: ▷ *'Mike's been and gone and done it now; old Jake must have seen him climbing on the school roof.'* Also shortened to *Gone and done it.*

7 **Well I'll be!** *see* **Blow 3**.

Bean
Old bean *see* **Boy 2**.

Beat
1 **Beat it!** *Slang* Go away: ▷ *The older boy hit the younger ones, shouting, 'Beat it, you lot, we don't want you playing with us.'*

2 **Can you beat that!** *Slang* I am surprised!; have you ever heard anything so strange?: ▷ *'Have you heard Carol's won that trip for two to California?' 'Well, can you beat that!'* The stress falls on *beat* and *that*.

3 **If you can't beat 'em, join 'em!** A saying used when a person fails in fighting for a particular idea or plan and therefore decides to move to the other, more successful side. *'em* is fixed in this phrase and is short for *them*.

Bedpost
Between you, me, and the bedpost *see* **Between**.

Bee
He (she, etc.) **thinks he's (she's, etc.) the bee's knees** He (she, etc.) thinks that they are the best person there is: ▷ *'Now that he's at university, he thinks he's the bee's knees!'*

Been
1 Have been and gone and . . . *see* **Be 5**.

2   Have been and gone and done it *see* **Be 6.**

Beg
I beg your pardon *see* **Pardon.**

Believe
1   **Believe it or not**   I am telling you the truth even if you don't believe me: ▷ *'They were great fans of the Beatles, so believe it or not, when they had children, they called them John, Paul, George and Ringo!'*

2   **Believe (you) me**   Please believe what I am saying: ▷ *'I feel like the United States president with his finger on the nuclear button—believe me, I take the responsibility of this job seriously.'*

3   **. . ., I believe?**   Am I right in thinking that you are (a particular person)?: ▷ *'Mr Ronson, I believe?' 'Yes.' 'Then do come in.'*

4   **I believe you, thousands wouldn't!**   A rather humorous expression used to show mild acceptance of what someone has just said: ▷ *'Excuse me, Kathy—don't think I'm not sitting next to you because I don't like you or anything—it's just that I've seen Ruth over there, and I've not spoken to her for ages!' 'I believe you, thousands wouldn't!'*

5   **If you believe that, you'd believe anything!**   An expression showing disbelief: ▷ *'Here's a racing tip:* Guide *in the three o'clock at York.' 'If you believe that, you'd believe anything!'*

6   **Would you believe**   A cry to catch and hold someone's attention: often used when there is some doubt about the truth of something: ▷ *'Ladies and gentlemen, this is, would you believe, the last rabbit of its kind in the world,' the man at the fair shouted as he held up what looked like an old rag!*

Bell
1   Hell's bells *see* **Hell 2.**
2   **That rings a bell**   That sounds familiar; I seem to have heard the name, phrase, etc., somewhere before: ▷ *'Patrick Mann, you say? That name rings a bell. Ah yes, did you go to Bristol University?'*

Belt
Belt up!   *Slang, becoming old-fashioned* Stop talking!: ▷ *'Belt up, I'm trying to work!'* Pat shouted impatiently.

Bennett

Gordon Bennett! *Old-fashioned* An expression showing great surprise: ▷ *'Gordon Bennett! It's old Jake—how are you keeping these days? We've not seen each other for ages, have we!'* Gordon Bennett was a proprietor of the *New York Herald;* his name is used as a euphemism to avoid calling upon the name of God directly.

Best

1 **All the best!** May everything go well for you: used when saying goodbye to someone or at the end of a letter to a friend: ▷ *'All the best then, Jean, and we'll see you in three weeks!'* Also used as a toast.

2 **The best of British!** Good luck!: used to wish someone well, especially when the speaker doubts whether someone will succeed: ▷ *'I'm off to take my driving test, and I've only had three lessons.' 'And the best of British to you—you'll need it!'* Originally, a phrase used in World War II, particularly when things were not going well for the British. The longer phrase *The best of British luck!* is also used.

Bet

1 **I bet**

a I'm sure; I should think: ▷ *'After swimming the Channel, you were glad to see the White Cliffs of Dover, I bet.'* ▷ *'I bet we run out of petrol before we reach Edinburgh! You last filled the tank up in Birmingham!'*

b I don't believe you: ▷ *'He promised faithfully to be here at seven!' 'I bet! I've heard too many of his promises before!'*

2 **What's the betting?** Is it likely?: ▷ *'What's the betting the bus will turn up late—it has done every day this week so far.'*

3 **You bet** *Slang* You can be certain: ▷ *'Were you frightened by that bull?' 'Frightened? You bet I was; I was scared out of my skin!'*

4 **You (can) bet your bottom dollar** *Slang, becoming old-fashioned* You can be absolutely sure: ▷ *'You can bet your bottom dollar that Roy will be away today, as we've got a history test.'* This idiom is American in origin. Alternatives to *You (can)* are *I will* and *I would* and alternatives to *bottom dollar* are *boots, life,* and *shirt.*

Betide

Woe betide *see* **Woe 1.**

Better

Had better *see* **Have 1**.

Between

Between you and me   An expression used with the telling of a secret that the speaker wants only the person being spoken to to know and no one else: ▷ *'Between you and me, I think Pete and Sarah's marriage is breaking up.'* This idiom is very commonly used wrongly in the form *Between you and I.* Also **Between ourselves; Between you, me, and the bedpost; Between you, me, and the gatepost.**

Big

That's big of you (him, etc.)   That's very generous, kind, of you (him, etc.): often said in a surprised tone, and used ironically: ▷ *'That's big of you to help me wash the car—I thought you were far too busy to care about other people.'*

Bind

I'll be bound *see* **Bound**.

Bird

1   **A little bird told me**   I heard indirectly or unofficially from someone: used to avoid saying the source of some information: ▷ *'A little bird told me you were moving soon!'* ▷ *'How did you know Marcia was expecting a baby?' 'Ah, a little bird told me!'*

2   **Kill two birds with one stone**   To do two things on one occasion: ▷ *'We'll go to Manchester to do the shopping and we'll pop in to see Aunt Madge—we'll kill two birds with one stone.'*

Birdie

Watch the birdie! *see* **Cheese 2**.

Birthday

Happy birthday!   An expression of greeting on someone's birthday, wishing a happy time: ▷ *As Sarah came down to breakfast, the rest of the family cried, 'Happy birthday!'* ▷ *'Let me be the first to wish you a happy birthday!'*

Bit

Not a bit   Not at all: often used as a reply: ▷ *'Do you mind if I read your newspaper?' 'Not a bit.'*

Bite

What's biting you (him, etc.**)?**   *Slang* What is worrying or annoying you (him, etc.)?:   ▷ *'What's biting Geoffrey? He seems so nervous today.'*

Blame

I don't blame you (him, etc.**)**   You were (he was, etc.) quite right: ▷ *'I told her I thought she was the biggest fool I'd ever met.' 'I don't blame you—I think so, too!'*   ▷ *'I don't blame him for walking out on her—I'd have done the same.'* Also **I can't say I blame you.**

Blast

1   **Blast it** (or **you)!**   *Slang, British* An expression of annoyance: ▷ *'I can't get this screw into the wall, blast it!'*   ▷ *'Blast you, can't you shut up while I'm trying to read?'*   ▷ *'Blast this sticky tape! Why doesn't it ever work when I want it to?'*

2   **Full blast**   At full power: ▷ *'Do you have to have your radio on full blast all the time?'*

Blaze

1   **Go to blazes!**   *Slang, old-fashioned* Go away!:   ▷ *'Can I have a word with you for a moment?' 'No, go to blazes!'*

2   **Like blazes**   *Old-fashioned* Very fast; very much: ▷ *She ran like blazes away from the scene of the explosion.*

3   **What (how, when, where, who, why) the blazes?**   *Old-fashioned* Whatever (however, whenever, wherever, whoever, why ever): used in questions to emphasise a strong feeling such as annoyance or surprise: ▷ *'What the blazes is going on here?'*   ▷ *'How the blazes did you get here? I thought you were on holiday in Canada!'*

Bleed

My heart bleeds for you *see* **Heart 4.**

Bless

1   **Bless you!**   An expression said to someone who has just sneezed.

2 **(God) bless my soul!** *Old-fashioned* An expression of surprise or pleasure: ▷ *'God bless my soul! You've won first prize again—well done!'* Also **Bless me!; I'll be blessed!; Upon my soul!; (Well) I'm blest!**

3 **God bless (you)** An expression said at saying goodbye to close friends, wishing them well: ▷ *As we stood at the gate, we shouted, 'God bless' to Johnny; he turned round and waved goodbye as he walked slowly down the lane.*

4 **(God) bless you (him,** etc.**)** An expression of thankfulness, fondness, or well-wishing: ▷ *'Bless you, Martha, you shouldn't have bothered to buy me these flowers, but it really is very kind of you.'* ▷ *'There were many of us who had good reason to be thankful, for the school, God bless it, had encouraged us greatly.'* Also **Bless your (his,** etc.**) heart,** and to small children **Bless his (little) cotton socks.**

Blind

It makes you go blind *see* **Make 3.**

Blow

1 **Blow it!** Used to express annoyance: ▷ *'Blow it! I just can't get this wallpaper straight! Will someone come and help me, please?'*

2 **Blow me (down)!** Used to express surprise: ▷ *'Blow me, if it isn't old Charlie—I've not seen you for years: how are you, old friend?'* ▷ *'I asked him twice to remember to post the letters, and blow me down if he didn't forget all about it!'*

3 **(Well) I'll be blowed!** *Slang* Used to express surprise or annoyance: ▷ *'I'll be blowed if I'll help him: he never helps me when I need him.'* Also shortened to **(Well) I'll be . . .!** (where . . . shows a pause) to express surprise: ▷ *'Well, I'll be . . ., the horse has won another race!'*

Board

Back to the drawing board We must go back to the beginning: used when an invention or design has gone wrong: ▷ *'Have you heard, the new car we're working on blew up this afternoon?' 'Well, it's back to the drawing board, then, I suppose!'*

Bob

(And) Bob's your uncle *Becoming old-fashioned* (And)

everything will work out well; everything will be all right: ▷ *'You turn left at the roundabout, go straight on for a little way, and, Bob's your uncle, you're at the motorway.'* The origin is unknown.

Body

Over my (his, etc.) dead body Not if I (he, etc.) can stop it happening: used to show opposition to what has just been said: ▷ *'Can I borrow the car tonight, Dad?' 'Over my dead body, son, you've crashed it once this week already.'* ▷ *'A wage freeze—over our dead body,' the trade union leaders cried.*

Bone

1 I've a bone to pick with you I've something I want to complain to you about: ▷ *'Ah, there you are, Audrey, I've a bone to pick with you—why didn't you tell me you'd be out all night? I was worried stiff about you!'*

2 Make no bones about it! *see* **Make 5.**

Book

That's a turn-up for the book! *see* **Turn 1.**

Boot

You (can) bet your boots *see* **Bet 4.**

Born

1 He must have been born in a barn *see* **Barn.**

2 I wasn't born yesterday I am not easily fooled: ▷ *'I won't let you take the car away till I know the money's actually paid into my bank account. I wasn't born yesterday, you know!'*

3 In all my born days *see* **Day 3.**

4 There's one born every minute There really are a lot of fools about: ▷ *'We were trying to sell our house for a long time and then suddenly someone came up and offered us thousands more than it's really worth: there's one born every minute!'*

5 You don't know you're born *see* **Know 24.**

Bottom

Bottoms up! An expression used when drinking with other people.

Bound

I'll be bound *Becoming old-fashioned* I'm quite sure: ▷ *'The bus will be late again, I'll be bound.'*

Boy

1 **(Oh) boy!** An expression of excitement, surprise, pleasure, etc.: ▷ *'Oh boy, our team's going to win! How fantastic!'* Also **Boy, oh boy!**

2 **Old boy** A familiar, friendly way of talking to a man or male animal: ▷ *'Well, Jim, how are you today, old boy?'* ▷ *'Come on, old boy, eat up your biscuits and then I'll take you out for a walk.'* Also **Old bean** *(British, old-fashioned);* **Old chap; Old fellow** *(British, old-fashioned);* **Old fruit** *(British, old-fashioned);* **Old man.** *Old man* is used especially to refer to a person's husband or father: ▷ *'The old man's just gone out.'*

3 **There's (or that's) my boy!** An expression of encouragement, approval, excitement, or delight: ▷ *'There's my boy! First again! Well done!'*

Break

1 **Break it up!** Stop fighting!; move!: ▷ *'Break it up! Move along there,'* the police called out to the rival gangs of teenagers milling around in the town square.

2 **You're breaking my heart** *see* **Heart 4.**

Breathe

As I live and breathe *see* **Live 1.**

British

The best of British! *see* **Best 2.**

Broad

As broad as it is long It makes no difference whichever way you consider it or whatever you do, it comes to the same thing: ▷ *'Whether we travel south first down the main road and then east along the motorway or east along the main road and south down the motorway is just the same: it's as broad as it is long.'*

Brother

Oh brother! *Becoming old-fashioned* An expression of

mild annoyance, impatience, or surprise: ▷ *'Oh brother, the phone's ringing again! That's the tenth time this morning—who can it be now?'*

Bully

Bully for you (him, etc.) *Slang, old-fashioned* An expression used in reply to someone's boasting, especially when the speaker is jealous; and in an ironical tone: ▷ *'We're flying to America for a month next week.'* *'Oh, bully for you. I suppose I've got to stay here and work all the time you're away.'*

Burn

Feel one's ears burning *see* **Ear 2.**

Business

1 **Business is business** A saying used to state that in commercial dealings, matters such as friendship should not be allowed to interfere with the aims of efficiency and making a profit: ▷ *'We shouldn't let the fact that we've just got engaged affect our relationship at work—business is business, you know.'*

2 **Mind your own business!** An expression used as a warning not to interfere in other people's concerns: ▷ *'Can you tell me what you're doing?'* *'No; mind your own business!'* This phrase is offensive in direct speech.

But

1 **But me no buts** *Rare* Don't give me any of your excuses: ▷ *'But me no buts this time, just do what I tell you and do it at once!'*

2 **There are no buts about it** There is no doubt about it: ▷ *'I saw you steal the money from the drawer. There are no buts about it. You can't defend yourself because I caught you in the act.'*

Butter

Butter wouldn't melt in his (or her) mouth He (or she) appears to be kind and well-behaved, but isn't really: ▷ *'She looks as if butter wouldn't melt in her mouth, but she's not so harmless really!'*

Buy

I'll buy it *Slang* I don't know the answer—you tell me: ▷

'What did the gum say to the glue?' 'Go on, I'll buy it.' 'Find a good thing and stick to it!'

Buzz

Buzz off!   *Slang, chiefly British, becoming old-fashioned* Go away!: ▷ *'Buzz off, I'm trying to work.'*

By

By and large *see* **Whole.**

C

Cake

1   A piece of cake *see* **Piece.**

2   **You can't have your cake and eat it**   You cannot have the benefit of the two things you want; only one is possible: ▷*'We won't let you work shorter hours and get more money—you can't have your cake and eat it.'*

Call

1   **Don't call us, we'll call you**   An expression humorously used to say that someone is not really interested in another person, especially having someone work for the other person: ▷*'I've been trying to get work from that firm for a long time, but they don't seem to like me.' 'Don't call us, we'll call you, you mean?' 'I suppose so.'* Also **Don't ring us, we'll ring you.**

2   Nature calls *see* **Nature.**

3   **(Now) that's what I call . . .**   An expression of great praise or admiration for (something or someone): often said in a surprised tone: ▷*'Now that's what I call a meal! It was delicious, dear!'* ▷*'Just look at that sunset! That's what I call beautiful!'*

Can

1   **Can I (you, etc.) . . . ?**   Used in making a request or asking for permission: ▷*'Can I have a cup of tea, please?' 'Yes, here you are.'* ▷*'Can you hold the ladder a minute please?'*

2   How can you . . . ? *see* **How 12.**

Care

1   **A (fat) lot you (I, etc.) care!**   You (I, etc.) don't care at all: ▷*'A fat lot you care about whether I've got a job or not—you don't help me to find one.'*

2   For all I (you, etc.) care *see* **All 16.**

3   For aught I care *see* **Aught.**

4   **Have a care!**   *Old-fashioned* Please be more careful: ▷*'Have a care, James, you nearly knocked over that pile of books!'*

5 **(I) couldn't care less** I am not in the least bit interested: often used when the speaker is angry, frustrated, or bored: ▷ *'I couldn't care less what you do with those old boxes. They've been there for months. Just get them out of here.'* ▷ *'Didn't you realise that was the headmaster you were so rude to?' 'Couldn't care less, I'm leaving next term, anyway.'*

6 **I didn't know you cared!** *see* **Know 9.**

7 Not care a damn *see* **Damn 4.**

8 **Take care!** Be careful!: often used (especially in American English) when saying goodbye to someone: ▷ *'Take care then, Nancy!' 'Yes, I will—cheerio, Amy!'* ▷ *'Do take care when you're crossing the road!'*

9 **Who cares?** It doesn't matter; I don't care: ▷ *'This is the problem, Sue—if you don't apply for college by January, you won't have a chance of a place!' 'Who cares? I'm not really interested in studying, anyway!'*

Carpet

Sweep something under the carpet To try to forget something bad: ▷ *'He wanted to sweep his years in prison under the carpet.'*

Cat

1 **(Has the) cat got your tongue?** *Old-fashioned* Can't you speak?: sometimes used to a child who refuses to say anything: ▷ *'What's the matter, Ronny? Has the cat got your tongue?'*

2 **Let the cat out of the bag** To give away a secret: ▷ *'Trust Malcolm to let the cat out of the bag and tell Jane we're having a party!'*

3 **Who's she? The cat's mother?** *Old-fashioned* Used when someone, especially a child, refers to a lady not by name, but with *she*: ▷ *'She comes and sees us every Saturday.' 'Who's she? The cat's mother?' 'Mrs Robinson, I mean.'*

Cease

Wonders will never cease *see* **Wonder 6.**

Chalk

Not by a long chalk (or shot) Not by any means: ▷ *'I've not given up my hopes of becoming a famous footballer, not by a long shot.'*

Chance

1 (A) fat chance! *see* **Hope 2.**

2 **Give me (him, etc.) a chance!** Give me (him, etc.) the opportunity to do something: used when what is being expected is thought unreasonable: ▷ *'Have you done the washing-up yet?' 'Give me a chance—I've only just finished my meal!'*

Change

1 **A change is as good as a rest** A saying that just a change in one's activities or environment is very valuable or has the same value as doing nothing; often said when one has a busy holiday, for example spent in decorating one's home, after one has worked hard in one's job.

2 **All change!** The train, bus, etc., ends its journey here, sometimes also meaning that passengers must board another one to continue travelling: ▷ *'All change!' the guard shouted as the train drew into Amersham station.*

3 **Change the subject** *see* **Subject.**

4 **It makes a change** Something different from the everyday routine is very pleasant: ▷ *'Having pizzas is nice! It makes a change from the usual pie and chips!'* ▷ *'We went to Bournemouth for our holidays. The sea air made a welcome change for Ruth and myself.'*

Chap

Old chap *see* **Boy 2.**

Cheer

1 **Cheer up!** An expression of encouragement; you can be happy: ▷ *'Cheer up, Pete, we're winning by three goals, and there's only ten minutes left!'* Sometimes a phrase is added, such as *Cheer up—the worst is yet to come!*

2 **Three cheers!** Three cries of *hurrah* said by a group of people to praise a person, event, etc.: ▷ *'Three cheers for the cricket team! Hip, hip, hurrah! Hip, hip, hurrah! Hip, hip, hurrah!'* The person leading the cheers cries *hip, hip* and everyone shouts *hurrah*; this all happens three times.

3 **Two cheers!** There is little enthusiasm for what is suggested: ▷ *'Two cheers for your plan to go to the National Park on a coach outing—we'd much rather watch the football on television!'*

Cheese

1 **Hard cheese!** *Becoming old-fashioned* An expression of sympathy at someone's misfortune; but usually now only used when the speaker does not really care about the other person's trouble: ▷ *'I failed my driving test again.' 'Oh, hard cheese—what went wrong this time?'* ▷ *'I've got to go out tonight.' 'Hard cheese! You've been in all day, so the fresh air will do you good!'*

2 **Say 'cheese'!** An expression used by a photographer when trying to get the people he is about to photograph to smile. This phrase is used because when one is saying the word *cheese,* one's lips spread to form part of a smile. Also **Watch the birdie!** This phrase is perhaps used so that the people will look at the camera in a lively, expectant way, as if gazing at a bird.

Chin

(Keep your) chin up! Keep cheerful; don't give up: ▷ *'Chin up, Freddie, it's not far to go now—we're almost home.'* Also *(slang, British)* **Keep your pecker up!**

Chip

He's (she's, etc.) got a chip on his (her, etc.) shoulder He (she, etc.) bears a grudge or feels bitter or resentful about something: ▷ *'He's got a chip on his shoulder because he can't read or write.'*

Christmas

Merry (or **Happy**) **Christmas!** An expression of greeting at Christmas, wishing a happy time: ▷ *'Merry Christmas, everyone!'* ▷ *'I wish you all a very happy Christmas!'*

Chuck

Chuck it (in)! *Slang* Stop what you're doing!: ▷ *'Chuck it in, Ted, or I'll go and tell your Dad.'*

Clear

1 **All clear** There are no obstacles in our way; we can now do what we want: ▷ *'The teachers have all gone now. All clear! We can climb over the fence!'*

2 **Clear off!** Go away!: ▷ *'You children are not supposed to come into this room—now clear off!'*

Club

Join the club! **Well done!**: said when something (usually bad) that has already happened to the speaker and to other people happens to the person being talked to: ▷ *'I've failed the exam!' 'Join the club! Lots of us have as well, don't worry!'*

Cobbleigh

Uncle Tom Cobbleigh and all *see* **All 11a.**

Cobbler

What a load of (old) cobblers! *see* **Load 2.**

Coin

To coin a phrase *see* **Phrase.**

Columbus

Christopher Columbus! *Old-fashioned* An expression showing great surprise: ▷ *'Christopher Columbus! What are you doing here? I thought you were still in Edinburgh!'* The name of the Spanish navigator and explorer (1451-1506).

Come

1 **As . . . as they come** *see* **Make 1.**

2 **Come again?** I didn't hear what you said, or I didn't understand what you said; could you say it again, please?: ▷ *'I hope this diagram is clear.' 'Come again?' 'I said, I hope this diagram is clear.'* ▷ *'Mum's won £100 in the lottery!' 'Come again?' 'You know that lottery Mum tries every week—well, she's just won £100!'* Also (*rare*) **Say again?**

3 **Come and get it!** The food is now ready for you to come to eat: ▷ *'Come and get it!' Jo called to the children, and they all came running downstairs to the dining-room.* Originally used in the army.

4 **Come back . . ., all is forgiven!** *Humorous* An expression used when (someone) has left a place or job and is missed: ▷ *'If only she were here now . . . Come back, Freda, all is forgiven!'*

5 **Come, come!** I don't believe what you've been saying; think again: let's settle the matter: sometimes used to express the speaker's annoyance or impatience: ▷ *'Come, come, what were you really doing behind the bicycle sheds? I think you've been telling me lies so far.'* Also **Come now**: ▷ *'Come* *now, let's not get angry about your results in the exams, but see if we can talk about them calmly.'*

6 **Come off it!** Stop trying to deceive people!; stop your boasting!: ▷ *'Come off it, Henry, we know you're only joking!'* ▷ *'As I was saying to the President only last week,'* Penny began. *'Oh, come off it, Penny, you've never even met him,'* Susie interrupted.

7 **Come on** Also **Come along**

a An expression used to encourage or persuade a person to do something: ▷ *'Come on, Rosalind, you can tell me—I promise I won't tell anyone else.'* ▷ *'Come along, boys, one of you must know who wrote* Macbeth.'

b Move more quickly; hurry up: ▷ *'Come on, Jackie, we've not got all day. The train's leaving in five minutes!'*

8 **Come to that** An expression used to add to and modify a previous statement: ▷ *'I remember we didn't have much money at the time. Come to that, none of us did.'* Also **If it comes to that:** ▷ *'I don't think I've seen Jim for ages now. If it comes to that, I've not seen his brother, either.'*

9 **. . . coming up** (Food or drink at home or in a café or restaurant) is ready to be served: ▷ *'Sausage and chips coming up!'* the lady behind the counter called out.

10 **How come . . .?** Why is it that . . .? How did it come about that . . .?: often used when the speaker is surprised: ▷ *'How come you're back from holiday a week early?'* ▷ *'You're late, Doris, how come? You're usually so punctual.'*

11 **If the worst comes to the worst** *see* **Worst.**

12 **(Now I) come to think of it** Now that (or when) I stop to think about it: ▷ *'Now I come to think of it, Robby does look like her mother, as you said.'* ▷ *'I've not had a letter from Hugh for a few weeks, but come to think of it, I've not written to him.'*

13 **What is . . . coming to?** What is happening to (something)?: ▷ *'What is this city coming to; people get mugged, women get raped—what's happening to us all?'*

Comment

No comment I don't want to answer your question; I've nothing to say on this subject: ▷ *After the important meeting, the minister firmly said, 'No comment' to the waiting reporters and quickly got into his car.* ▷ *'For the moment I'm still an honest businessman.' 'For the moment?' 'No com-*

ment!' ▷ *'I'm a bit impatient at times, aren't I?' 'No comment!'*

Company

1 **Present company excepted** Not including the people who are here now: used as a polite comment by a speaker to tell his listeners that his unfavourable or critical comments do not apply to them: ▷ *'Present company excepted, I don't think many people realise the full significance of this project.'*

2 **Two's company, three's a crowd** It is all right to have two people together by themselves, but a third person is not wanted; said for example by a boyfriend and girlfriend to a third person who wants to join them.

Complain

Can't complain A reply to a greeting such as 'How are you?', saying that one's health and well-being are really not too bad: ▷ *'How are you, Carol?' 'Can't complain, I suppose, but I've got a lot of shopping to do today.'* Also **Mustn't grumble:** ▷ *'How's things?' 'Mustn't grumble—I've finished most of my work and I'm just about to go home.'*

Compliment

1 **My (or our) compliments to the chef** *Formal* An expression of praise to be passed on to the person who has cooked a good meal in a restaurant: ▷ *'My compliments to the chef; that fish was very tasty!'* Also **Please present (or give) my (or our) compliments to the chef.**

2 **The compliments of the season** Best wishes for a particular time of year: mostly used at Christmas: ▷ *'The compliments of the season to you, Jack!' 'Thank you, sir, and I wish you the same.'*

Concern

As far as I'm concerned What I think is this: used to give a personal view; sometimes used in a situation which the speaker finds unpleasant: ▷ *'As far as I'm concerned, you're welcome to come to the lecture, but the Head of Department may not agree.'* ▷ *'As far as I'm concerned you can leave now—we've got nothing more to say to each other.'*

Confess

I must confess I freely acknowledge or admit: ▷ *'I must* *confess I'm glad the holidays are over and the children are back at school.'* ▷ *'I must confess I cried a bit in that film—it was all too sentimental for me.'*

Confound

Confound it (you, etc.)! *Old-fashioned* An expression used to show anger or annoyance: ▷ *'Confound this nail! Why won't it go into the wall?'*

Confucius

Confucius, he say . . . *Humorous, becoming old-fashioned* An expression used before relating a traditional wise thought: ▷ *Confucius, he say, 'You take no umbrella—it rains, you get wet!'* Unorthodox grammatical verb forms are used to imitate Chinese grammar.

Cook

What's cooking? What is happening?; what is everyone thinking of doing?: ▷ *'What's cooking? Where are we going this evening, then?'*

Cookie

That's the way the cookie crumbles That is the state of affairs and nothing can be done about it: used (often humorously) when something unfortunate has happened: ▷ *'Sorry to hear you've failed your exam again, Sarah, but that's the way the cookie crumbles.'* This phrase is American in origin. Also **That's the way it goes.**

Cool

Cool it! *Slang* Stop getting so excited or angry: ▷ *'Cool it, you two, let's see if we can discuss this more calmly.'* This phrase is American in origin.

Cotton

Bless his (little) cotton socks *see* **Bless 4.**

Could

1 **Could I (you, etc.) . . .?** Used in making a polite request or asking permission: ▷ *'Could you open the window slightly, please—it's very hot in here.'* ▷ *'Could I ask you to help me if you've got time?'* This is rather more hesitant than using *can*.

2   How could I have . . .? *see* **How 8.**
3   How could you . . .? *see* **How 12.**
4   If you could *see* **If 4.**
5   You could . . .   Used in making a polite suggestion, invitation, etc.: ▷ *'You could always try the library to see if they might be able to help you.'*

Count

Count to ten (before you lose your temper)!   Don't lose your temper!: ▷ *Colin looked furious, but Josh tried to calm him down and told him, 'Count to ten!'*

Country

It's a free country!   Surely I can do what I am suggesting!; I am certainly within my rights: ▷ *'But it's a free country, Mum, why shouldn't I stay out all night if I want to?'*

Course

Of course

a   Certainly: ▷ *'Are you taking me into town?' 'Of course!'* ▷ *'Of course Pete's coming—he always comes to our parties!'*

b   As expected; what I am saying is true: used when the speaker knows that the other person knows what he is saying already, and sometimes said before adding some modification to the opinion: ▷ *'The orchestra was good, of course, but it was hardly worth the price we paid for the tickets!'* ▷ *'The weather's bad again, so the buses are late, of course.'*

Court

The ball is in your court *see* **Ball.**

Cow

1   Holy cow! *see* **Holy.**
2   . . . till the cows come home   For ever: ▷ *'You could argue with him till the cows come home, but he'll never change his mind.'*

Crack

Get cracking!   Start doing the job quickly; do the job more quickly: ▷ *'Get cracking, Mary, you've got all your packing to do by six o'clock and it's five o'clock now.'* ▷ *'I'd better get cracking on the painting, as it'll take me a long time.'* Also **Get weaving!**

Crime
Crime doesn't pay A saying that crime is not worthwhile, because criminals may well get caught.

Cross
1 **Cross one's fingers** *see* **Finger 1.**
2 **Keep one's fingers crossed** *see* **Finger 2.**

Crow
Stone the crows! *see* **Stone.**

Crumble
That's the way the cookie crumbles *see* **Cookie.**

Cry
1 **A far cry** Something very different: ▷ *Preparing a speech in your study is a far cry from delivering it in front of hundreds of people.*
2 **For crying out loud!** An expression of impatience, anger, etc.: ▷ *'For crying out loud, please shut the door!'* ▷ *'For crying out loud, why do you worry about the children all the time?'*

Curious
Curiously enough *see* **Enough 5.**

Curiosity
Curiosity killed the cat Don't interfere in affairs that do not concern you or you will suffer harm yourself: ▷ *'Where were you two last night?' 'I'm not saying. Remember curiosity killed the cat!'*

Curse
1 **Curse it (you, etc.)!** An expression used to show anger or annoyance: ▷ *'Curse it, why does the phone always ring just when we're eating our meal?'*
2 **Not care (or give) a tinker's curse** *see* **Damn 4.**

Customer
The customer is always right A motto that the customers in

a hotel, bank, shop, etc., are important, and are to be considered right in any dispute, even when they may be wrong.

Cut

1   **Cut it (or that) out!**   Stop what you're doing: ▷ *'Cut it out, you two, or one of you will get hurt,' Adam said, as he tried to stop the fight.*

2   **To cut a long story short** *see* **Story 4.**

d

Damage

What's the damage? *Slang* What is the price of a service given or an article that is being bought?: ▷ *'Thanks for mending the car; what's the damage?'*

Damn

1 **Damn all** *Slang, chiefly British* Absolutely nothing: ▷ *'You men sit around all day, doing damn all, and expect to get paid for it!'*

2 **Damn it (you,** etc.**)!** *Slang, chiefly British* An expression used to show annoyance, impatience, etc.: ▷ *'I can't remember his name, damn it! What did you say it was?'* ▷ *'Damn that fool who left his bike in front of the door!'*

3 **Damn me!** *Slang, chiefly British* An expression used to show surprise, anger, etc.: ▷ *'Well, damn me, if it isn't my old schoolmate, Peter; I wonder what he's doing here in California!'* Also **I'll be damned!; I'm damned!:** ▷ *'I'll be damned if I'll help him: he never helps me when I need him.'* ▷ *'Well, I'm damned, it's started snowing!'*

4 **Not care (or give) a damn** Not to care in the slightest: ▷ *'Shall I come by car or walk here tomorrow?' 'I don't care a damn how you come here, on foot, in a car, or by jet plane: just make sure you're here by nine o'clock!'* ▷ *'Ken couldn't give a damn about what other people think of him, he's only interested in himself.'* Alternatives (*old-fashioned*) to *a damn* are *a fig, a tinker's curse, two hoots,* and *two pins.*

Dare

1 **How dare you!** How can you be so rude!: ▷ *'How dare you speak to me like that! You must apologise at once!'*

2 **I dare say** *see* **Say 9.**

3 **(Just) you dare!** Used to discourage someone from doing something: ▷ *'Can I jump off that tree?' 'You dare!'* Also **Don't you dare!:** ▷ *'Mummy, look—I'm going to fly through the air!' 'Don't you dare!'*

Darken

Never darken my (our, this, etc.**) door again!** *see* **Door.**

Darn

1 Darn it! *Slang, chiefly British, becoming old-fashioned*
Used to express annoyance, impatience, etc.: ▷ *'Darn it!*
I've missed the last bus home!'

2 I'll be darned Used to express anger, surprise, dissatisfaction, etc.: ▷ *'It's not me I'm worried about, but I'll be darned*
if my children have to grow up in such a world of inequality
and injustice!' In both **1** and **2**, *darn* was originally a
euphemism for *damn*.

Dash

Dash it! *Slang, chiefly British, old-fashioned* Used to
express annoyance, impatience, etc.: ▷ *'Dash it all, old*
chap, when I say I'll pay you back, I mean it!' *Dash* was
originally a euphemism for *damn*.

Day

1 Any day of the week Always and under any conditions:
used to show what one would prefer to do or when one is sure
of one's opinions: ▷ *'I'd rather be on holiday in Florida any*
day of the week than stuck in this office all of the time.' ▷ *'I'm*
a far better footballer than he is, any day of the week.'

2 Good day *see* **Good 4.**

3 In all my (his, etc.) born days In the whole of my (his, etc.)
life: used to add emphasis to what the speaker says and often
to show surprise: ▷ *'I've never heard such nonsense in all my*
born days.'

4 (It's) all in a day's work These things are unpleasant but
have to be accepted as part of life: ▷ *'Don't you mind*
running round town with all these messages that Mr Brown
gives you?' 'Oh no, it's all in a day's work.'

5 It's not my (his, etc.) day So many unfortunate things have
happened to me (him, etc.) today: ▷ *'The washing-machine*
flooded this morning; I burnt the dinner; it's just not my day.'

6 One of these (fine) days Some time in the future: ▷ *'One of*
these fine days, I'll get round to decorating the living-room.'

7 One of those days A day on which many things go
wrong: ▷ *'I lost my purse in town, missed the bus, and got*
soaked walking home: it's been one of those days.'

8 That'll be the day! I will be very surprised when what you
say actually happens: used when the speaker does not really
believe what the other person says will happen: ▷ *'I'll get*

round to putting that shelf up soon.' 'That'll be the day!' ▷
'Me get married? That'll be the day!'

9 **Those were the days!** There were good or happy times in
the past: ▷ *'I used to go to school by steam train.' 'Ah—those
were the days!'* ▷ *'Those were the days when you could buy a
big bar of chocolate for half the price it costs now!'*

Dead
1 **Drop dead!** *see* **Drop 1.**
2 **Strike me dead!** *see* **Strike.**

Deal
Big deal! *Slang* I do not think what you're saying is important; I am not impressed by it: used to take away a person's
boasting, excitement, or keenness: ▷ *'I'm going to America
for three months next summer.' 'Big deal! I was a student there
for two years!'*

Dear
1 **My dear** A way of addressing someone in a friendly
way: ▷ *'How lovely to see you, my dear!'* Also used in more
formal, humorous, or condescending situations: ▷ *'My dear
sir, may I take your coat?'* The phrase is *My dears* when used
to more than one person: ▷ *'My dears, come in and tell me
all your news.'*
2 **Oh dear!** An expression of sadness, sympathy, or anxious
surprise: ▷ *'Oh dear, where can Harry be? He should have
been here an hour ago.'* Also **Dear, dear!; Dear me!; Dear, oh
dear!; Deary me!:** ▷ *'Dear me, where have I put my keys?'*

Death
. . . will be the death of you (him, etc.) (Some bad experience, a naughty child, etc.) is or will be very terrible for you
(him, etc.); often used in an annoyed tone or humorously: ▷ *'Going out without a coat will be the death of
you!'* ▷ *'That child will be the death of me!'*

Declare
Well I (do) declare! An expression of surprise, annoyance,
or disbelief: ▷ *'Well I do declare, this is an awful mess you've
got us in!'*

Deliver

Stand and deliver! *see* **Stand 2**.

Depend

1 **It (or that) all depends** I am not sure about it (or that): ▷ *'Can you come to the party tonight?' 'It all depends when I finish my work.'*

2 **(You can) depend on it** You can be quite certain about this: ▷ *'We'll be there at six, you can depend on it.'* ▷ *'Depend on it, I'll finish making the bookshelves by Monday.'*

Deuce

What (how, when, where, who, why) the deuce? *Rare, old-fashioned* Whatever (however, whenever, wherever, whoever, why ever): used in questions to emphasise a strong feeling such as annoyance or surprise: ▷ *'Where the deuce did I put my keys? I can't seem to find them anywhere.'*

Devil

1 **Be a devil!** An encouragement for someone to be bold on this one occasion: ▷ *'Come on, Joe, be a devil and have another drink!'*

2 **Be the very devil** To be very difficult, awkward, or annoying: ▷ *'My new car is super to drive, but it's so big it's the very devil to find a parking place for it.'*

3 **Go to the devil!** *Slang, old-fashioned* Go away!: used to express annoyance with someone: ▷ *'Go to the devil, Jo. I'm sick of your questions all the time.'*

4 **Talk (or speak) of the devil!** A phrase used when a person who has just been discussed unexpectedly appears: ▷ *'Peter really is a bit of a fool, isn't he?—Oops, talk of the devil, here he is!'*

5 **The (or a) devil of a . . .** *Slang* (Something) that causes great difficulty: ▷ *'We had the devil of a job to get the wardrobe upstairs!'*

6 **The devil you (he, etc.) do (will, have, etc.)!** Used as an answer to a statement to express anger, disbelief, or other strong feeling: ▷ *'I came first in the exam.' 'The devil you did!'* ▷ *'Peter said I'd drive him into town—the devil I will!'*

7 **There'll be the devil to pay** There will be trouble to be faced because of an action: ▷ *'There'll be the devil to pay if we're caught breaking into this room, you know!'*

8 **To the devil with you (it, etc.)!** *Old-fashioned* I do not care at all about you (it, etc.): ▷ *'To the devil with you all! You amateurs don't know how to run a gardening club at all!'*

9 **What (how, when, where, who, why) the devil?** *Slang* Whatever (however, whenever, wherever, whoever, why ever): used in questions to emphasise a strong feeling such as annoyance or surprise: ▷ *'How the devil do I know where your book is! When were you last reading it?'*

Dice

No dice *Slang* No: used when refusing to do something or when there has been no success or luck: ▷ *'Did you get him to drive you into town?' 'No dice.'* ▷ *'I tried to get him to back us with £1000. But no dice. He just wasn't interested.'*

Dickens

What (how, where, who) the dickens? Whatever (however, wherever, whoever): used in questions to express surprise or anger in a strong but fairly polite way: ▷ *'What the dickens are you doing here?'* Originally, a euphemism for *devil*, *dickens* is an altered form of *devilkins,* a small devil.

Die

Never say die! *see* **Say 23.**

Do

1 **. . . and have (or be) done with it** And finish the job completely: often used in a humorous suggestion: ▷ *'You've broken four out of the six windows—why don't you smash the other two and be done with it?'*

2 **Anything doing?** *see* **Anything 2.**

3 **Did you ever?** A way of expressing surprise, amazement, etc.: ▷ *'Well, did you ever! Mary's finally marrying Dave after all!'*

4 **Do me (or us) a favour!** *see* **Favour.**

5 **Don't do anything I wouldn't do!** *see* **Anything 5.**

6 **Don't . . . me!** Used to show annoyance at (the use of a particular word in addressing the speaker, originally said by the other person and repeated by the speaker): ▷ *'Come on, dear!' 'Don't "dear" me, you nasty man!'*

7 **Easy does it** Do it slowly and carefully: ▷ *'Easy does it!' Steve said as he and Leslie lifted the wardrobe through the narrow door.*

8 **Fair do's**

a Let's have fair shares: ▷ *'I want a bigger slice of cake, Mummy.' 'So do I, Mum.' 'Fair do's, children; you can each have a piece the same size.'*

b Please be fair with me: ▷ *'Fair do's, Jane, I only said I might phone you, not that I definitely would.'*

9 **Have been and gone and done it** *see* **Be 6.**

10 **How are you doing?** *see* **How 6.**

11 **How do you do** A polite conventional way of greeting someone when people meet each other, especially for the first time: ▷ (John talking to Peter) *'Peter, I'd like you to meet Mr Duckworth.'* (Peter to Mr Duckworth) *'How do you do, Mr Duckworth.'* (Mr Duckworth to Peter) *'How do you do.'* The stress falls on *do*. Very informally, the expression may be shortened to *How do*.

12 **How do you do it?** How is that done?: often said with a note of surprise: ▷ *'How do you do it, Tony? You travel long distances every day—I just don't know where you get the energy from!'*

13 **I (he,** etc.**) could do with . . .** I need (he needs, etc.) or can make use of (something): sometimes used as an indirect way of asking someone to do something: ▷ *'I could just do with a nice cup of tea.'* ▷ *'I think the car could do with a good clean.'*

14 **Nothing doing**

a Nothing is happening: ▷ *'Nothing doing tonight—there's only an old film on at the cinema, the bowling alley's closed down, so we're staying at home.'*

b No; I refuse: ▷ *'Will you help me with the washing-up?' 'Nothing doing. I must go and get my work done.'* ▷ *'I've got no money. Have you got a bed for tonight?' 'Sorry, nothing doing unless you've got some money.'*

c A way of reporting failure, refusal, or a lack of success: ▷ *'I tried to get a job at the factory but every time I rang, it was always nothing doing.'*

15 **Sure do!** Yes please: ▷ *'Do you want an ice-cream?' 'Sure do!'* This phrase is American in origin.

16 **That does it!** I cannot bear any more!; I am now going to take some action: said after a series of unfortunate events have happened: ▷ *'That does it! You've been rude so many times tonight that I'm sending you straight up to bed!'* The stress falls on *does*.

17 **That will do** No more is needed or wanted; enough has already been done: used to express a wide range of feelings from politeness to anger: ▷ *'I think that will do, Mr Smith. Thank you very much for coming to speak to us.'* ▷ *'Children, that will do! How many more times do I have to tell you to be quiet?'* When expressing anger, the stress falls on *do*.

18 **That's done it!** Something bad has been done now!: ▷ *'Why did you have to break the window? That's done it now! Mum'll be furious with us.'* The stress falls on *done*. Also **Now you've (he's,** etc.**) done it!**

19 **Well done!** An expression of praise and congratulation: ▷ *'I came first in the history exam!' 'Well done!'*

20 **Well I never did!**

a An expression of surprise or astonishment; what I've heard or seen is amazing: ▷ *'Ros went to America for the weekend, you say? Well I never did!'* Sometimes shortened to *Well I never!*

b An expression of surprise mixed with disapproval: ▷ *'After all the nasty things he's said about me, he now wants me to help him!' 'Well I never did!'*

21 **What can I do for you?** *see* **Help 1.**

22 **What do you do (for a living)?** What is your job?: ▷ *'What do you do, Martin?' 'I write dictionaries.'*

23 **What's . . . doing . . .?** Why is (something) (in a particular place)?: often expressing disapproval: ▷ *'What's that coat doing on the floor?'*

24 **Why don't . . .?** Used in making a request, invitation, etc.: ▷ *'Why don't you shut up?'* ▷ *'Why don't you come round for dinner one evening?' 'I'd love to, but I'm rather busy at the moment.'*

25 **Will do!** I will do that: ▷ *'Can you go upstairs and get my jacket?' 'Will do!'*

26 **You do that** Yes, do it: ▷ *'Shall I try some of your chicken pie?' 'You do that.'* This phrase can also be used to discourage someone from doing something: ▷ *'Mummy, I'm going to turn on the television!' 'You just do that!'* The stress falls on *do*.

27 **You know what you can do with . . .** *see* **Know 27.**

Dog

It's a dog's life *see* **Life 3.**

Dollar

You (can) bet your bottom dollar *see* **Bet 4.**

Door

Never darken my (our, this, etc.) **door again!** *Old-fashioned* Stay away from here!; you must never come back again!: ▷ *'Go away and never darken my door again.'* ▷ *'You must promise never to darken these doors again, as long as you live.'*

Doubt

No doubt I am sure; I suppose; probably: ▷ *'You must be hungry after your journey. No doubt you'd like something to eat.'* ▷ *'You've no doubt heard the news that the president's been shot.'* No doubt can also be used as a polite way of persuading people to do something: ▷ *'No doubt you'll be paying us your rent soon, Mr Bannister?'*

Down

Down with . . .! A slogan used to show disapproval of something or someone: ▷ *'Down with school!'* ▷ *'Down with the king!'* ▷ *'Down with the government!'*

Dozen

Six of one and half a dozen of the other There is no difference between two things or two ways of dealing with a difficulty; both sides seem equal: ▷ *'It's six of one and half a dozen of the other—the fares on the bus or the coach are the same.'* ▷ *'Aunt Edith's been complaining about her neighbours talking about her behind her back, but if you ask me, it's six of one and half a dozen of the other!'*

Drat

Drat it (you, etc.)! An expression used to show anger or annoyance: ▷ *'Drat this pen, it never writes when I want it to!'* Drat it was originally a euphemism for *God rot it.*

Dream

1 **I wouldn't (or shouldn't) dream of it** Certainly not: ▷ *'Would you ever think of smoking inside a church?' 'I wouldn't dream of it!'*

2 **Sweet dreams!** Sleep well: said especially to children when

wishing a good night's rest: ▷ *'Sweet dreams!' Mummy whispered, as she kissed Hannah goodnight.*

Drop

1 **Drop dead!** *Slang* Go away!; stop bothering me!: ▷ *'Drop dead!' shouted John to his older brothers who were interfering with his electronics kit.*

2 **The penny dropped** *see* **Penny 2.**

Dry

Dry up! Be quiet!: ▷ *'Dry up, Rick! I'm fed up with hearing your voice!'*

Duck

1 **Lovely weather for ducks!** *see* **Weather 1.**

2 **Take to (something or someone) like a duck to water** To find something such as learning a language easy to learn or do; get to know a person very quickly: ▷ *'He took to German like a duck to water.'*

e

Ear

1 (Could I have) a word in your ear? *see* **Word 1**.

2 **Feel one's ears burning** To think that other people are talking about one: ▷ *'We talked last night for a long time about you and Jim.' 'That's funny—I thought I felt my ears burning!'* Also **My ears are** (or **must be**) **burning**.

3 **Play it by ear** To decide something at the moment you need to and not before: ▷ *'We'll play it by ear what time we should leave.'*

Earth

1 **Cost the earth** To cost a lot of money: ▷ *'Our new car cost the earth, I can tell you!'*

2 **What (how, where, who, why) on earth?** Whatever (however, wherever, whoever, why ever): used to add strength in questions: ▷ *'How on earth can you wear that hat? It looks awful!'* ▷ *'Why on earth did we have to go out this evening—I'd much rather have stayed at home!'*

Earthly

Not have an earthly Not to have the slightest chance at all; not have any real idea about something: ▷ *'Do you think John will get through the exam?' 'No, he hasn't an earthly; he's not worked all term.'* ▷ *'Have you any thoughts on what you'd like to do after you finish college?' 'Not an earthly.'*

Ease

At ease! A command, especially to soldiers, to stand in a relaxed manner with feet apart: ▷ *When the ceremony had finished, the officer shouted, 'At ease!' and the men could move again after standing still for so long.*

Easy

1 **Easy does it** *see* **Do 7**.

2 **Go easy (on . . .)** *see* **Go 5**.

3 **I'm easy** *Chiefly British* I have no special desire for any of the choices offered; I will accept whichever you want to do: ▷ *'Francis, would you like to go to the cinema or go out for a meal tonight?' 'I'm easy—which would you like to do?'*

4 **Take it easy!** *see* **Take 7.**

Eat

1 **I'll eat my hat** *see* **Hat 1.**

2 **What's eating you (him, etc.)?** What is worrying you (him, etc.)?; why are you (is he, etc.) so unhappy and worried?: ▷*'What's eating you, Anne? You look so miserable.'*

Egg

Good egg! *Old-fashioned* I am pleased!: used to express delight: ▷*'We thought of going out for a drive in the car this afternoon, Jamie.' 'Oh, good egg, Mother, I'd love that!'*

Elbow

More power to your elbow! *see* **Power.**

Elementary

Elementary, my dear Watson! *Old-fashioned* An expression used in connection with an explanation that makes something clear and that is obvious to the speaker: ▷*'I can't get this tape-recorder to work. Can you help me?' 'Ah! You've not plugged it in! There you are—elementary, my dear Watson!'* From the *Sherlock Holmes* stories by Sir Arthur Conan Doyle, though this exact phrase is not found in the original texts.

Else

Or else! Or something terrible will happen!: used after a command as a threat or warning: ▷ *'Hand over the money or else!'* ▷*'Do what I say or else!'* The phrase may also be followed by a verb: ▷ *'Do as I say or else leave the room!'*

End

1 **It's not the end of the world** It's not really as bad as it seems: used to bring comfort when someone has suffered a misfortune: ▷ *'It's not the end of the world, Suzie. You'll soon forget Peter and there are lots of other nice boys around!'* ▷ *'We'd like to have won, but losing in the first round isn't the end of the world.'*

2 **The (absolute) end** The limit of what I can endure: ▷ *'This* *car of mine is the end. I've had nothing but trouble with it since I bought it.'* Also **The (absolute) limit**: ▷ *'That child is the absolute limit! He howls every night and keeps us awake all the time!'*

Enough

1 **Enough is enough!** I cannot bear what is happening, being done, etc., any more: ▷*'Enough is enough. Can't you talk about anything else but politics?'* Often shortened to *Enough's enough!*

2 **Enough of . . .** Stop (something); I cannot bear it any more: ▷ *'Enough of your rudeness! Come here at once and apologise!'*

3 **Enough said** *see* **Say 25.**

4 **Fair enough!** That is reasonable; all right; I agree: ▷ *'I'll give Pat and Judy a lift home if you take Charlotte and Margaret.' 'Fair enough.'*

5 **Funnily enough** It is strange, but . . .: ▷ *'Funnily enough, Alan, we were just talking about you and here you are!'* Also **Curiously enough; Oddly enough; Strangely enough**: ▷ *'Oddly enough, Peter hasn't said anything about it.'* ▷ *'No one, strangely enough, has ever noticed this mistake before.'*

6 **Right enough** *see* **Sure 8.**

7 **Sure enough** *see* **Sure 8.**

8 **That's enough!** No more is needed or wanted; stop!: ▷ *'That's enough now, children! Stop playing and put your toys away, please.'*

Evening

1 **Evening all!** *see* **All 14.**

2 **Good evening** *see* **Good 5.**

Ever

1 **Did you ever?** *see* **Do 3.**

2 **Ever so** *Slang, chiefly British* Very much: ▷ *'That was a smashing tea! Thanks ever so!'* Also **Ever so much**.

3 **. . . for ever!** A slogan used to show support and approval: ▷ *'Scotland for ever!'* ▷ *'QPR for ever!'*

Everything

1 **Everything in the garden is lovely** *Becoming old-fashioned* A saying that everything is just as one could want and needs

no improvement: ▷ *'We've just moved to a lovely house;
Roger's settled in his job, and Ruth is doing well at school.
Everything in the garden is lovely.'*

2 Hold everything! *see* **Hold 1a.**

Except

Present company excepted *see* **Company 1.**

Excuse

1 Can (or may) I be excused? May I leave the room?: used,
especially by children at school, when they want to go to the
lavatory: ▷ *'Can I be excused please, Miss?' 'Yes, Jason.'*

2 Excuse me Often pronounced *'scuse me.*

a An expression used before the speaker does or says something that could annoy someone else; used to attract
someone's attention: ▷ *'Excuse me, could I come past?'* ▷
'Excuse me, is this the way to the post office?'

b An expression used to apologise for expressing a disagreement with someone else; forgive me: ▷ *'Excuse me, but I
think you're wrong.'*

c An expression showing annoyance: ▷*'Excuse me, but isn't
that my parking place you've put your car in?'*

3 Excuses, excuses! You always make excuses!: used to show
disbelief at what has just been said: ▷*'The bus was late, Mr
Faversham. Honest, sir!' 'Excuses, excuses, my boy!'*

Expect

Expect me when you see me I'm not sure when I'm coming
back: ▷ *'Expect me when you see me, Mum,'* Pete said as he
walked out of the door. The person who is staying behind may
say: *'We'll expect you when we see you,'* meaning that the
person leaving may return whenever he wants.

Eye

1 Eyes down! A call to start playing the game of bingo or said
by schoolchildren as the teacher approaches.

2 Here's mud in your eye! *see* **Mud 1.**

3 My eye! *Old-fashioned* What you are saying is nonsense!:
used to express disagreement, surprise, or astonishment: ▷
*'I'll have finished my work by seven o'clock.' 'My eye! You'll
still be working at midnight!'* Also (*old-fashioned*) That's all
my eye!; That's all my eye and Betty Martin!: ▷ *'I'm going to*

climb the Empire State Building!' 'That's all my eye! You won't even climb a ladder by the side of the house!' It is not certain who Betty Martin was.

4   **You must have eyes in the back of your head!**   You've got a good instinct or intuition: said when the speaker discovers that someone is aware of something that could not normally be known: ▷ 'You must have eyes in the back of your head—how did you know I'd come in!' 'I just knew you had!'

f

Face

1   **Let's face it**   Let us look at the matter, problem, etc., as it really is; let us accept a fact honestly: ▷ *'Let's face it, Jim, you never were very good at playing the guitar.'* ▷ *'This country has, let's face it, been going downhill for years.'*

2   **Not just a pretty face**   Used humorously to describe a person who is more intelligent and able than others might think: ▷ *'Gone to university, got a BA and a doctorate—not just a pretty face, are you!'*

3   **Shut your face!** *see* **Shut**.

4   **Was my face red!**   Used to express embarrassment or shame that the speaker felt: ▷ *'I got into the compartment on the train and a few minutes later saw that it was for "Ladies only"! Was my face red!'*

Fact

As a matter of fact

a   Used to introduce an answer that the previous speaker is not expecting and will find surprising: ▷ *'I hear Mr Duckworth is leaving. I wonder who will get his job.' 'I am, as a matter of fact.'*

b   Used to add strength to what is said, by making it more definite or giving more details; indeed: ▷ *'I didn't go to the club on Saturday. As a matter of fact, I've not been for months.'* Also **For that matter; In actual fact; In fact; In point of fact; The fact is; The fact of the matter is**: ▷ *'This book will fascinate all students of the English language, and for that matter, all speakers of the language, too.'* ▷ *'I could come and see you tonight, or I could come now, in fact.'* ▷ *'I've not read the books, and the fact is neither has anyone else.'*

c   In reality; actually: ▷ *'Was the play good?' 'Yes, as a matter of fact, it was fantastic.'* Also **In actual fact; In fact; In point of fact**: ▷ *'It was a very cold day. In fact, it was −10° Centigrade.'*

Fail

Words fail me *see* **Word 13**.

Faint

Not have the faintest idea *see* **Foggiest**.

Fair

1 Fair do's *see* **Do 8**.
2 **Fair's fair** What is being suggested really is just and right: ▷ *'Fair's fair, children; Paul can stay up late tonight because I let Roger stay up late last night.'*

Fall

1 Fall between two stools *see* **Stool**.
2 It (or they) fell off the back of a lorry *see* **Lorry**.

Fancy

Fancy that! An expression used to indicate surprise or disbelief, often as a reply: ▷ *'I met Elsie Griffiths the other day. I'd not seen her for years!' 'Fancy that!'* Also **Just fancy!**

Far

1 **Far be it from me** Although I really should not; I am unwilling: ▷ *'Far be it from me to interrupt your conversation, but I couldn't help overhearing what you were saying.'* ▷ *'Far be it from me to correct you, but I think you've made a serious mistake.'*
2 **Far from it** Not at all: ▷ *'Are you cold in here?' 'Far from it — we're boiling!'*
3 **Far out!** *Slang* That's wonderful!; that's fantastic!: an expression of amazement or delight: ▷ *'Far out, man! This music's great!'* This phrase is American in origin.
4 **So far, so good** Up to now all has gone well: usually said when difficulties or trouble may be coming: ▷ *'The new president has been in office for a year now—so far, so good; but I don't know whether he'll last another year.'*

Fast

Not so fast Wait a moment: often used when the speaker thinks something may be wrong: ▷ *'Not so fast, young man, let me check your ticket.'*

Father

Like father, like son A saying that a son behaves just like his father.

Favour

Do me (or us) a favour!   *Slang*

a   Please (do something)!: ▷ *'Do us a favour, Ken, go and annoy someone else!'* ▷ *'Do me a favour, John, sit still and stop messing about!'*

b   I (or we) can't possibly believe what you're saying!; do you think I am (or we are) foolish enough to believe you?: ▷ *'Do you expect me to pay £100 for this heap of old metal that you call a car? Do me a favour!'*

Fear

1   **Never fear!**   That is not likely; don't worry: ▷ *'I won't tell him you came, never fear!'* Also **Have no fear!**: ▷ *'Have no fear, I'm not going yet!'*

2   **No fear!**   Not likely; certainly not!: ▷ *'You didn't agree to go to the States with him did you!' 'No fear! I'm staying right here in London!'*

Feather

A feather in his (her, etc.**) cap**   Something to be proud of that brings honour or respect: ▷ *Being promoted to Senior Salesman was a real feather in his cap.*

Feel

1   **Feel free**   Please do as you want: ▷ *'May I sit down?' 'Feel free.'* ▷ *'Feel free to come and go as you want.'*

2   **I feel**   I think: used to make an opinion sound less strong: ▷ *'I really feel you're making a big mistake.'*

Feeling

1   **I know the feeling**   I've had the same thought or experience: ▷ *'I realised that the other people being interviewed were more qualified than me.' 'I know the feeling. It was like that when I went for a job once.'*

2   **No hard feelings**   I have no feelings of anger or bitterness towards you: used to be friendly to an opponent after a competition, race, etc.: ▷ *'Sorry we treated you so badly last night!' 'Oh, no hard feelings!'* ▷ *'At last I've finished in front of you after all these months of running—no hard feelings are there?'*

Fellow

Old fellow *see* **Boy 2.**

Fig · 52

Fig

Not care (or give) a fig *see* **Damn 4.**

Fight

Be looking for a fight *see* **Look 1.**

Figure

That figures!

a That seems reasonable and logical; it is as I expected: ▷ *'He said he wouldn't come if the weather was bad. It's pouring with rain and he's not here.' 'That figures!'*

b An expression said disparagingly of someone: ▷ *'He missed the first train, then he missed the next one because he went for a cup of coffee.' 'That figures, knowing him!'*

Finder

Finders keepers Whoever finds something has the right to keep it: said when someone, especially a child, finds something by chance: ▷ *'Finders keepers, I don't have to give the pen back, do I, Mum?'* Also **Finding's keeping**.

Finger

1 **Cross one's fingers** To put one finger over the next one on the same hand (especially behind one's back), as a sign of excusing one from the lie being told: used mainly by children: ▷ *Perry had his fingers crossed when he told his dad the lie.*

2 **Keep one's fingers crossed for (someone or something)** To wish someone well for a particular event; hope that something will be successful: said sometimes at the same time as actually putting one finger over the next one on the same hand: ▷ *'We're keeping our fingers crossed for you on Thursday with the exam.'* ▷ *'Now let's see if the light works. Keep your fingers crossed and I'll switch it on.'*

Finish

When you've quite finished! *see* **Quite 3.**

Fire

Fire away! Start speaking; start asking questions: ▷ *'Can I ask you something?' 'Yes, fire away!'*

First

1 **First off** Before anything else: ▷ *'First off, let's find out how much money we've got to spend.'*
2 **First things first** *see* **Thing 2.**
3 **Not have the first idea** *see* **Foggiest.**

Fish

Like a fish out of water Awkward and uncomfortable, because you are in strange surroundings: ▷ *When he first joined the company he felt like a fish out of water because he didn't know anybody.*

Flat

(And) that's flat That's my final decision: used to add strength to a (usually negative) statement: ▷ *'I will not go to your mother-in-law's, and that's flat!'*

Flatter

You flatter yourself You think too highly of yourself: ▷ *'Look, don't I look great in this new outfit! Won't they all be looking at me tonight!' 'You flatter yourself, Henrietta! You look just like you always do!'* ▷ *'I wonder if they'll invite me to the cocktail party.' 'You flatter yourself—why should they invite you?'*

Fly

1 **Go fly a kite!** *see* **Kite.**
2 **Pigs might fly** *see* **Pig.**
3 **There are no flies on him (her, etc.)** He (she, etc.) is not a fool and is not easily deceived: ▷ *'You can't get through without showing your ticket to old Parkey, you know—there are no flies on him!'*

Foggiest

Not have the foggiest (idea) Not to have any idea at all: ▷ *'Where's old Sam these days?' 'I haven't the foggiest idea.'* Also **Not have the faintest (idea)**; **Not have the first idea**; **Not have the remotest idea**: ▷ *'How long will it take you to do this work?' 'I haven't the faintest.'*

Follow

Follow that! Say something that will be as significant as what the last speaker has just said, when the previous speaker has just done something very well that will be difficult for the next person to follow: ▷ *'That's the answer to the problem. I'm sure you're all surprised at how easy it all was.' 'Follow that, Jim!' called out a number of people.* Sometimes the phrase is *I can't follow that*: ▷ *'The plan I am proposing is undoubtedly the best scheme ever put forward for this redevelopment. Peter, let's hear your plan in similar detail.' 'I'm afraid I can't follow that, but here are a few of my rough ideas.'*

Fool

More fool you (him, etc.)! I think you were (he was, etc.) stupid to do that: ▷ *'More fool you for believing him: you should have known he only wanted your money.'* ▷ *'Darren's just eaten some strange berries.' 'More fool him. They could be poisonous!'*

Foot

My foot! An expression used to show disagreement, surprise, or disbelief: added at the end of a comment, usually repeating the particular word that the speaker disagrees with: ▷ *'This is glass, isn't it?' 'Glass, my foot! It's made of plastic—can't you see?'* ▷ *'He didn't know, my foot! Of course he knew!'*

For

Oh for . . .! I would very much like (something)!: rather old-fashioned, but also used humorously: ▷ *'Oh for a good drink!'* ▷ *'Oh for spring to come!'*

Forbid

God (or **heaven**) **forbid** *Becoming old-fashioned* I hope it will not happen; I hope that is not true: ▷ *'God forbid that something should happen to Jackie; she's our only child.'* ▷ *'I'm sorry to have to tell you that your son is one of the missing people.' 'Oh no, heaven forbid!'*

Forget

Forget it! Let everything stay as it is; there is no need for an apology, paying money back, thanks, etc.: ▷ *'I'm sorry, I've broken a cup. Let me pay for it.' 'Oh, forget it, they were*

only very cheap ones.' ▷ *'What about the money I owe you?'*
'Forget it.' ▷ *'How can I thank you enough for a lovely time
this weekend, Jennifer?'* *'Oh, that's all right, forget it!'* Also
used when it is clear that the person being spoken to has not
understood something: ▷ *'If you're after the manager's job,
when you've only been here two months, forget it!'*

Forgive

1 **Forgive me, but . . .** A polite way of asking a question or
disagreeing with what someone has done or said: ▷ *'Forgive
me, but I think you're wrong.'* Also in the form *Forgive my
. . .*: ▷ *'Forgive my ignorance, but just who is it you're
talking about?*

2 **May you be forgiven!** An expression used to excuse
someone after they have done or said something bad: ▷
'Sheila really is a very nasty piece of work!' *'May you be
forgiven—she's one of the nicest people I know!'*

Free

1 **Feel free** *see* **Feel 1.**

2 **Free, gratis, and for nothing** Absolutely free: often used
humorously: ▷ *'Yours for free, gratis, and for nothing, this
set of wooden spoons when you buy this bowl!'*

French

Pardon my French Please excuse my bad language: often
used humorously: ▷ *'Pardon my French, but can you turn
that . . . radio down a bit, please?'* (. . . indicates a swear
word.)

Friend

1 **Some of my (your, etc.) best friends are . . .** *Humorous* An
expression said in reply to and often to excuse unreasonable
criticism of (a group of people), but often not when one's
friends really are as stated: ▷ *'I can't stand Spaniards!'*
'Some of my best friends are Spaniards!'

2 **(To) absent friends!** An expression used when taking a
drink with other people, wishing the prosperity of the
missing friends of those gathered: ▷ *At the college reunion,
the president called a toast, 'To absent friends!'*

3 **We're just good friends!** Our relationship has no physical
or sexual element: sometimes said as a public statement to

stop rumours to the contrary: ▷ *At the airport, as the two filmstars flew off to Brazil together, they told the waiting reporters, 'We're just good friends!'*

4 **What's . . . between friends?** (A difficulty or the spending of time or money) does not really matter when compared to our friendship: ▷ *'Let me pay for the petrol.' 'What's a few pounds between friends?'*

5 **Your friend and mine** Our good friend: used in announcing or presenting an actor, singer, etc.: ▷ *'Here he is, your friend and mine, the greatest comedian in the world, Dickie Duckworth!'*

Frog

Have a frog in my (his, etc.**) throat** To speak in a husky voice because a small amount of mucus is lodged in your throat: ▷ *'I'm sorry I've a frog in my throat. It's this cold I've had all week.'*

Fruit

Old fruit *see* **Boy 2.**

Funeral

It's your (his, etc.**) funeral** That is your (his, etc.) concern; if you do that, you will have to accept the consequences: ▷ *'If you break into the factory it's your funeral—don't expect us to help you if you're caught.'*

Funny

1 **Funnily enough** *see* **Enough 5.**
2 **Funny peculiar or funny ha-ha?** When you say 'funny', do you mean amusing or strange?: ▷ *'A funny thing happened to me today!' 'Funny peculiar or funny ha-ha?'*

g

Gad

By Gad! *Old-fashioned* An expression of surprise, disbelief, anger, etc.: ▷*'By Gad, it's time for dinner already!'* Also **By gum!** *Gad* and *gum* are euphemisms for *God*.

Game

1 **It's anyone's game** *see* **Anyone 2.**

2 **(So) that's your (his, etc.) little game** I have now discovered the trick, etc., that you are (he is, etc.) trying to do without being noticed: ▷*'So that's your little game, Smith: stealing other boys' textbooks and selling them back to them. Well, we've caught you now!'*

3 **The game is up** What you were trying to do without anyone noticing has been discovered; there is no chance of success: ▷*'We've discovered your plan to escape! The game is up!'*

4 **Two can play at that game** I can also do the unpleasant thing you are doing to me, and I can do it better than you and will beat you in the end: used as a threat or warning: ▷*'Two can play at that game,' said Rick as he was tripped up playing football, so later in the game he tackled the boy in the other team viciously.*

5 **What's the game?** What is happening; what are you doing: ▷*'I thought we were all supposed to meet at six, and there's only you and me here. What's the game?'*

6 **What's your (his, etc.) little game?** What trick are you (is he, etc.) planning?: ▷ *'What's his little game now? How is he going to stop them beating us this time?'*

Garden

Everything in the garden is lovely *see* **Everything 1.**

Gatepost

Between you, me, and the gatepost *see* **Between.**

Gee

1 **Gee up!** Go on; go faster: used as an encouragement to a horse.

2　**Gee whiz!**　An expression of surprise, excitement, etc.: ▷ *'Gee whiz, I never thought I'd pass that exam!'* A distortion of the word *Jesus*.

Gentleman

Ladies and gentlemen *see* **Lady 1.**

George

By George!　*Old-fashioned* An exclamation of surprise, disbelief, excitement, etc. ▷ *'By George, you're right. How amazing!'*

Get

1　**Don't get me wrong**　Don't misunderstand me: ▷ *'Don't get me wrong, Charles, I wasn't trying to do your job for you. I just worked out some of the figures for last year's trading for the report I'm writing.'*

2　**Get a load of this!** *see* **Load 1.**

3　**Get a move on!** *see* **Move.**

4　**Get along with you!**　An exclamation expressing slight annoyance, impatience, disbelief, etc.: ▷ *'Get along with you! I've heard that excuse before and I just don't believe you!'* ▷ *'Get along with you! You don't really mean all those nice things you've said about me, do you?'* Also **(Get) away!**; **(Get) away with you!**; **Get on!**; **Go along with you!**: ▷ *'We walked twelve miles today.' 'Get away! It seemed like nearer twenty!'* ▷ *'Away with you! What nonsense you do come out with!'*

5　**Get cracking!** *see* **Crack.**

6　**Get it?**　Do you understand?: also used as a request to obey what has been said: ▷ *'You're to sit here and keep quiet, get it?'*

7　**Get knotted!** *see* **Knot.**

8　**Get lost!** *see* **Lost.**

9　**Get off and milk it!**　An expression shouted at someone who is riding a bicycle slowly.

10　**Get off my back!** *see* **Back 3.**

11　**Get stuffed!** *see* **Stuff 1.**

12　**Get weaving!** *see* **Crack.**

13　**Get you!**　*Slang* I don't believe what you're saying: used as a reply to someone who is boasting: ▷ *'I went to America for three months this summer and stayed on a cowboy ranch!' 'Get you!'* The stress falls on *you*.

14 **I get it** I understand what you're trying to say; I understand the joke: *'I get it. You mean if we go earlier, we'll have time to do some shopping.' 'Yes, that's right!'* Also **I have it.**

15 **I've got it** I know the answer: ▷ *'I've got it! I've worked out how to open the safe!'* Also **I have it.**

16 **You've got me there** Also **You have me there**

a Your idea in the argument is a good one, and I will have to think about how I can answer it: ▷ *'Why did you decide to put a fifth leg on the table?' 'You've got me there, I was hoping you wouldn't ask me that!'*

b I don't know: ▷ *'How many goals did your team score two years ago?' 'Ah, you've got me there—I'll have to look that up.'*

Girl

1 **Old girl** A familiar, friendly way of talking to a woman or usually female animal: ▷ *'Come on, old girl, you can look happier!'*

2 **Who's the lucky girl, then?** *see* **Lucky 1.**

Give

1 **Don't give me that** Don't expect me to believe that: ▷ *'Would you like to go out for a meal on Saturday?' 'Don't give me that! You've been saying you'd take me out for months now, and you've not done so yet!'*

2 **Give it a rest!** *see* **Rest 2.**

3 **Give me . . .** I like (something) most of all: ▷ *'Give me a nice old-fashioned cup of tea any day!'*

4 **Give me (him, etc.) a chance!** *see* **Chance 2.**

5 **Give or take** Plus or minus: ▷ *'I'll be there at one o'clock, give or take ten minutes.'* ▷ *'Give or take a few minor mistakes, your essay is very good.'*

6 **Give over!** *Slang* Stop (doing something); be quiet: ▷ *'Do give over! I can't work with all that noise!'* ▷ *'Give over eating all my chocolates, will you?'*

7 **I give up** I'm stopping trying to guess what the joke, story, etc., means: ▷ *'OK, I give up; you tell me what happened to the princess!'*

8 **I wouldn't have it if you gave it to me!** *see* **Have 5.**

9 **Not give a damn** *see* **Damn 4.**

10 **What gives?** *Chiefly American* What's happening?: ▷ *'What gives? What's everyone looking at?'*

Glad

Glad to meet you! *see* **Meet 1.**

Glory

Glory be! *Old-fashioned* An expression of surprise or pleasure: ▷ *'Glory be! The coat that woman is wearing looks just like mine!'* ▷ *'Glory be! All the flowers are for me—what a delight!'*

Go

1 As the saying goes *see* **Saying.**

2 Go along with you! *see* **Get 4.**

3 Go (and) jump in the lake! *see* **Lake.**

4 Go back to sleep   I can see that you are not interested in what I am saying and you can return to your state of not being alert: ▷ *'Go back to sleep, Catherine—it's useless trying to explain things to you when your mind is somewhere else.'*

5 Go easy

a Be moderate (with something): ▷ *'Go easy on the milk— that's all we've got till Monday.'*

b Do not exert yourself too much physically: ▷ *'Go easy while you feel strong, so you'll have strength left later when you're tired.'* Also **Go easy (with . . .).**

6 Go fly a kite! *see* **Kite.**

7 Go man, go! *see* **Man 2.**

8 Go on

a I don't believe you; don't exaggerate: ▷ *'I'm sixty on Sunday.' 'Go on—you only look about forty-five!'* Also **Go on with you:** ▷ *'I'm sure there were over 10,000 people at the demonstration.' 'Oh, go on with you—it looked like a few hundred, that's all.'*

b I dare you to (do something): used as an encouragement: ▷ *'Should I ring him or not?' 'Oh, go on, you'll never make any friends if you don't.'*

9 Go to it   Do something with much energy and effort; begin something: ▷ *'Go to it, Robert—if you work hard, you'll have it finished by lunchtime!'*

10 Going, going, gone

a The announcement by an auctioneer that the bidding for a particular article is closing: ▷ *'Any more offers for this fine vase, then? Going, to the man in the black suit, going, going, gone!'*

b   An expression used to describe a thing or person that is disappearing, especially below the surface of the water: ▷ *'My little boat's sinking! Going, going, gone; now it's sunk!'*

11   **Here goes!**   I am about to do something: used before starting something that needs courage: ▷ *'Here goes then! I'll see you in three hours, after the exam!'* ▷ *'Now you've mended the television, let's try it.' 'OK, here goes!'*

12   **Here we go again**   The same events are happening again: used especially of things that are unpleasant: ▷ *'Here we go again,' muttered Sue as she left the waiting-room to go into the dentist's surgery for the sixth time that year.*

13   **How's it going?**   An informal greeting; how are you?; what's happening?: ▷ *'How's it going, Jane?' 'OK, thanks. And how are you?'* Also **How are things going?**; **How goes it?**

14   **(It's) no go**   It's impossible; it can't happen: ▷ *'It's no go, I'm afraid—that plan will never work.'* ▷ *'Will the boss let you have next week off?' 'No go, I'm afraid.'*

15   **My heart goes out to you** *see* **Heart 4.**

16   **Off we go!**   Let's go; now we're going: ▷ *'Off we go, then,' said Dad as he drove off at the beginning of the family holiday.*

17   **That's the way it goes** *see* **Cookie.**

18   **There you go again**   You are doing what you usually and repeatedly do: ▷ *'There you go again, chewing your food loudly—I've told you not to do that lots of times, now stop it!'* Also used with *he, she,* etc.: ▷ *'There she goes again, telling stories about other people!'* The stress falls on *there.*

19   **Where do we go from here?**   What do we do next?: ▷ *'We've cut all the pieces of card out. Where do we go from here? Do we stick them all together or paint them first?'*

20   **Who goes there?**   The words of challenge by a soldier standing on guard: ▷ *'Halt! Who goes there?' shouted the guard at the front of the palace.*

God

1   **For God's sake!** *see* **Goodness 1.**

2   **For the love of God** *see* **Love 1.**

3   **God bless my soul!** *see* **Bless 2.**

4   **God bless (you)** *see* **Bless 3.**

5   **God bless you (him, etc.)** *see* **Bless 4.**

6   **God forbid** *see* **Forbid.**

7   **God grant**   *Formal* May it happen: ▷ *'God grant you much happiness in your marriage!'* ▷ *'God grant that I never have to see this essay again once I've finished writing it!'*

8 God help him (you, etc.) *see* **Help 2.**

9 God knows *see* **Know 8.**

10 God preserve us! *see* **Preserve.**

11 **God save . . .** May God keep and protect (a person): ▷ *'God save the Queen!'* ▷ *'God save the Prince!'*

12 **God save me (him,** etc.) **from . . .** May I (he, etc.) be protected from (the interference of other people): ▷*'I know her approaches are well-meant but may God save me from her constant offers of help!'*

13 **God willing** If circumstances allow it; if all goes well: an expression of hope: ▷ *'I'll see you again next Tuesday, God willing.'* Also the Latin phrase *Deo volente* or *DV*, used especially in church announcements.

14 **Good God!** *see* **Good 7.**

15 **Honest (to God)** Honestly: used to add strength to a statement of the speaker's truthfulness: ▷ *'Honest to God, sir, I wasn't anywhere near the garden at the time of the accident.'* Also **Honest to goodness.**

16 **In God's name** *see* **Heaven 9.**

17 **Oh God!** An expression of surprise, disbelief, fear, etc.: ▷ *'Oh God! I wish this pain would stop!'* Also **God almighty!**; **My God!**; **Oh Lord!**

18 **Please God** I hope; if all goes well: ▷ *'We'll be married this time next year, please God.'* ▷ *'If everything works as I've planned it, we should have enough money one day to retire to the country, please God.'*

19 **So help me God** *see* **Help 5.**

20 **Ye gods!** *Old-fashioned* An expression of surprise: ▷ *'Ye gods! I didn't expect to see you here—I thought you were on the other side of the world!'*

Golly

1 **By golly!** *Old-fashioned* An expression of surprise, disbelief, etc.: ▷ *'By golly, that's Pete Bates over there!'* ▷ *'Be quick about it or, by golly, you'll be punished!'* ▷ *'By golly, if you buy a present, you certainly buy expensive ones, don't you!'*

2 **Golly gumdrops!** *see* **Gumdrop.**

Gone

1 Have been and gone and . . . *see* **Be 5.**

2 Have been and gone and done it *see* **Be 6.**

Good

1 **A good one** Sometimes written (*slang*) *a good 'un*.

a That is unbelievable: ▷ *'My dad earned £100,000 last year!'* *'That's a good one—I suppose he'll earn twice that much this year!'* ▷ *'The bus never turned up, sir!' 'That's a good one, Smith—I was on it myself, so where were you?'*

b That is a good joke!: ▷ *'A good 'un, Freddie!' they cried, as they bent double with laughter.*

2 **(And a) good job** (or **thing**) **too** Used as a reply, expressing approval of what has just been said: ▷ *'I complained about the broken bag they'd sold me and the shop gave me my money back.' 'A good job too!'* ▷ *'Pete's rung to tell me not to come this weekend.' 'And a good thing too—if you'd driven all that way and found no one there, you'd have been very annoyed.'* Also **It's a good job** (or **thing**).

3 **Good afternoon** An expression used when greeting or leaving people in the afternoon.

4 **Good day** *Formal, becoming rare* An expression used when greeting or leaving people during the day.

5 **Good evening** An expression used when greeting, or, less commonly, leaving people in the evening.

6 **Good for you** (**him,** etc.)! An expression of congratulations; well done!; well said!, etc.: ▷ *'I got three grade A's, you know!' 'Good for you!'* ▷ *'Good for Pete—I'm glad he's beaten John at the long jump at last!'* An alternative in British English for *for* is *on*: *Good on you!*

7 **Good gracious!** An expression of surprise, disbelief, annoyance, etc.: ▷ *'Good gracious, you should have done your homework by now! It's ten o'clock already!'* Also **By heaven!** (*old-fashioned*); **Good God!**; **Good heavens!**; **Good Lord!**; **Goodness gracious (me)!**; **Goodness me!**; **My goodness!**

8 **Good grief!** *see* **Grief.**

9 **Good morning** An expression used when greeting or leaving people in the morning: used especially on the speaker's first meeting of the day with the person spoken to.

10 **Good night** An expression used when leaving people in the late afternooon, evening, or at night, especially when going to bed or to sleep.

11 **If you can't be good, be careful!** *see* **Anything 5.**

12 **It's a good thing** *see* **Thing 6.**

13 **So far, so good** *see* **Far 4.**

14 Very good   Yes; of course: used as a polite way of showing agreement: ▷ *'Get my suit out, please!' 'Very good, sir!'*

15 Would you be so (or **as**) **good as to . . .?**   *Formal* Would you please (do something)?: ▷ *'Would you be so good as to open the door for me?'* Also **Would you be good enough to . . . ?**

Goodness

1 For goodness' sake!   An expression of impatience, anger, surprise, etc.: often used in questions or requests: ▷ *'For goodness' sake, man, pull yourself together!'* ▷ *'Be quiet, for goodness' sake!'* Also **For God's sake!**; **For heaven's sake!**; **For mercy's sake!**; **For Pete's sake!**; **For pity's sake!**; ▷ *'Yes, you can see some of the most famous pictures in the world. They're all on show at your local gallery, right here, now, in Wolverhampton, for heaven's sake!'*

2 Goodness gracious (me)! *see* **Good 7.**

3 Goodness knows *see* **Know 8.**

4 Honest to goodness *see* **God 15.**

5 My goodness! *see* **Good 7.**

6 Thank goodness! *see* **Thank 3b.**

7 . . . to goodness   An expression used to add strength to (a wish or hope): ▷ *'I hope to goodness James will be back soon.'* ▷ *'I wish to goodness you'd shut up!'* Also **Surely to goodness**: ▷ *'Surely to goodness, you don't expect me to believe that!'*

Gracious
Good gracious! *see* **Good 7.**

Grant
God grant *see* **God 7.**

Grape
Sour grapes   An expression used to describe the bitterness a person feels, prompted by envy, when pretending to dislike something that he likes really but cannot do or get himself: ▷ *'He said that the book I wrote is not worth reading, but that is sour grapes because he'd like to write one himself!'*

Grass
The grass is (always) greener on the other side   A saying that life is more comfortable, pleasant, etc., in a different place or situation from the one a person is in at the moment.

Gratis

Free, gratis, and for nothing *see* **Free 2.**

Great

That's great! That's fantastic!; that's excellent!: ▷ *'I've just passed my driving test!' 'That's great!'* Also used sarcastically: ▷ *'It's just started to rain.' 'That's great—what are we going to do now?'*

Greek

It's all Greek to me It's too difficult for me to understand: ▷ *'That lecture on biochemistry—I'd no idea what he was saying; it's all Greek to me!'*

Grief

Good grief! An expression of surprise and sometimes horror: ▷ *'Good grief! It's Jill Winter—how are you? We've not seen each other for years, have we?'* ▷ *'Good grief! How am I going to manage now my wife's left me?'*

Grin

1 **Grin and bear it** To accept and suffer difficulty, hardship, or pain without complaining: ▷ *'I'm not sure how I'll fit in this extra work when I'm so busy already, but I suppose I'll just have to grin and bear it.'*

2 **Take** (or **wipe**) **that grin** (or **smile**) **off your face** Stop laughing at what I'm saying: ▷ *'Take that grin off your face for a start, Jones—this is serious. I'm going to find out who broke that window!'*

Groan

Groan, groan! An expression of humorous disapproval: used as a reply to a joke that is not very funny: ▷ *'Call me a taxi!' 'Right oh—you're a taxi!' 'Groan, groan!'*

Grow

Grow up! Stop behaving like a child!: ▷ *'Grow up, Michael—when are you going to stop hitting boys younger than yourself?'*

Grumble

Mustn't grumble *see* **Complain.**

Guess

1 **Guess what** Here is something that I think you will find surprising: ▷ *'He's a great fan of the Beatles—and, guess what, he's called his boys John, Paul, George, and Ringo!'*

2 **I guess** *Chiefly American* Used to show reluctant agreement: ▷ *'Mummy, can I play with Snoopy?' 'Sophie, you know dinner's nearly ready. But I guess it's all right.'*

3 **It's anybody's** (or **anyone's**) **guess** It is difficult to predict; there is no certain way of knowing: ▷ *'It's anybody's guess who will win the next race!'* Also note that *anybody's* (or *anyone's*) *guess* can stand on its own: ▷ *'What will happen next is anyone's guess!'*

4 **Your guess is as good as mine** I know as little as you do about it; I don't know either: ▷ *'When is the bus coming?' 'Your guess is as good as mine! They seem to turn up whenever they want to!'*

Guest

Be my guest! Please feel free to do as you like; I do not mind if you do: often used in reply to a question: ▷ *'May I use your phone?' 'Be my guest!'* ▷ *'Can I have another piece of cake?' 'Be my guest!'*

Gum

By gum! *see* **Gad.**

Gumdrop

Golly gumdrops! *Old-fashioned* An exclamation of surprise or wonder: ▷ *'Golly gumdrops! You're back already— that was quick!'*

Gun

1 **Jump the gun** Do or say something before you should: ▷ *'We jumped the gun by saying that you could buy televisions more cheaply. There is a plan to do this, but it is not yet in operation.'* The phrase comes from athletes beginning a race before the starter's gun goes off.

2 **Son of a gun** *see* **Son 2.**

h

Hair

1   **Keep your hair on!** *see* **Shirt 1.**

2   **Let your hair down!**   Relax and enjoy yourself; behave as you want: ▷ *'Go on, let your hair down this evening. You deserve it after the busy week you've had at work!'*

Half

1   **A . . . and a half**   A very big or good example of (a thing or person): ▷ *'That's a car and a half you've got there—it's far too large for the two of you and it'll never fit in your garage!'*

2   **Half a moment** *see* **Just 2a.**

3   **Half a tick** *see* **Just 2a.**

4   **My better half**   My wife; my husband: usually used humorously: ▷ *'I'll have to talk to my better half about that.'*

5   **Not half**   *British*

a   Very: ▷ *'It isn't half cold in this room.'* ▷ *'That chicken wasn't half nice!'*

b   Very much: ▷ *'He doesn't half swear!'* ▷ *'It didn't half rain!'*

c   Yes; certainly: used as a reply to a question: ▷ *'Would you like to come with us?' 'Not half!'* ▷ *'Did you like the film?' 'Not half I did!'*

6   **Not half bad** *see* **Bad 3.**

7   **The half of it**   Only part of the whole story, trouble, etc.: ▷ *'I went out of the house this morning, lost my keys at the shops, got soaked walking to school, and that's not the half of it—I've had an awful day!'*

8   **Too . . . by half**   *British* Far too (something): ▷ *'He's too cocky by half!'* ▷ *'I'm no chef.' 'You're too modest by half.'*

Hand

1   **A big hand for . . .**   Please welcome (usually a famous person) by clapping: ▷ *'A big hand for Toby Tootall, the greatest circus acrobat of all time!'*

2   **All hands on deck!**   Everyone must play their part with the work to be done: ▷ *'All hands on deck! We need everyone's help to get us out of this mess!'* Also **All hands to the**

pumps!: ▷ *'We've got so much work to do, it'll be all hands to the pumps for weeks now!'* Both these expressions were originally used on ships.

3 **Hands off!** Don't touch; don't interfere: ▷ *'Hands off that machine—it's dangerous, you know!'* ▷ *'Hands off! She's my girlfriend, if you don't mind!'* ▷ *'Hands off our schools!'*—the slogan had been painted on the wall by the protesters against cuts in government spending on education.

4 **Hands up!**

a Please raise your hands if you . . .: used to ask members of a group (to agree to something): ▷ *'Hands up all those who want to go swimming,'* the teacher said. ▷ *'Hands up if you know the answer.'*

b Put your arms above your head: used by gunmen to the people they want to rob, etc., to get them to surrender: ▷ *The armed men burst into the shop. 'Hands up everyone! Hand over the money!'* Also **Put** (or **stick**) **'em up!**

5 **I've only one pair of hands** *see* **Pair.**

6 **On the one hand . . . and** (or **but**) **on the other . . .** Used to contrast two ideas, statements, etc.: ▷ *'On the one hand, it's a very economical car, but on the other, it's not much to look at, is it?'*

7 **Shake hands** To take hold of another person's hand and move it up and down when greeting or coming to an agreement or reconciliation: ▷ *When I was introduced to Mr Page, we shook hands.* ▷ *They shook hands after their quarrel.*

Hang

1 **Hang in there!** *Chiefly American* Keep at it!: an expression of encouragement to persevere when things are difficult.

2 **Hang it (all)!** Used to express annoyed dissatisfaction, disappointment, etc.: ▷ *'I've forgotten my keys, hang it—how am I going to get in?'* ▷ *'Hang it all! You've had three weeks to plant the seeds and you say you've not even started?'*

3 **Hang on**

a Please wait a moment: used especially to someone on the telephone but also in other contexts: ▷ *'Hang on—I'll just get a pencil and jot down the details.'* ▷ *'Can I speak to Mr Jones, please?' 'I'll see if he's in—just hang on.'*

b Be reasonable; I want to make a comment or objection: ▷ *'Hang on, old chap, who are you calling a liar?'* Also **Hang about.**

c An expression of surprise or amazement: ▷ *'Hang on—don't I know you? Weren't we at school together?'*

4 **I'll be hanged** Used to express anger, surprise, dissatisfaction, etc.: ▷ *'I'll be hanged if I'll apologise this time—he should say he's sorry first.'* Also **I'm hanged**: ▷ *'I'm hanged if I know the answer!'*

5 **Let it all hang out** *Slang* Be completely free to express yourself as you want: ▷ *'We're just off to the party.' 'Enjoy yourselves—let it all hang out!'*

6 **Thereby hangs a tale** *see* **Tale.**

Happen

It's all happening There's a lot of successful activity: ▷ *'It's all happening here today!'* ▷ *'It's all happening in Birmingham at the moment: it's got a new shopping centre, good concert halls, and an excellent library—what more could you want?'*

Hat

1 **I'll eat my hat** *Becoming old-fashioned* I will be proved wrong; I will be surprised: used to show that the speaker does not really believe that something is true or that something will happen: ▷ *'If that old horse of yours does come first in the race, I'll eat my hat!'* ▷ *'If it wasn't Richard who broke the window, I'll eat my hat!'*

2 **My hat!** *Old-fashioned*

a What nonsense!: ▷ *'Seventy, my hat! Surely you're only around fifty!'* ▷ *'My hat! You don't expect me to believe that story, do you? Where were you really last night?'*

b An expression of surprise: ▷ *'My hat, it's cold today, isn't it!'*

Hatch

Down the hatch! An expression used when taking a drink with other people.

Hate

I hate to mention it, but . . . *see* **Mention 2.**

Have

1 **. . . had better . . .** (Someone) ought to (do something): ▷ *'I'd better check that I've locked all the doors* *before I go out.'* ▷ *'You'd better not go there this evening—I think he'll be busy.'* Sometimes used as a threat: ▷ *'I'll pay you back on Friday.' 'You'd better!'* ▷ *'I promise I'll return the car.' 'You better had!'*

2 **Have . . ., will . . .** An expression used to show a willingness or ability (to do something, especially go somewhere), because you have (something): ▷ *' "Have car, will travel!" as the saying goes—so we've been to Scotland for the weekend!'*

3 **I have and I haven't** An ambiguous, rather defensive, reply to a question, showing that the speaker has partly done or undertaken something, and often used when the speaker purposely does not want to be clear: ▷ *'Have you spoken to Mr Smith about a pay rise?' 'I have and I haven't—not directly, yet, but I promise to tomorrow.'* ▷ *'Have you got any work for me to mark?' 'Well, I have and I haven't.'*

4 **I have it** *see* **Get 14, 15.**

5 **I wouldn't have it if you gave it to** (or **paid**) **me!** I'm not accepting what you're offering: ▷ *'That car of yours is so old, I wouldn't have it if you gave it to me!'*

6 **Let's be having you** A firm request to move somewhere quickly: used by attendants at a public place, foremen to workers, and supposedly by policemen: ▷ *'Come along now, let's be having you, please!'* ▷ *'Ladies and gentlemen, let's be having you: the museum closes in ten minutes.'*

7 **Thanks for having me** *see* **Thank 7.**

8 **You have me there** *see* **Get 16.**

9 **You shouldn't have** It is very kind of you: used in accepting a gift: ▷ *'Auntie, we've brought you some flowers, and all the family hope you'll get better soon.' 'Oh, you shouldn't have! Aren't they lovely!'*

Head

1 **Heads or tails?** An expression used when throwing a coin into the air to decide who will start a game, etc., the result depending on which side shows upwards: ▷ *'Heads or tails?' Gerald called. 'Tails!' said Pat, but it was heads, so Gerald decided that his team should play downhill.* ▷ *'Let's toss for it—heads or tails?' 'Heads!' 'Heads it is!'* Also used in the phrase *Heads I win, tails you lose,* a false bet, as whatever the result, the speaker will benefit.

2 **Mind your head(s)!** Be careful; something may hit your head or you may hit your head on something: ▷ *'Mind your heads!' the workmen shouted to the people below as the tiles fell off the roof.* ▷ *'Mind your head! It's a low ceiling!'*

3   **Off with his (or her) head!**   Execute him!; execute her!: ▷ *The women sat knitting in front of the guillotine. 'Off with his head!' they shouted.*

Health

Your health!   An expression used before drinking to wish that someone will remain well and be successful: ▷ *'Your health, Pat—may you have a prosperous time in Scotland!'* Also **Good health!**; **Your good health!**; **Your very good health!** : ▷ *The whole gathering raised their glasses and the chairman spoke, 'Your very good health, Colonel Digby!'*

Hear

1   **Hear! hear!**   An expression of agreement and approval: called out by someone at a public meeting: ▷ *'The government may decide in certain circumstances to reduce the amount of tax paid.' 'Hear! hear!'* Also used in more informal contexts: ▷ *'I think I'd better go and do the washing-up!' 'Hear! hear!'*

2   **I've heard that one before!**   I don't believe you: often used in reply to an excuse that has just been given: ▷ *'The bus didn't turn up.' 'I've heard that one before! Be honest now, why were you late?'* ▷ *'Let's go to the disco on Friday!' 'I've heard that one before—you always say that and then forget about it later!'*

3   **You heard!**   Used to add force to a command, especially when the speaker is impatient: ▷ *'Get this lorry out of the car park. You heard—move it!'*

Heart

1   **Bless your (his, etc.) heart** *see* **Bless 4.**

2   **Cross my (your, etc.) heart**   I (you, etc.) promise; I swear that I am telling the truth: used to express emphatically one's sincerity: ▷ *'Are you sure you don't know who broke the window? Cross your heart?'* Also **Cross my (your, etc.) heart and hope to die** Often used by children: ▷ *'I won't tell your secret to anyone else, cross my heart and hope to die!'*

3   **Have a heart**   Be kind or sympathetic: ▷ *'Have a heart, Dick! I've been ill for six months—can't you give me a bit*

more time to catch up on the work?' ▷ *'I think you could have been more reasonable with Jane for being late; have a heart—after all, she has travelled all day to get here.'*

4 **My heart bleeds for you (him,** etc.) *Often humorous* I feel very sorry for you (him, etc.) but often used when the feelings are not really of sorrow: ▷ *'I've got to be up by seven tomorrow morning to get to work early.' 'My heart bleeds for you—I get up at six every day at the moment.'* Alternatives to *bleeds* are *aches* and *goes out.* The phrases may also be used in the plural: ▷ *'Our hearts went out to her when she had a miscarriage, just after we'd had a baby.'* Also **You're breaking my heart.**

5 **Put your (his,** etc.) **heart and soul into (something)** To give a full commitment to some work or activity; make the strongest possible effort: ▷ *'I put my heart and soul into writing that speech, so don't tell me it wasn't worth it!'*

Heave

Heave ho! The cry of sailors when lifting the anchor up, and, more widely, to encourage someone when pushing or pulling something.

Heaven

1 **By heaven!** *see* **Good 7.**
2 **For heaven's sake!** *see* **Goodness 1.**
3 **Good heavens!** *see* **Good 7.**
4 **Heaven forbid** *see* **Forbid.**
5 **Heaven help him (you,** etc.) *see* **Help 2.**
6 **Heaven knows** *see* **Know 8.**
7 **Heaven preserve us!** *see* **Preserve.**
8 **Heavens above!** An expression of surprise, disbelief, annoyance, etc.: ▷ *'Heavens above! That's Jane Mitcham over there—I've not see her for years!'* ▷ *'Heavens above, child! Can't you be quiet for two minutes?'* Also (*slang, old-fashioned*) **Heavens to Murgatroyd!**
9 **In heaven's name** An expression used to add strength to a question, request, etc.: ▷*'Where in heaven's name did you put my keys?'* Also **In God's name.**
10 **Thank heavens!** *see* **Thank 3.**

Heck

1 **What (how,** etc.) **the heck?** *see* **Hell 5.**

2 **What the heck!** *see* **Hell 6.**

Hell

1 **Go to hell!** Go away!; stop talking!: a strong expression: ▷ *'Can I have a word with you for a moment?' 'No, I'm tired of you annoying me all day—go to hell!'*

2 **Hell's bells!** *Becoming old-fashioned* A strong expression of anger, annoyance, etc.: ▷ *'Hell's bells! How many more times do I have to tell you to shut up?'* Also **Hell's teeth!**

3 **Like hell**

a Very much, fast, etc.: ▷ *'He always works like hell before exams.'* ▷ *'We ran like hell to get away from the police.'*

b An expression of strong disagreement: said as a reply to the previous statement, request, etc.: ▷ *'Will you buy me that book I wanted?' 'Like hell I will: you never get me things when I ask you!'* ▷ *'Like hell he paid for the holiday! We had saved for months and months to pay for it ourselves.'* Also *(slang)* **The hell you will** (or **won't**); **The hell he can** (or **can't**), etc.: ▷ *'Mary says she'll help you learn to drive.' 'The hell she will—she's only just passed the test herself!'*

4 **To hell with . . .** I (or we) do not care about; I'm fed up with (something or someone): ▷ *'To hell with this essay—I've spent hours on it already, but I don't seem to be getting anywhere!'* ▷ *'To hell with the lot of you—we're going home!'*

5 **What (how, where, who, why, etc.) the hell?** Whatever, (however, wherever, whoever, why ever): used in questions to emphasise a strong feeling such as annoyance or surprise: ▷ *'What the hell are you doing in my workshop?'* ▷*'How the hell are we going to get out of this mess?'* An alternative to *hell* in these expressions is *heck* : ▷ *'Who the heck do you think you are, coming in here without even knocking?'*

6 **What the hell!** An expression used to reject a difficulty or problem, showing that the speaker does not care: often used in a resigned tone: ▷ *'What the hell, the company's paying for the meal, so let's have the most expensive dish!'* ▷ *'So Jo's not in—what the hell—we can come back tomorrow instead!'* ▷ *'OK—so I failed the exam. What the hell, I can always try again!'* Also **What the heck!**: ▷ *After he'd crashed the car, Pat just said, 'What the heck—my Dad'll buy me another one.'*

Hello

1 **Hello, hello, hello!** *British* An expression supposedly used by policemen on finding something strange: but used humorously in real life: ▷ *'Hello, hello, hello! What's all this then? A pot of gold hidden in the bushes!'* This phrase is pronounced and often written *'ello, 'ello, 'ello.*

2 **Hello, stranger!** *see* **Stranger.**

3 **Hello there!** A cry for attention when entering a house or when you cannot see: ▷ *'Hello there! Is anyone in?'* Jean called out as she went through the door of the dark old house.

Help

1 **Can I help you?** An expression used by a shop assistant in serving a customer: ▷*'Can I help you, sir?'* *'Two boxes of matches, please.'* Also **What can I do for you?**

2 **God** (or **heaven**) **help me** (**you,** etc.) A cry requesting help from God: ▷ *'God help us all at this time of national disaster.'* ▷ *'Heaven help Mary in this crisis in her life.'* Also used humorously to express mild sympathy: ▷ *'Heaven help the man who marries Kitty!'*

3 **Not if I can help it** Only against my agreeing to it: ▷ *'I won't pay the money on time, not if I can help it.'* ▷ *'I'm coming round this evening to put an end to our arguments once and for all!' 'Not if I can help it, you won't!'* Also **Not if I know it** : ▷ *'Not if I know it, you won't borrow my car!'*

4 **So help me** Used in emphasising a promise: ▷ *'I'll get revenge on you, so help me!'* ▷ *'If you're not at the theatre tonight, so help me, I'll resign as your agent!'*

5 **So help me God**

a Although this may seem strange, I am speaking the truth: ▷*'I really did see a flying-saucer, so help me God.'* Sometimes shortened to *So help me.*

b Used to emphasise a hope or wish: ▷ *'I never want to see you again, so help me God!'*

Here

1 **Here goes!** *see* **Go 11.**

2 **Here we go again** *see* **Go 12.**

3 **Here you are**

a An expression used when giving something to someone; this is what you wanted: ▷ *'Here you are, madam, what you ordered, roast chicken and peas.'*

b An expression used to call attention to something: ▷ *'You say you want to go to the States in July but, here you are, it's January already and you've still not got any money—you'd better start saving, my lad!'* Also **Here we are.**

4 **Here's how!** An expression used when taking a drink with other people.

5 **Here's to . . .** An expression used when drinking, to wish (someone or something) well: ▷ *'Here's to the bride and groom.'* ▷ *'Here's to your new job!'*

Hey

Hey presto!

a An expression a conjuror says as he comes to the main part of a trick: ▷ *'Do you see this smart top hat? Hey presto, here are two rabbits jumping out of it!'*

b Used to announce a surprising change or sudden appearance: ▷ *The doorbell rang. I went to see who it was. Hey presto! It was my brother, Jason, who I'd not seen for years!* ▷ *No one had arrived for the party—the room was empty. But hey presto, in five minutes all my friends were suddenly there!*

Hint

Hint, hint! An expression used when making a small, indirect suggestion to do something: ▷ *'It's ten o'clock, hint, hint!' muttered Sue quietly. Sam understood. 'Yes, I think it's time we went,' he said.* ▷ *'A cup of tea would be nice—hint, hint!'*

Hip

Hip, hip, hurrah! An expression used to introduce cheers: ▷ *'Congratulations to the team for coming first in the competition! Hip, hip, hurrah! Hip, hip hurrah! Hip, hip, hurrah!'* The expression is usually called out with the person leading the cheers crying *Hip, hip* and everyone shouting *hurrah.* This all happens three times.

Hit

Hit it off To have a good friendly relationship with someone: ▷ *'From the first time they met, they hit it off.'*

Hold

1 **Hold it!**

a   Stop everything!; stop what you're doing, wait a moment: ▷ *'Hold it, son, where do you think you're going with that picture under your coat?'* ▷ *The armed men made their way into the bank. 'Hold it, everyone—don't anyone move: now tell us where the safe is!'* Also **Hold everything!**

b   Keep still: said by a photographer who wants people to stay in the same position: ▷ *We stood around chatting to one another after the ceremony. 'Hold it!' Ian shouted, as he took a picture of us all.*

2   **Hold on!**   Please wait a moment: used especially to someone on the telephone, but also in other circumstances: ▷ *'Is Mr Jackson there, please?' 'Hold on, I'll see if he's available.'* ▷ *'Hold on a minute! Aren't you the man the police are looking for in connection with the robbery?'*

3   **Hold your horses!** *see* **Horse.**

Hole

Top hole!   *British, rare, old-fashioned* Excellent!; splendid!: ▷ *'We're going to take you to the circus at Christmas!' 'Top hole!' cried Andrew with delight.*

Holy

Holy smoke!   *Old-fashioned* An expression of strong feeling such as surprise, delight, or anger: ▷ *'Holy smoke! What are you doing here? I thought you were in America still!'* Also **Holy cow!**; **Holy mackerel!**; **Holy Moses!**: ▷ *'Holy mackerel! Can't you children ever learn to be quiet?'*

Home

1   **. . . go home!**   A slogan used to show the speaker's disapproval of (someone): ▷ *'Prime Minister go home!'* ▷ *'Foreign troops go home!'*

2   **Home, James!**   A humorous way of asking the driver to drive the car home: ▷ *The children got into the back of the car and called out, 'Home, James!' to their father.* Originally, *Home, James, and don't spare the horses!*, an order to the driver of a carriage or coach, and later the chauffeur, to return home.

3   **Make yourself at home!**   Please relax and do as you would in your own home: ▷ *'Do come in and make yourself at home! Would you like something to eat?'* ▷ *'Sit down and make yourself at home, while I put the kettle on for a cup of tea.'*

4 **Who's . . . when he's (she's,** etc.) **at home?** I've never
heard of (someone): used to ask who the person just mentioned really is: ▷ *'I'm off to see Tracy Rossiter.' 'Tracy
Rossiter? Who's she when she's at home?'*

Honest
Honest to God *see* **God 15.**

Honour
1 **Do the honours** To act as host or hostess by doing something such as pouring drinks or serving food: ▷ *'Will you do
the honours and carve the meat, while I go and bring in the
vegetables?'* ▷ *'Patrick, you do the honours and propose the
toast.' 'All right, then. Ladies and gentlemen; here's to your
new job, Elizabeth!'*

2 **God's honour!** Used to strengthen a promise, agreement,
or statement: ▷ *'God's honour! I'm telling the truth!'* Also
(old-fashioned) **Scout's honour!**; **Honour bright!** *(British
school slang)*: ▷ *'I really am going to finish my work tonight,
Scout's honour!'*

3 **On my honour** I assure you: used to emphasise a
promise: ▷ *'On my honour, we will do all we can to help
you.'*

Hoot
Not care (or **give**) **two hoots** *see* **Damn 4.**

Hop
Hop it! *Slang, British* Go away!: ▷ *'Hop it, Pete, we don't
want you around!'*

Hope
1 **I hope you feel proud of yourself!** I hope you feel pleased
with yourself: but used when the person has nothing to be
proud of and has, in fact, in the speaker's opinion behaved
badly: ▷ *'I hope you feel proud of yourself, Sarah! Your silly
behaviour in the restaurant really made your mother and me
feel embarrassed!'*

2 **Some hope(s)!** There is little or no chance that what you
want will actually happen: ▷ *'Some hopes of playing games
today—it's been raining since early this morning!'* ▷ *'I want
to sail around the world one day!' 'Some hope!'* Also **(A) fat
chance!**; **Not a hope!**

Horse

    Hold your horses! Don't be too hasty to do something; be more patient!: ▷ *'Hold your horses! We don't need to ring for the ambulance—it's only a slight cut.'* ▷ *'Why do you have to get so angry about something as unimportant as that? Hold your horses!'*

Host

    Mine host A humorous way of talking to one's host or, often, the landlord of a pub.

How

1   **And how!** Very much so: used to express strong agreement with what has just been said, but sometimes also used to express the opposite of this: ▷ *'Goldie's beautiful, isn't she?' 'And how!'* ▷ *'So you had a good time in London?' 'And how! It was all so dirty, the hotel was expensive, the trains were all late—we're never going back there!'*

2   **Here's how!** *see* **Here 4.**

3   **How . . .!** Used to introduce an exclamation: ▷ *'How kind you are!'* ▷ *'Treacle tart! How lovely!'* ▷ *'How she's grown!'* ▷ *'How polite her behaviour is these days!'*

4   **How about . . .?** *see* **About 1.**

5   **How about that!** *see* **About 2.**

6   **How are you** A conventional greeting, often also a definite enquiry about someone's health and welfare: ▷ *'How are you, Paula?' 'Very well, thanks, and you?' 'OK, thanks.'* ▷ *'How are you, Mr Dickson?' 'Fine, thank you; how are you?' 'Fine, thank you.'* When used as a question, the stress falls on *are* ; if used in a reply, the stress falls on *you.* Also **How are you doing?**; **How are** (or **how's**) **things?**; **How are you keeping?** *(becoming old-fashioned)*; **How's yourself?** *(slang)* : ▷ *'How are you doing, Vic? I've not had a chance to talk to you for ages!'*

7   **How come . . .?** *see* **Come 10.**

8   **How could I have . . .?** Used in an apology when one has (done something foolish): ▷ *'How could I have been so stupid? I'm sorry I stepped on your toe!'*

9   **How do you do** *see* **Do 11.**

10 **How is it?** Why?; what is the reason?; ▷ *'How is it you always arrive late on Mondays?'*

11 **How is it for . . .?** Is this satisfactory regarding (a particular feature): ▷ *'Do you want to try on this coat?' 'Yes, let's.'* *'How is it for size?'*

12 How (or **however**) **could** (or **can**) **you . . .?** You shouldn't have (done something): used to express sorrow and surprise that someone has acted in a certain way: ▷ *'How could you have said such rude things to him?'* ▷ *'How can you speak to her like that?'* ▷ *'However could you have forgotten my birthday?'*

13 How so? Why?, why is it like that?: ▷ *'I thought the concert was very disappointing.' 'How so?' 'The lead singer didn't turn up, and the understudy couldn't reach the high notes properly.'*

14 How's it going? *see* **Go 13.**

15 How's that?

a What do you think of that?: ▷ *'There, the picture's on the wall—how's that?' 'I don't think you've got it quite straight.'*

b Why?; what is the reason?: ▷ *'I'm not sure I'll be able to come and visit you again.' 'How's that?'*

c *Cricket* Is the batsman out?: said to an umpire: ▷ *The shouts of 'How's that?' were loud enough to be heard outside the cricket ground.* Sometimes written and pronounced *(slang)* **Howzzat?**

d Please repeat what you said: ▷ *'I'm going to be an astronaut when I grow up.' 'How's that?' 'I said I'm going to be an astronaut when I grow up.'*

16 How's that for . . . An expression used to praise or draw attention to (a particular feature of something): ▷ *'How's that for economy! It's the cheapest small car available!'* ▷ *'How's that for the best float in the parade!'*

17 That's how it is *see* **That 16.**

18 This is how it is *see* **This 1.**

However

However could you . . .? *see* **How 12.**

i

Ice

Break the ice To make the shyness and embarrassment less, for example when people meet for the first time: ▷ *'Fortunately, we had the baby with us when we went round there for tea, so that helped to break the ice.'*

Idea

1 **Not have the foggiest (idea)** *see* **Foggiest.**
2 **Not my (his, etc.) idea of . . .** This is the opposite of what I (he, etc.) think of as (something): ▷ *'Sitting on a beach all day is not my idea of a holiday—I prefer doing something active like looking round the area or climbing mountains.'* ▷ *'Camping in the rain is not my idea of fun!'*
3 **That's an idea** What you are suggesting is worth considering: ▷ *'Shall we go to Ilfracombe for the day?' 'That's an idea! I'd never thought of that!'*
4 **That's the idea** That's about right: ▷ *'Listen, Mum, to me playing this piece by Mozart.' . . . 'Yes, that's the idea! You're coming on very well now.'*
5 **The (very) idea!** What you are suggesting is most unreasonable: ▷ *'The very idea of you staying out late makes me shudder!'* ▷ *'The very idea! You thought you could just take my car without asking me first!'* Also **What an idea!**
6 **What's the (big) idea?** Why are you doing that?; how dare you do that!: used as an accusation: ▷*'What's the idea—coming into my workshop without even knocking?'* ▷ *'What's the big idea of gossiping about me behind my back?'*

If

1 **As if . . .** *see* **As 2.**
2 **If I were you** An expression used in giving advice: ▷ *'If I were you, I'd accept that job.'* ▷ *'If I were you, I'd be thinking about getting rid of that old car.'* A rather rude reply to this is sometimes *but you're not*: ▷ *'I'd think about resigning, if I were you.' 'But you're not, so shut up!'*
3 **If only . . .** I wish: often used about (something that is very unlikely) or to express a regret: ▷ *'If only I'd known, I*

wouldn't have done it!' ▷ *'If only Pete were here, it would all be different!'* ▷ *'If only he didn't snore!'*

4   **If you could** (or **would**)   Used in polite requests: ▷ *'Pass me that glass, if you could.'*

5   **(Well) if . . .**   Used to introduce (an exclamation): ▷ *'If it isn't spotty Brian from London! What are you doing here in Ibiza?'* ▷ *'Well, if this doesn't beat everything!'*

6   **What if . . .** *see* **What 15.**

Imagine

(Just) imagine (that)!   An expression of surprise: sometimes expressing disapproval of what is being mentioned: ▷ *'Just imagine! After all these years of buying British, he's now bought a foreign car!'* ▷ *'My dad's a driver on one of the new fast trains!' 'Imagine that! I thought he was a ticket-collector!'*

Incline

I'm inclined to . . .   An expression used to make an opinion sound less strong: ▷ *'I'm inclined to think you're right and Sheila's wrong.'*

It

1   **It's me**   I am at the door; it is me speaking: ▷ *There was a knock on the door. 'Who's there?' Kitty asked. 'It's me,' replied Annette, as she came in.*

2   **That's it** *see* **That 17.**

3   **This is it** *see* **This 2.**

4   **Who is it?**   Who is at the door?; who is speaking?: ▷ *There was a knock at the door. 'Who is it?' Bill called out. 'Cathy!' 'Come in, then.'* ▷ *'75311,' John answered the phone, 'who is it?'*

j

Jack

1 Before you can say Jack Robinson *see* **Robinson**.

2 I'm all right, Jack   I'm doing very well: used to show that you care only about yourself and not at all about other people: ▷ '*We're going to make sure that our union gets the highest pay settlement this year. Workers in other industries don't count; it's "I'm all right, Jack" that's important.*' The phrase comes from the title of a film *I'm All Right, Jack* (1960).

Jeeper

Jeepers (creepers)!   *Slang, chiefly American* An expression of surprise, sometimes also used for emphasis: ▷ '*Jeepers creepers, Aaron's coming down the drive—we'd better move!*' *Jeepers* is a euphemism for *Jesus*.

Jiffy

Just a jiffy *see* **Just 2a**.

Jigger

I'm jiggered!   *Old-fashioned* Used to express surprise, anger, etc.: ▷ '*It's Pete! Well, I'm jiggered! Who would have thought of meeting you here!*' ▷ '*I'm jiggered if I'll let him get away without being punished!*'

Jiminy

By Jiminy!   *Old-fashioned* An expression showing surprise, also used to add force to a statement: ▷ '*By Jiminy—you're right, that is Margaret over there! I wonder what she's doing here!*' *Jiminy* is a shortened form of *Jesus Domine*, Jesus Lord.

Jingo

By jingo!   *Old-fashioned* An expression of surprise, excitement, etc.: ▷ '*By jingo, the bus is on time!*' ▷ '*By jingo, Mary's passed her driving test!*' Originally, perhaps a euphemism for *Jesus*.

Job

1 (And a) good job too *see* **Good 2.**

2 (That's) **just the job** That is exactly what is needed: ▷ *'A glass of cold milk! Just the job on a hot day like this!'* ▷ *'So I could stay with you in Birmingham and then drive up to Edinburgh the next day? That's just the job!'* Also (*old-fashioned*) **That's (just) the ticket.**

Join

1 If you can't beat 'em, join 'em! *see* **Beat 3.**

2 Join the club! *see* **Club.**

Joke

1 **It's** (or **it was**) **no joke** It is (or was) something serious: ▷ *'It's no joke walking along a country lane in the dark.'* ▷ *'It was no joke carrying all your suitcases from one side of the station to the other—what did you put in them?'*

2 **Joking apart** (or **aside**) Seriously: ▷ *'Joking aside, has anyone got any real suggestions as to what we might use the patch of ground for?'*

3 **You must be joking!** I cannot seriously believe what you're saying; I am very surprised: ▷ *'Goldie's just won first prize in the beauty competition!' 'You must be joking!'* Also **You're joking!**: ▷ *'Have I told you we're emigrating?' 'You're joking!'*

Jove

By Jove! *Old-fashioned* An expression of surprise, excitement, or sometimes approval; also used to add force to a statement: ▷ *'Isn't that plane Concorde?' 'Yes, by Jove, I think you're right!'* ▷ *'By Jove, I'll get you back for what you've done to me, if it's the last thing I do!' Jove* comes from Old Latin *Jovis*, Jupiter. Also **By thunder!**

Joy

1 **Full of the joys of spring** Very happy and bright; sometimes said to someone who is obviously very cheerful when you yourself are not feeling at all like this: ▷ *'You're full of the joys of spring this morning, aren't you?'*

2 **No joy** *British* No success or luck: ▷ *'Did you manage to find the book you were looking for?' 'No joy!'* Also, more fully, *I got no joy; I didn't get any joy.*

Judgement

Judgement on you *School slang, becoming old-fashioned* It is as if you were being punished by God: said when something bad happens to a person after they have done something bad themselves: ▷ *'I got my homework back. The mark was only three out of ten.'* *'Judgement on you!'* Carol replied, *'you shouldn't have cheated and copied it!'* ▷ *'I've just got absolutely soaked running for the bus!'* *'It's a judgement on you for breaking Mrs Jones' window!'*

Jump

1 Go (and) jump in the lake! *see* **Lake.**

2 **Jump to it!** Get going on something; hurry; show that you are willing to obey: ▷ *'You'd better start cleaning the office! Jump to it! The manager will be here in half an hour!'* ▷ *'We'll have to jump to it to get our work finished by the time Pete comes round for us!'*

3 **Take a running jump!** Go away: used as a rude expression when you are very annoyed with someone: ▷ *'You've really got on my nerves this morning!'* *'Yes, and you've got on mine!'* *'Why don't you take a running jump!'* ▷ *'And then she told him to go and take a running jump—you can imagine what sort of an effect that had!'*

Just

1 **Isn't (wasn't, etc.) it (he, etc.) just!** Yes, I agree; very much so: used to express complete agreement, but sometimes also indicating the opposite: ▷ *'Wasn't that book interesting?'* *'Wasn't it just! Once I started it, I couldn't put it down!'* ▷ *'Isn't Perry helpful around the home?'* *'Helpful? Isn't he just—he sits there all the time, watching the television, and never even asks if he can help at all!'*

2 **Just a moment**

a Wait a moment, please: ▷ *'Just a moment, please—I'm still dealing with another customer!'* Also **Half a mo** *(very informal)*; **Half a moment**; **Half a tick** *(very informal, British)*; **Just a jiffy** *(old-fashioned, very informal)*; **Just a minute**; **Just a sec** *(very informal)*; **Just a second**; **Just a tick** *(very informal, British)*; **One moment**: ▷ *'I'll be with you in just a minute.'*

b I wish to make a comment or objection: ▷ *'Just a moment! What about the plans for the other side of the building? Has everyone forgotten them?'* Alternatives to *moment* are *minute* and *second*.

c An expression of surprise or amazement: ▷ *'Just a moment! Aren't you the chap we met in the bank? Yes, look, your beard's falling off!'* Alternatives to *moment* are *minute* and *second*.

3 **Just as well** *see* **Well 3.**

4 **Just so** *British* It is exactly as you say; I agree; that's right: used to express complete agreement: ▷ *'I'll come and pick you up at six o'clock and then we can drive on to Ralph's together.' 'Just so!'* Also **Quite (so)**: ▷ *'I always think that a cup of tea is the most refreshing drink there is.' 'Quite so!'* ▷ *'I'm sure Harvey's the best tennis-player we've ever had, isn't he?' 'Quite!'*

5 **Just the thing!** *see* **Thing 8.**

k

Keep

1   How are you keeping? *see* **How 6.**

2   Keep one's fingers crossed *see* **Finger 2.**

3   **Keep smiling!**   Take things easy; don't worry!: used to describe an optimistic approach to life even when things are going wrong: ▷ *'Whatever troubles you may be going through, remember, "Keep smiling".'*

4   Keep taking the tablets! *see* **Tablet.**

5   Keep your shirt (or hair) on! *see* **Shirt 1.**

6   **You (he, etc.) can keep . . .**   I do not want (what is being offered) in the least: often said in a rude tone: ▷ *'You can keep your burnt pie—I'm going out for a take-away!'*   The stress falls on *keep.*

7   You can't keep a good man down *see* **Man 10.**

Keeper

Finders keepers *see* **Finder.**

Kettle

1   That's a different kettle of fish *see* **Story 2a.**

2   **That's (or it's) a fine kettle of fish**   That's an awkward situation: ▷ *'It's a fine kettle of fish you've got us in—stuck way out in the country with no petrol!'* Alternatives to *fine* are *nice* and *pretty.*

Kick

For kicks   Just for the excitement: ▷ *The boys stole the car and drove it round town just for kicks.* Also **For the hell of it.**

Kid

1   **(And) no kidding!**   I mean exactly what I say!; I am not joking: ▷ *'I'll beat you in the long jump today—no kidding!'*

2   **No kidding?**   I'm surprised at what you're saying; is it really true?: ▷ *'Have you heard, Janet? My cousin's going to work in the States for the whole of next year.' 'No kidding?' 'Yes—she goes in January.'* ▷ *'I've lived here all my life!' 'No kidding? Then how come you don't know where the railway station is?'*

3 **You're kidding!** I don't believe you!: ▷ *'Pearl's just won first prize in a swimming competition!' 'You're kidding! She's about as athletic as an apple pudding!'* ▷ *'You're kidding! You say you heard the Beatles at a concert—live? You're not old enough, surely?'*

Kill

Kill two birds with one stone *see* **Bird 2**.

Kind

1 **A kind (or sort) of . . .** A vague or unusual type of (something): ▷ *'I had a kind of feeling you'd be offered the job.'* ▷ *'He always has a sort of mental blockage when it comes to buying other people presents.'*

2 **Kind of thing** *see* **Thing 9**.

3 **Kind (or sort) of . . .** An expression used to make a statement or opinion sound less certain or definite; rather; to some degree: ▷ *'That kind of explains it.'* ▷ *'We felt kind of sorry for him.'* ▷ *'It was sort of the size of that bag.'* Also written and pronounced (*slang*) *kinda, sorta*. These phrases are American in origin.

Kite

Go fly a kite! *Slang, chiefly American* Go away!: ▷ *'I'm tired of you telling us what to do, Goldie. Go fly a kite!'*

Knife

Before you can say knife *see* **Robinson**.

Knob

And the same to you with brass knobs on *see* **Same 2b**.

Knock

1 **Knock it off!** *Slang* Stop it!: ▷ *'Knock it off, you two. Can't you see I'm trying to work?'*

2 **Knock, knock** Used as the first set of words of a joke (*a knock-knock joke*): ▷*'Knock, knock!' 'Who's there?' 'Lettuce!' 'Lettuce who?' 'Lettuce in and you'll know!'*

Knot

Get knotted! *Slang* An expression of contempt, used to show that you disapprove of something or that you do not want to do something: ▷ *'Can I borrow your pen?' 'Get knotted! You never gave me back the last one you took!'* ▷ *'I told her to get knotted!'*

Know

1 **And I don't know who** (or **what**)   And many other people (or things) also: ▷ *'There was the mayor, the school governors, the chaplain, and I don't know who at the dinner.'* ▷ *'In the room, books, packs of cards, empty boxes, and I don't know what, had just been thrown about.'*

2 **As you know**   You know this already, but I am telling you again: used to introduce further information: ▷ *'As you know, Pete's got a place at university. Well, he starts next month.'*

3 **Don't I know it**

a Unfortunately, I know it: used when the speaker has to do or has done something unpleasant: ▷ *'I've got to wash all those dishes, don't I know it.'* ▷ *'I got up at five o'clock this morning to finish my work, and don't I know it.'*

b Yes; I agree; I know it already: ▷ *'She's angry with you!'* ▷ *'Don't I know it! She just threw something at me!'*

4 **Don't you know**   *Becoming old-fashioned* An expression used to show strong emotion: ▷ *'It's such a nuisance, don't you know, travelling by train.'*

5 **For all I** (**you**, etc.) **know** *see* **All 16.**

6 **For aught I know** *see* **Aught.**

7 **He didn't want to know** *see* **Want 1.**

8 **Heaven knows**   Also **God knows; Goodness knows; (The) Lord knows**

a I do not know; it is impossible to say: ▷ *'Heaven knows where Leslie's got to—he should have been here two hours ago!'* Often used with *only* : ▷ *'God only knows how I'm going to explain why I'm late!'*

b Certainly: used to add force to a statement or opinion: ▷ *'I hope you pass the exam. Heaven knows, you've tried hard enough!'* ▷ *'Goodness knows, we were poor enough already before we were robbed!'*

9 **I didn't know you cared!**   *Humorous* I had no idea that I meant something to you!; used between friends: ▷ *'Here are some chocolates for you, Julie!' 'I didn't know you cared!'*

10 **I don't know**

a A cry of exasperation or surprise: ▷ *'I don't know! You*

children are really getting on my nerves this morning!' ▷
'Well, I don't know! Imagine her entering a beauty competition with a figure like that!' The stress falls on *I*.

b I'm not sure: ▷ *'I don't know that I care for the colours of that room.'* ▷ *'I don't know if I can be home for six, but I'll do my best.'*

11 **I don't know about that** Used to show disagreement with what has just been said: ▷ *'Robert's getting on very well at school these days, isn't he?' 'I don't know about that—though he's certainly not bottom of the class any more.'* The speaker can also use words used by the previous speaker: ▷ *'That new dictionary looks very helpful.' 'I don't know about helpful, though it's certainly got lots of details about the words: it's just that it's all too difficult for me to understand.'*

12 **I don't know, I'm sure** I don't understand what is happening: said with an impatient tone: ▷ *'What's this country coming to?—I don't know, I'm sure!'*

13 **I don't know that** I think that is not really true: ▷ *'Tom's quite a good friend, isn't he?' 'I don't know that—he's never helped me much.'*

14 **I knew it** I was sure this would happen: ▷ *'I knew it! As soon as I left the room, you stopped working!'*

15 **I know the feeling** *see* **Feeling 1.**

16 **I know (what)** Used to introduce a new idea or suggestion: ▷ *'I know what, let's go and see Pat tonight.'* Also **(I) tell you what; I'll tell you what:** ▷ *'I tell you what, we'll have a cheap holiday and stay at home this year—that'll save us some money.'* ▷ *'Tell you what,'* I said to encourage her, *'let's go and watch a film.'*

17 **I (you, etc.) wouldn't know** As is to be expected, I am (you are, etc.) not in a position to know: sometimes used to show scorn: ▷ *'Is this the way to the station?' 'I'm sorry, I wouldn't know—I'm a stranger here myself.'* ▷ *'Of course you wouldn't know what it was like spending all day at home doing the housework, would you?'*

18 **I'd have you know** Used to add emphasis to a statement, and also often to contradict what has just been said: ▷*'The car doesn't look too clean, does it?' 'I'd have you know I've just spent an hour washing it!'*

19 **Knowing you (him, etc.)** Because I am familiar with your (his, etc.) real character, I am sure that: ▷ *'Knowing Shirley, she'll be late.'* Also **If I know you (him, etc.); You know**

what he (it, etc.**) is:** ▷ *'If I know the weather, it'll rain on sports day—it does every year.'* ▷ *'You know what Perry is, he always has some excuse for missing a French test.'*

20 Not if I know it *see* **Help 3.**

21 **That's all you know (about it)** You are more ignorant about it than you think: ▷ *'Pete's started to go out with my sister!'* *'That's all you know about it! It's been going on for weeks!'*

22 **There's no knowing (or telling)** No one can say: ▷ *'There's no knowing what we could do to help, if we had more money.'* ▷ *'You'd better take your boots with you. There's no telling how deep the snow will be if it keeps falling like this.'*

23 **Well, what do you know (about that)!** An expression of surprise: ▷ *'I've been to America for the weekend!' 'Well, what do you know!'* Sometimes written: *Well, what d'you know!* This phrase is American in origin.

24 **You don't know when you're well-off** You are more fortunate than you realise: ▷ *'You don't know when you're well-off. You've got a good job, a house, a colour television; just think of what the rest of the world has got compared with you!'* Also **You don't know you're alive** (or **born**): ▷ *'Why are you moaning? You've passed your exams, got into college, and you're doing pretty well—you don't know you're alive!'*

25 **You know**

a An expression used while the speaker is thinking about what to say next or about what has already been said: ▷ *'I sort of kept asking myself, you know, if only Karen hadn't married Derek, what might have happened . . .'* ▷ *'Then this car came along, you know, and well, just knocked her over.'* ▷ *'Paul started off the game well enough, you know, he scored a goal in the opening minutes.'*

b An expression used to introduce a suggestion, to make it seem less strong: ▷ *'You know, I think we should be going.'* ▷ *'You know, we could always try the other supermarket down the road.'*

c An expression used to add emphasis to part of what is said: ▷ *'You'll have to work harder, you know, if you want to pass your exams.'* Also **Do you know:** ▷ *'Do you know, that's the sixth time this morning that the phone has rung.'* ▷ *'Do you know, I think I will go to her party after all, in spite of the way she's treated me.'* The stress in both these phrases falls on *know*.

d An expression used to make what the speaker is saying less definite: ▷ *'I think it's more or less a crime, you know, to kill those seals.'*

e An expression used to remind the hearer of something he already knows or should know: ▷*'How can a chap like me get another job? I'm over fifty-five, you know.'* ▷*'Which book are you talking about?' 'You know, the one you borrowed from the library last week.'*

f An expression used to introduce an explanation or a subject which the speaker assumes is known by the hearer: ▷ *'You know the road going up the hill? Well, the post office is up there on the right.'* ▷ *'You know the difference between a gorilla and an ape? Well, which one's that, then?'*

26 **You know something** (or **what**)? Used to introduce something that the speaker thinks important: ▷ *'You know what? I've never told you this before, but this is my second marriage.'*

27 **You know what you can do with . . .** *Slang* A rude expression indicating contempt towards (someone or something): ▷ *'I'm fed up with your Aunt Agatha! You know what you can do with her!'* ▷ *'Your pen never works! You know what you can do with it!'*

28 **You never know** Things in the future are uncertain; perhaps: ▷ *'Do you think you'll be able to come and stay with us in Malaysia sometime?' 'You never know! My firm might give me a job there!'* Also **You never can tell**: ▷ *'You'd better take an umbrella; you never can tell if it's going to rain.'*

29 **You never know your luck** *see* **Luck 11**.

l

Lady

1 **Ladies and gentlemen** An expression used to address a meeting of adults of both sexes: ▷ *'Ladies and gentlemen, we welcome to our gathering tonight Miss Jane Hunt, President of the local horticultural society.'* ▷ *'Before your very eyes, ladies and gentlemen, these rabbits will disappear as I say these magic words.'*

2 **Ladies first** An expression used by a polite man who wants to allow a woman to go through a door before him: ▷ *'Ladies first,'* said Mr Harrington, holding the door open for Mrs Giles.

3 **Your good lady** *Chiefly humorous* Your wife: ▷ *'How's your good lady?'* Also **Your (good) lady wife.**

Lake

Go (and) jump in the (or a) lake! Go away!: used when you are very annoyed with someone: ▷ *'How dare you speak to me like that!' 'Go and jump in a lake!'*

Landing

Happy landings! *Old-fashioned* An expression used when drinking with others; good health.

Large

By and large *see* **Whole.**

Last

Last but not least Used to introduce an important item that comes last in a list: ▷ *'The group included Harriet, June, and last but not least, Avril.'*

Laugh

1 **Don't make me laugh!** I don't believe you for one moment; what you're saying is ridiculous: used with a rather critical or even scornful tone: ▷ *'Did I tell you I'm going to buy a brand new sports car?' 'Don't make me laugh! You've not got enough money for your bus fare into town!'*

2 **Have** (or **get**) **the last laugh** To be successful at the end of a competition, etc., or be proved right in the end: ▷ *'Everyone made fun of John's invention, but he's had the last laugh—think of the money he's made out of it!'*

3 **You're** (or **you'll be**) **laughing!** You will be in a fortunate position, with no further worries: ▷ *'If you get that amount of money for your new job in Saudi, you're laughing!'*

Lay

1 **Lay it on (thick)** To exaggerate, often when you are praising: ▷ *'I know you think he's a good musician, but there's no need to lay it on.'* Also **Pile it on (thick).**

2 **Lay off!** Stop being annoying!; leave alone!; stop!: ▷ *'Lay off me, will you!'* ▷ *'Lay off or I'll hit you!'* ▷ *'You'll have to lay off smoking or it will kill you.'*

Least

To say the least *see* **Put 3.**

Leave

1 **Leave it at that** To say or do nothing more; take a matter no further: ▷ *'I think I've given you a strong enough warning; we'll leave it at that for the moment.'* ▷ *'Let's leave it at that; we've worked hard enough today.'*

2 **Leave off!** Stop!: ▷ *'Leave off doing that, will you?'* ▷ *'Leave off interrupting me whenever I'm talking!'*

3 I must love you and leave you *see* **Love 3.**

4 Take it or leave it *see* **Take 8.**

Leg

1 **Not have a leg to stand on** To have no reasons, defence, or other support for an opinion or action: ▷ *'Some friends of mine saw you take the watches so you haven't got a leg to stand on.'*

2 **Shake** (or **show**) **a leg!** *Slang* Hurry up!: ▷ *'Shake a leg, there! We've got to get this work done soon, you know!'*

Less

Less of . . . Stop (something): ▷ *'Less of your cheek, young man!'* Also **Less of that** (or **it**)!; **None of . . .:** ▷ *'We'll have none of that sort of thing in this class, thank you!'*

Liberty

What a liberty!   An expression used when someone does something improper or rude: ▷ *'What a liberty! He's taken my car without even asking my permission!'* ▷ *'Who does she think she is? She just walked past me without even saying a word! What a liberty!'*

Lie

I tell a lie   An expression used to correct what the speaker has just said: ▷ *'I saw him yesterday—no, I tell a lie—it was the day before.'*

Life

1 **For dear life**   With great force, as if despairing: used when something is important or urgent: ▷ *'He ran for dear life away from the scene of the crime.'* ▷ *'When the horse began to gallop, she held on to the reins for dear life.'*

2 **For the life of me (him,** etc.)   Though trying very hard: ▷ *'I can't for the life of me remember her name.'*

3 **It's a dog's life**   It's a life full of unhappiness and worries: ▷ *'It's a dog's life running a small business—no holidays, so many forms to fill in, little money in the end—I sometimes wonder why I bother.'*

4 **Not (or never) on your life!**   Most certainly not!: ▷*'Would you ever think of disobeying a commanding officer?' 'Not on your life!'* ▷ *'Surely you'd like to be our new representative for the Arctic region, John?' 'Never on your life!'* Also *(slang, old-fashioned, British)* **Not on your nelly!:** ▷ *'Do you really expect me to believe that excuse?' 'Not on your nelly!'* *Nelly* is short for *Nelly Duff,* which is rhyming slang for *puff,* itself a slang word for *life.*

5 **Run for your life!** *see* **Run.**

6 **That's life!**   That's the way things happen!; ▷ *'It's a pity Colin and Rowena got divorced, but then that's life!'* A translation of the French *c'est la vie!*

7 **This is the life!**   An expression of contentment with one's present state: ▷ *'A sandy beach, plenty of hot sun, lots of nice people! This is the life!'* The phrase dates from the early 1900s and became more current in World War I.

8 **To save his (her,** etc.**) life**   Despite every attempt or consideration: ▷ *'He couldn't play cricket to save his life.'*

9 **Upon my life!**   *Old-fashioned* Used to express surprise or to strengthen a statement or command: ▷ *'Upon my life, I didn't realise how stubborn you could be!'* ▷ *'Upon my life, we were lucky to come out of that crash with only a few cuts!'*

10 **What a life!** An expression of discontent: ▷ *'What a life! I get up at half-past five every day, work solidly for eight hours, come home, have my meal and go to bed. It's all so monotonous!'*

11 **You (can) bet your life** *see* **Bet 4.**

Light
Strike a light! *see* **Strike.**

Like
1 **I (we, etc.) should** (or **would**) **like to** I (we, etc.)want to: ▷ *'I should like to thank you very much for coming to speak to us this evening, Miss James.'* ▷ *'Would you like to drink a cup of coffee yet?'*

2 **I'd like to see . . .** I'd be surprised if (something actually happened): used to express impatience: ▷ *'If he thinks he's so smart, I'd like to see him come round and mend this bike; I can't.'*

3 **If you like**
a If you do not want anything else: used to express agreement with or approval of a suggestion: ▷ *'I'd thought of asking Julie to give me some driving practice. What do you think she'd say?' 'I'll ask her, if you like.'*

b An expression used to emphasise a statement: ▷ *'I may be mean with money, if you like, but my wife certainly isn't.'* In this sense, the stress falls on *like*.

c If I may express this in a rather strange way: ▷ *'This is our house, if you like, but we've not yet made it into our home.'*

4 **That's more like it!** That is better; that is nearer what is needed: used to express satisfaction that things have improved or that what was wanted has actually happened: ▷ *'I got sixty per cent in my history test this week.' 'That's more like it! That's a lot more than you've had recently.'*

5 **(Well) I like that!** An expression showing annoyance, dislike, or surprise: ▷ *'I said this department store wouldn't have what we were looking for!' 'Well, I like that! It was you who suggested that we come here!'* The stress falls on *like*.

Likely

1   A likely story! *see* **Story 1.**

2   **Not likely**   Certainly not; that is impossible: ▷ *'Would you be willing for your name to be put forward as chairman of the committee?' Pete asked. 'What, me? Not likely!' Bob exclaimed and walked out of the room.*

Limit

The (absolute) limit *see* **End 2.**

Line

1   **All** (or **right**) **down** (or **along**) **the line** Completely; in every part: ▷ *The politician supported the government's actions all down the line.*

2   Hard lines! *see* **Luck 1.**

Lip

My lips are sealed   I will not say anything about it: ▷ *'OK—it's a secret, remember—don't tell anyone!' 'Right, my lips are sealed!'*

Live

1   **As I live (and breathe)**   *Old-fashioned*

a   An expression of surprise: ▷ *'As I live and breathe, if it isn't Josh Harrington! I've not seen you for years!'*

b   An expression of firmness or boldness: ▷ *'As I live and breathe, this will be the last time I come through these gates again!'*

2   **Long live . . .**   May (someone or something) live or last a long time: an expression of loyalty, but sometimes used in a humorous way: ▷ *'Long live the Queen!'* ▷ *'Long live the party!'* ▷ *'Long live anarchy!'*

3   **You've (he's, etc.) not** (or **never**) **lived**   You (he, etc.) have not really known life to the full: used in connection with a particular experience, place, or person: ▷ *'You've never flown in an aeroplane before? You've never lived!'* ▷ *'You've not lived until you've seen the Niagara Falls—they're magnificent!'* ▷ *'She'd not lived before she met him.'*

Lively

Look lively! *see* **Look 5.**

Lo

Lo and behold! *Often humorous* An expression of surprise at the appearance of an unexpected person or thing: ▷ *'I'd just come in, when, lo and behold, your old friend Mandy came to the door!'*

Load

1 **Get a load of this!** *Slang* Listen to this!; look at this!: ▷ *'Get a load of this—it's the new record I've just bought!'*

2 **What a load of (old) cobblers!** *Slang, British, old-fashioned* What nonsense!: ▷ *'Our car goes much faster than yours!' 'What a load of old cobblers! Ours will beat yours anyday!'* Often shortened to *Cobblers!*

Loaf

Use your loaf! *Slang* Be sensible; show some common sense: ▷*'Use your loaf! Can't you be more tactful?'* *Loaf* is from *loaf of bread,* which is rhyming slang for *head.*

Long

1 **As broad as it is long** *see* **Broad.**

2 **So long** Goodbye until we next meet: used between friends: ▷ *'So long, Tom! See you next week!'* ▷ *'I'm going now, but I'll be back again tomorrow. So long!'*

Look

1 **Be looking for a fight** (or **trouble**) To behave in such a way that may provoke an offensive or violent response: ▷ *'Are you looking for a fight?' 'No!' 'Then shut up!'* ▷ *Three youths were going round the streets late at night—you could tell from their faces that they were looking for trouble.* Also **Be spoiling for a fight.**

2 **It's** (or **that's**) **your** (**his,** etc.) (**own**) **look-out** That is something that you (he, etc.) alone is responsible for: ▷ *'If you don't do any revision for the exams, it's your own look-out.'* ▷ *'That's her look-out, cycling without any lights at night.'*

3 **Look after yourself!** Take care!; said when saying goodbye to someone: ▷ *'Look after yourself, Julia!' 'Yes, I will, thanks. Cheerio.'*

4 **Look here!** An expression used to introduce a complaint, warning, or suggestion: ▷ *'Look here, young man, I've had* *about enough of all this noise; now turn that radio down, or I'll report you.'* ▷ *'Look here, why don't we go to Blackpool for the day? We've got some money and I've always wanted to see the lights.'* Also **See here!**: ▷ *'Now see here! I won't have you speaking to my daughter like that! Apologise at once!'*

5 **Look lively** (or **smart**)! Be quick; hurry up!: ▷ *'Look lively—teacher's coming!'* ▷ *'You'll just catch the bus if you look smart.'*

6 **Look out!** Be careful; take care!: used as a warning: ▷*'Look out, Colin, that ladder's not secure.'* Also used on a grander scale: ▷ *'Look out world, here I come!'* the great stunt man used to cry as he performed his daring acts. ▷ *'Look out, prime minister, these new parties mean business!'*

7 **Look sharp!** *see* **Sharp 1.**

8 **Look what you've done!** An expression of mild rebuke: ▷ *'Look what you've done! You've woken baby up after we've spent an hour trying to get him to go to sleep.'*

9 **Look who's talking!** *see* **Talk 4b.**

10 **Look you!** Pay attention to what I am saying!: ▷ *'Look you, take my advice, or you'll regret what you're about to do.'*

Lord

1 **Good Lord!** *see* **Good 7.**

2 **Oh Lord!** *see* **God 17.**

3 **(The) Lord knows** *see* **Know 8.**

Lorry

It (or they) fell off the back of a lorry *Euphemistic* It was (or they were) stolen: ▷ *'Where did you get those coats from?' 'Oh, they just fell off the back of a lorry!'* Also in the form of a question *Did it fall off the back of a lorry?*

Lose

1 **Get lost!** *see* **Lost.**

2 **What you lose on the swings you gain on the roundabouts** *see* **Swing.**

Loss

. . . is a dead loss (Someone or something) is very bad or useless: ▷ *'You're a dead loss, I must say, coming now that I've finished all the work.'*

Lost

Get lost! *Slang* Go away! stop annoying me (us, etc.)!: ▷ *'Get lost, I'm trying to work!'*

Lot

1 **A fat lot . . .** Very little; none at all: ▷ *'A fat lot of good you are!'* ▷*'He gave us a pat on the back. That's a fat lot of encouragement. His time and money are more important to us than his words!'* ▷ *'Have you read Roland's book?' 'Roland's written a book? A fat lot he knows about anything!'*

2 **A (fat) lot you care!** *see* **Care 1**.

3 **That's your (or the) lot** You have had all you are going to have; there is no more; this is the end: ▷ *'Well, that's the lot for today—I'm off home now.'* ▷ *'Well, that's your lot. I've checked all the lists for you and the total amount is correct.'*

Love

1 **For the love of God (or Mike)** *Old-fashioned* An expression used to add strength to a question, request, etc.: ▷ *'Where for the love of God are my keys? I can never find them when I want them!'* ▷ *'For the love of Mike, stop complaining, and get on and do some work!'* *Mike* comes from *St Michael*.

2 **I love you, too!** An expression used to show displeasure at something that someone has said or done that is unkind: ▷ *'I'll have my meal now and you can wait for yours!' 'I love you, too!'* ▷ *'You're absolutely hopeless, aren't you!' 'I love you, too!'*

3 **I must love you and leave you** I have to go now: ▷ *'Time's getting on—I must love you and leave you!' 'OK; see you next week!'*

4 **My love** A way of addressing one's husband or wife, or very close friend: ▷ *'You are beautiful, my love!'* ▷ *'My love, shall we go out for a meal on Saturday?'*

Luck

1 **Bad luck!** An expression of sympathy about someone's misfortune: ▷ *'Bad luck! How awful that you didn't pass the exam!'* Also **Hard luck!**; **Tough luck!**; **Hard lines!** *(British, old-fashioned)*: ▷ *'I've just heard they're not picking me for the football team.' 'Hard luck!'*

2 **Better luck next time** I'm sorry that you didn't do well this time and wish you success when you try again: ▷ *'Sorry to* *hear you failed your driving test, Harry. Better luck next time!'*

3 **For luck** To be lucky: sometimes offered as the supposed reason for doing something extra: ▷ *'I used to put a little coin in my handkerchief for luck before I took an exam.'* ▷ *'I've already eaten two pieces of cake, but I think I'll have another one for luck!'*

4 **Good luck!**

a I wish you well: ▷ *'Good luck, Andy!' my friends all shouted as the train pulled out.* ▷ *'Good luck to you at college!'*

b An expression used before drinking: ▷ *Mary raised her glass, 'Good luck!' she said.*

5 **It's the luck of the draw** You must take things as they come: ▷ *'I wish I hadn't been chosen to be in John's team!'* *'You'll just have to accept it—it's the luck of the draw!'*

6 **Just my (his, etc.) luck!** This is typical of my (his, etc.) misfortune: ▷ *'Just my luck! The day I wanted to travel by train was the day of the national rail strike.'* ▷ *'Just our luck to choose a hotel that was still only half built when we arrived!'*

7 **No such luck** Unfortunately not: ▷ *'Can you take this Saturday off to help me move some furniture?'* *'No such luck—I'm sorry but I've got to work.'*

8 **Some people have all the luck!** *see* **People.**

9 **With any luck** An expression showing hope: ▷ *'With any luck we should be there by two o'clock.'* Alternatives to *any* are *a bit of* and *a little bit of*: ▷ *'With a little bit of luck I'll have finished the painting this afternoon.'*

10 **Worse luck** Unfortunately: ▷ *'Do you know Robert Hampshire?'* *'Yes, I have met him before, worse luck.'*

11 **You never know your luck** You may be lucky: ▷ *'Let's have another go on the space invader! I may beat you this time!'* *'You never know your luck!'*

Lucky

1 **Who's the lucky girl (or man), then?** Who have you just become engaged to?: an expression used on hearing that someone has got engaged: ▷ *'Who's the lucky man, then, Cathy?'*

2 **You should be so lucky!** Why ever should something as good as that happen to you!: used as a humorous reply: ▷ *'When I got there I thought you were going to give me some money.'* *'You should be so lucky!'*

3 **You'll be lucky!** Good luck; I wish you well: used when the speaker doubts whether something will really happen: ▷ *'I'm going to ask the manager for a pay rise.' 'You'll be lucky! At the moment the firm hasn't any extra money for its employees!'*

m

Mackerel

Holy mackerel! *see* **Holy.**

Mad

Like mad   Very fast: very much: ▷ *'We ran like mad away from the scene of the explosion.'*

Make

1   As . . . as they make 'em   Used to express an extreme degree of quality of someone or something, usually of bad characteristics: ▷ *'Your new girlfriend's as cheeky as they make 'em, isn't she?'* In this phrase *'em* is almost always used instead of *them.* Also **As . . . as they come:** ▷ *'That chap's as stupid as they come.'*

2   Don't make me laugh! *see* **Laugh 1.**

3   It makes you go blind   An expression used humorously to describe the results of over-indulgent actions: ▷ *'I wouldn't drink too much, if I were you—it makes you go blind, you know!'*

4   Make it snappy!   *Slang* Be quick!: ▷ *'Pie and chips, please, and make it snappy: I'm in a hurry!'*

5   Make no bones (or mistake) about it!   Do not doubt this at all; this is certainly true: used to emphasise a statement or promise expressed plainly and directly: ▷ *'Make no bones about it, my boy, I'm going to see you're punished properly this time!'* ▷ *'Make no mistake about it, you're bound to have an accident if you drive so fast down the motorway.'* ▷ *'I shall be coming back, make no mistake about it!'*

6   Make yourself at home! *see* **Home 3.**

7   That makes two of us!   The same applies to me; that is true of me, too: ▷ *'I'm going up to Birmingham University in October!' 'That makes two of us—I am as well!'*

Man

1   Be a man!   Act in a manly way: used especially to emphasise such qualities as a brave or independent spirit: ▷ *'Be a man! You can beat him easily!'* ▷ *'Go on, be a man, accept the bet!'*

2 **Go man, go!** An expression of encouragement: ▷ *'You can beat Perry—go man, go!'* Originally, from the language of American jazz.

3 **I'm** (or **he's**) **your man** I am (or he is) the person needed to do that particular job: ▷ *'I'm your man! I'll accept that offer and start immediately!'* ▷ *'If you want any plumbing work done, then he's your man.'*

4 **Man alive!** An exclamation showing amazement, surprise, or pleasure: ▷ *'Man alive! What are you doing here?'*

5 **May the best man win!** An expression wishing that the better or best person in a group might be the successful one: ▷ *'I'd like to wish you every success!' 'Thank you, and may the best man win!'*

6 **My good man** An offensive expression used to show that the speaker thinks he is more important than the man he is speaking to: ▷ *'Look here, my good man! How dare you speak to me like that!'*

7 **Oh man!** *Slang* An exclamation expressing excitement, surprise, pleasure, etc.: ▷ *'Oh man, was I pleased to see her!'* ▷ *'Oh man, you really get on my nerves, you know!'*

8 **Old man** *see* **Boy 2.**

9 **Who's the lucky man, then?** *see* **Lucky 1.**

10 **You can't keep a good man down** A saying that you can't stop a man with firm, determined intentions from doing what he wants: sometimes used ironically: ▷ *'I hear Bill's company have launched yet another new product.' 'Yes—you can't keep a good man down!'*

Marine

Tell it (or **that**) **to the marines!** *Old-fashioned* I don't believe what has just been said: ▷ *'I've just been to tea at Buckingham Palace!' 'Tell that to the marines!'* The phrase comes from the fact that at one time marines were thought to be stupid by regular sailors, and therefore likely to believe something obviously foolish.

Mark

1 Mark you *see* **Mind 12.**

2 On your mark(s), (get) set, go! *see* **Ready 1.**

Matter

1 As a matter of fact *see* **Fact.**

2   For that matter *see* **Fact b.**

3   **No matter!**   It is not important: ▷ *'I've just broken one of your mugs!' 'No matter! They were only cheap ones!'*

4   **No matter how (who, what,** etc.)   It makes no difference how (who, what, etc.): ▷ *'No matter who phones, say I'm not in.'* ▷ *'No matter how hard I try, I still can't do crossword puzzles.'* ▷ *'I'm going tomorrow, no matter what.'*

5   **What matter?**   That need not worry or upset us: ▷ *'What matter if there's a strike, we'll muddle through somehow.'*

6   **What's the matter?**   What is wrong?; what is causing you trouble or pain?: ▷ *'What's the matter with you?' 'Nothing.'* ▷ *'What's the matter with her this morning? She's so grumpy with everyone.'* ▷ *'What's the matter with having a good time once in a while?'*

May

May I (we, etc.**) . . .?**   Used in making a polite request or asking for permission: ▷ *'May I come in for a minute, please?' 'Yes, of course you can.'* ▷ *'May I make a suggestion? Why don't we vote now rather than continuing the discussion further?'*

Maybe

That's as maybe! *see* **That 13.**

Mean

1   **And I don't mean maybe**   *Chiefly American* I mean exactly what I say: ▷ *'I want this work done for ten this evening, and I don't mean maybe!'*

2   Do you mean to say? *see* **Say 4.**

3   Do you see what I mean? *see* **See 3.**

4   **I mean**   An expression used to keep the attention of a listener, and making a slight pause; often the speaker wants to clarify what has just been said or give additional information, and rephrases the sentence: ▷ *'It's no good just saying we're suffering from the recession. I mean, the people we do business with are only interested in seeing our products.'* ▷ *'To rehearse for the concert . . ., I mean . . . we had to play for two hours.'*

5   I mean (to say) *see* **Say 11.**

6   I see what you mean *see* **See 5.**

7   **What do you mean by . . .?**   What is the purpose of (doing something)?: used to ask the reasons or justification for some behaviour; sometimes said in an annoyed tone: ▷ *'What do you mean by getting me up in the middle of the night?'* ▷ *'What do you mean by that? Please explain, as I'd like to know!'*

Means

1 **By all means**   Certainly; yes; of course: ▷ *'Can we come aboard?' 'By all means! You're most welcome!'* ▷ *'By all means use my name when you apply for the job.'*

2 **By no means**   Not at all: ▷ *'That's by no means the last you've heard of this.'*

Meet

1 **Pleased (or glad) to meet you!**   An expression used as a reply in an introduction of one person to another: ▷ (Robert talking to William) *'William, I'd like you to meet Mr Jones.'* (William to Mr Jones) *'Pleased to meet you, Mr Jones.'* (Mr Jones to William) *'Pleased to meet you!'* ▷ (Colin talking to John) *'How do you do, John.'* (John to Colin) *'Glad to meet you, Colin!'*

2 **Until (or till) we meet again!**   *Rather formal or literary* An expression used when saying goodbye to someone: ▷ *'Until we meet again, farewell!'* Also *(more informal)* **Until (or till) the next time!**

Memory

If my memory serves me right . . .   If I am remembering (something) correctly: ▷ *'If my memory serves me right, Harold Wilson became Prime Minister in 1964.'*

Mention

1 **Don't mention it!**   *Polite* There is no need to thank me or apologise: ▷ *'Thanks so much for lending me your typewriter!' 'Don't mention it!'* ▷ *'I'm so sorry I trod on your toe!' 'Oh, don't mention it!'*

2 **I hate to mention it, but . . .**   A polite expression used to draw attention to (something that the person being spoken to has, perhaps deliberately, forgotten or not noticed): ▷ *'I hate to mention it, but what about the money you owe me?'* Also **If you don't mind my mentioning it**: ▷ *'If you don't mind my mentioning it, your tie isn't quite straight.'*

3 **Not to mention . . .** To say nothing of (something very obvious that it only needs to be named); in addition: ▷ *'It was an awful hotel, with poor meals, hopeless service, not to mention the noise outside.'* Also **To say nothing of . . .**

Mercy
For mercy's sake! *see* **Goodness 1.**

Might
Might I (you, etc.**) . . .?** Used in making a request or asking permission for something: ▷ *'Might I be able to leave a little earlier tonight, please?'* ▷ *'Might it not be helpful to look at last year's figures and compare them with this year's?'* This is rather more hesitant than *may.*

Mike
For the love of Mike *see* **Love 1.**

Mild
To put it mildly *see* **Put 3.**

Milk
Get off and milk it! *see* **Get 9.**

Mind
1 **Do (or would) you mind . . .?** Used in making a polite request: ▷ *'Do you mind if I smoke?' 'No, that's quite all right.'* ▷ *'Would you mind opening the window, please?' 'Yes, it is a bit hot in here, isn't it?'* Also **Would you . . .?** ▷ *'Would you be quiet a moment, please?'*

2 **Do you mind!** Please stop that!: used to show annoyance when one has been offended: ▷ *'Do you mind! That's my parking space you've taken!'*

3 **Don't mind me (him**, etc.**)**

a Don't pay any attention to or worry about me (him, etc.): ▷ *'Just carry on working! Don't mind her!'* ▷ *'Don't mind me—I can manage quite well while you're away!'*

b An expression used when one is annoyed at someone's rudeness, thoughtlessness, or when one thinks one is not being fairly treated: ▷ *'Don't mind me, will you? I just type your letters, make you drinks, wait on you hand and foot, and you pay me next to nothing for all this!'*

4   **Great minds think alike**   *Humorous* An expression used to praise oneself when two people both have the same idea, opinion, etc.: ▷ *'Let's go to Brighton this afternoon!' 'Great minds think alike—I was just about to suggest that myself!'* A common reply to this phrase is *Fools seldom differ.*

5   **(I) don't mind if I do**   Yes, I would like that, thank you: ▷ *'Have another cake.' 'Thank you. I don't mind if I do.'*

6   **I wouldn't mind . . .**   Used in making a polite request: ▷ *'I wouldn't mind a nice cup of tea.' 'All right, I'll go and make one for you.' 'Thank you.'*

7   **If you don't mind my mentioning it** *see* **Mention 2.**

8   **If you don't (or won't) mind**   An expression used in making a request or command: ▷ *'Please wait over there, if you don't mind.'* ▷ *'If you won't mind, I'll see you in a few minutes.'*

9   **It's all in the mind**   What is happening to you is all in the imagination: ▷ *'I think Jane's in love with me!' 'It's all in the mind!'* ▷ *'I feel awful with this stomach ache.' 'It's all in the mind; you're perfectly all right really.'*

10   **Mind how you go**   Take care of yourself!; be careful: often used when saying goodbye: ▷ *'Mind how you go! See you next week!'*

11   **Mind (out)!**   Be careful: ▷ *'Mind out! Don't go too near the edge!'* ▷ *'Mind! The plate's hot!'*

12   **Mind (you)**   Note what I'm saying: an expression used to qualify, disagree with, or emphasise something that has just been said: ▷ *'Our baby's very sweet, but mind you, we do have a lot of nappies to wash.'* ▷ *'I wouldn't help everyone, mind.'* Also **Mark you.**

13   **Mind your back(s)!** *see* **Back 4.**

14   **Mind your head(s)!** *see* **Head 2.**

15   **Mind your own business!** *see* **Business 2.**

16   **Mind your step!** *see* **Step 1.**

17   **Never mind**   Don't worry or be troubled about; take no notice of: ▷ *'Do what the doctor says; never mind the advice of your friends.'* ▷ *'Never mind about yesterday; it's today I'm interested in!'* ▷ *'I've hurt my finger.' 'Never mind, I'll kiss it better.'*

18   **Never you mind**   It is no concern of yours and you are not going to be told: ▷ *'Where did you two go last night?' 'Never you mind!'*

19   **The mind boggles**   I am surprised, confused, or overwhelmed (by something): ▷ *'The mind boggles at how she managed to bring up seven children by herself.'* ▷ *'Three bathrooms and seven bedrooms in that house! The mind boggles!'*

Minute

1 **. . . in a minute!** An expression used to show annoyance or anger at something that has just been said: ▷ *'Your hair needs cutting!' 'I'll cut you in a minute!'* The particular part that is found annoying is repeated before the phrase *in a minute!*

2 **Just a minute** *see* **Just 2.**

3 **There's one born every minute** *see* **Born 4.**

4 **Wait a minute** *see* **Wait 4.**

Mirror

It's all done by (or with) mirrors An expression used when something clever or ingenious has been done: ▷ *'You see that new machine I've made for brewing tea?' 'Yes, how does it work?' 'Ah! It's all done by mirrors, you know!'*

Missis

The missis My (or your) wife: ▷ *'How's the missis?'* Also **The wife.**

Mist

Scotch mist *Old-fashioned* The very thing you are talking about, that you are pretending is not there: used in stating firmly that something does in fact exist, despite the other person's ignorance or disbelief: ▷ *'I've lost my keys again!' 'What do you think these are, then? Scotch mist?'*

Mistake

1 **And no mistake** Without any doubt: used to emphasise what has just been said: ▷ *'It's boiling hot today, and no mistake!'* ▷ *'This is the biggest orange I've ever seen, and no mistake!'*

2 **Make no mistake about it!** *see* **Make 5.**

3 **There's no mistake about it!** There is no doubt about it; it is certain: ▷ *'There's no mistake about it—this is quite simply the best car on the market, sir!'*

Moment

1 Just a moment *see* **Just 2.**
2 **Never a dull moment!**   Life is so busy: an expression used in times of much action, excitement, or danger: ▷ *'As a teacher, it's all go from the moment I come into school to when I leave.' 'Yes, never a dull moment!'*
3 One moment *see* **Just 2a.**
4 Wait a moment *see* **Wait 4.**

Money

You pays your money and you takes your choice   There are a number of different ways of doing something, courses of action, or opinions, that could be followed, any of which is as good as any other: often used humorously: ▷ *'You could go to London or Manchester to study for your degree—you pays your money and you takes your choice!'* Originally, the words of a nineteenth-century rhyme.

Moon

Over the moon   Very happy and excited: ▷ *'Rosalind's over the moon about her new job!'*

More

1 **And what's more**   Used to add something to what has just been said; moreover: ▷ *'The price is too high, and what's more the style is too old-fashioned.'*
2 **More or less**   Used to make an opinion sound less strong: ▷ *'This is more or less the best book on the market on that subject.'* ▷ *'It's more or less a day's journey to see the grandchildren.'*
3 That's more like it! *see* **Like 4.**

Morning

1 Good morning *see* **Good 9.**
2 Morning all! *see* **All 14.**
3 The top of the morning (to you)! *see* **Top 2.**

Moses

Holy Moses! *see* **Holy.**

Mother

1 **Be mother**   To act as host or hostess by doing something,

especially pour out the tea: ▷ *'Who's going to be mother?'* ▷ *'I'll be mother!'*

2 **Oh mother!** *Becoming old-fashioned* An exclamation of surprise, distress, etc.: ▷ *'Oh mother! What are we going to do now?'* ▷ *'Oh mother! Those children have broken another pane of glass!'*

3 **Some mothers do 'ave 'em!** An expression used when someone has made a silly or foolish mistake or blunder: ▷ *'Trust Jim to be so clumsy! Some mothers do 'ave 'em!'* The phrase was made popular by a television comedy series, *Some Mothers Do 'Ave 'Em*, which began in 1974. Also **We've got a right one 'ere.**

4 **Who's she? The cat's mother?** *see* **Cat 3.**

Mouth

Shut your mouth! *see* **Shut.**

Move

Get a move on! Hurry up!: ▷ *'Get a move on or you'll miss the bus!'*

Much

1 **It's a bit much** Your expectations are too high: ▷ *'It's a bit much that you want this shirt now, when you know I've not done the ironing.'* ▷ *'You come in late and want your dinner immediately—it really is a bit much, you know!'*

2 **So much for . . .** This is now the end of (an idea): used when finishing talking about something, and often said in a resigned tone: ▷ *'So much for my idea of going to town. It's snowing hard again, so we'd better stay in.'*

3 **Too much** *Slang, chiefly American* Used to express the speaker's enjoyment of or delight at something: ▷ *'This music's too much, man!'*

Mud

1 **Here's mud in your eye!** *Old-fashioned* An expression used when taking a drink with other people: originally, referring to the muddy conditions of the soldiers fighting in Flanders in World War I.

2 **(It's) as clear as mud** *Humorous* What you have said is not at all clear: ▷ *'Is my explanation clear?' 'Yes, as clear as mud, thanks!'*

Muggins

Muggins here *Slang, British* A way of referring to oneself: ▷ *'Go on, you go out and enjoy yourselves, while muggins here stays at home and does all the work!'* ▷ *'Who's going to do the washing-up?' 'Muggins here, I suppose, as usual!'* Muggins was probably originally a surname.

Mum

Mum's the word Don't say anything to anyone: ▷ *'I don't want her to know about the present till Christmas Day!' 'OK! Mum's the word!'* Mum comes from the sound made when one's lips are closed.

Murgatroyd

Heavens to Murgatroyd! *see* **Heaven 8.**

Music

Face the music To have to meet the unpleasant effects that your own actions have brought about: ▷ *'Joe was caught taking Petra's bike, and now he's got to face the music.'*

My

1 **My, my!** An expression of surprise, pleasure, etc.: ▷ *'My, my! How nice to see you again after all these years!'* ▷ *'My, my! Who's grown so much, then? You're a big boy now, aren't you?'*

2 **Oh my!** An expression of surprise, disbelief, or annoyance: ▷ *'Oh my, it must be all of five years since we last saw you!'* ▷ *'Oh my, when are you going to turn that radio down?'*

n

Name

1   **In heaven's name** *see* **Heaven 9.**

2   **. . . is my middle name**   I am noted for my (characteristic): often used in humorous contexts: ▷ *'I gave a good speech tonight!' 'Modest, aren't you?' 'Yes, modesty is my middle name!'*

3   **. . . or my name's not. . .**   I'm certain of (something): ▷ *'I'll do that for you immediately, sir, or my name's not Peter Perkins!'*

4   **Take my (your, etc.) name in vain**   *Humorous* To mention my (your, etc.) name to someone else, sometimes disrespectfully, without that person's knowledge: ▷ *'Yes, when we came to discussing the photographs, I heard them taking your name in vain.'* ▷ *'Hello, Ken!' Pete called out. Ken turned round to see who it was and said, 'I thought I heard my name being taken in vain!'* Originally, *take God's name in vain,* to use the name of God without proper reverence.

5   **The name of the game**   *Slang* The main point: ▷ *'The name of the game in this business is speed—if we can get our offer to the client before everyone else, then we're more likely to get the contract.'*

6   **What name shall I say?**   What is your name?: used at reception desks, on the telephone, etc.: ▷ *'I'll put you through to Mr Longfield. What name shall I say?'*

7   **What's in a name?**   It is not what a thing is called that matters, its character or quality is far more important. From *Romeo and Juliet,* by William Shakespeare, Act 1, Scene 4.

8   **You name it**   Whatever you need, mention, etc.: ▷ *'This is one of the best-stocked department stores in the country. You name it, we'll have it!'* ▷ *'Pete's an expert on films: you name it, he's seen it!'*

Nameless

    . . ., who shall be (or remain) nameless   An expression used when you don't want to mention someone's name although you know it: used when someone has done something wrong or when you don't want to embarrass them: ▷ *'And*

someone, who shall remain nameless, broke that window!'
Also . . ., without mentioning any names.

Nature

Nature calls   I must go to the lavatory: ▷ *'Sorry, nature calls, I must leave you for a moment.'* Also **Answer** (or **obey**) **the call of nature:** ▷ *'I must answer the call of nature—I'll be back in a minute.'*

Naughty

Naughty, naughty!   An expression used to show annoyance or impatience when criticising a child: ▷ *'Naughty, naughty, Eric—why did you have to empty all your toys out of the box?'* Also used humorously to show disapproval of something: ▷ *'Naughty, naughty! We know what you two are up to!'*

Need

That's all I needed!   This is the last thing I wanted!; this is the worst thing in a series of bad events or circumstances: ▷ *'What a day it's been—Rod had an accident on the way to school, the car's broken down, and now you say you're leaving me! That's all I needed!'* Also **That's all I need.**

Nelly

Not on your nelly! *see* **Life 4.**

Nerve

What a nerve!   What cheek or impudence!: ▷ *'What a nerve! She's the richest person I know and now she asks me if she can borrow some money!'* Also **He's (she's,** etc.) **got a nerve!; Some nerve!; The nerve of it!:** ▷ *'He's got a nerve, hasn't he, coming in here, taking my car keys off the desk without even asking!'*

Never

1   Now or never *see* **Now 3.**
2   Well I never did! *see* **Do 20.**

News

1   **I've (or we've) news for you**   I'm going to tell you something that will surprise you: ▷ *'You know we'd invited one or two friends for a small celebration drink tonight—well, we've got*

news for you—we've invited the whole class and we're all going out for a slap-up meal!'

2   **That's news to me!**   I've not heard that!; often showing some disbelief: ▷ *'Did you know Rob's just got engaged to Susie!' 'That's news to me—I thought he was going out with Sheila!'*

Next

1   **Next please!**   Ask the next question; the next person can come now, please: ▷ *'Next please,' the man behind the counter in the post office called out.* ▷ *'Thank you for raising such an interesting subject. And now, next please!'*

2   **Who's next?**   Who's got the next question?; whose turn is it next?: ▷ *'Who's next?' the chairman asked. 'Yes, I'd like to ask our speaker what he thinks about the state of the economy.'*

Night

1   **Good night** *see* **Good 10.**

2   **Night, night**   An expression used to children to wish a good night's rest: ▷ *'Night, night, darling; sleep well!'*

No

1   **I wouldn't say no** *see* **Say 16.**

2   **No, repeat, no** *see* **Repeat.**

3   **Oh no!**   An expression of sorrow at someone's misfortune, a disappointment, etc.: ▷ *'Harry's had to go back into hospital, I'm afraid.' 'Oh no, how awful—I am sorry.'* ▷ *'Oh no, that's the third time the line's engaged; how can I get in touch with him?'*

None

None of . . . *see* **Less.**

Nose

It's no skin off your nose *see* **Skin.**

Nosey

Nosey got shot!   *British school slang, old-fashioned* Don't interfere in affairs that do not concern you or you will suffer harm yourself: ▷ *'What were you saying about me to June?' 'Mind your own business! Nosey got shot!'* Often said touching the nose with one's forefinger. *Nosey* comes from *nosey parker,* a person who pries into other people's affairs; *Parker* as a surname seems to have been freely chosen.

Not

1 **Not at all!** *Polite* There is no need to thank me or apologise: ▷ *'Thank you for a lovely meal!' 'Not at all; we enjoyed having you!'* ▷ *'I'm sorry I'm a bit late.' 'Not at all—do come in!'*

2 **Not half** *see* **Half 5.**

Nothing

1 **It was (or it's) nothing** There is no need to thank me or praise me: often said in either a self-effacing or an embarrassed way: ▷ *'Thank you for all the help you've given us over the last few days— you've been tremendous!' 'It was nothing—all I've done is cook a few meals and tidy up a bit.'* ▷ *'I thought you acted the star role marvellously!' 'Oh, it was nothing, really!'*

2 **Nothing doing** *see* **Do 14.**

3 **Nothing like** *see* **Anything 3.**

4 **Nothing ventured, nothing gained** A saying that if you are not prepared to make an effort or take risks, you cannot expect to get results: ▷ *'I'm not sure whether Pete will let me borrow his motorbike.' 'Ask him—nothing ventured, nothing gained.'*

5 **Thank you for nothing** There is nothing to thank you for: used after someone has unexpectedly been snubbed or received a refusal or rebuff: ▷ *'I can't get that coat cleaned for you by tonight, I'm afraid.' 'Well, thank you for nothing!'*

6 **There's nothing for it** An expression of resignation, used when the speaker has reluctantly to do something: ▷ *'There's nothing for it—we'll just have to sell the car to pay off our debts, that's all.'*

7 **There's nothing in it**

a The story, rumour, etc., is untrue: ▷ *'Have you heard about Rob and Sheila?' 'Yes, but there's nothing in it, I'm sure!'*

b The competitors in the race are very close to each other: ▷ *'There's nothing in it as they're coming up to the last hedge!'*

8 **There's nothing to it** It really is very easy: ▷ *'This is how you ride a bike . . . You see, there's nothing to it. Now you try!'*

9   **Think nothing of it!**   *Polite* There is no need to thank me: ▷ *'Thank you very much for all your help!' 'Think nothing of it! I'd do the same for you!'* Also used to apologise when someone thinks they have been rude: ▷ *'I really am very sorry I forgot your name just now!' 'Think nothing of it—it happens to all of us!'*

10   **To say nothing of . . .** *see* **Mention 3.**

Now

1   **Now for . . .**   And now let us have, see, or concern ourselves with (something else): ▷ *'I think we've finished with that point. Now for the next item on the agenda.'*

2   **Now, now!**

a   An expression of comfort or sympathy, as to a child: ▷ *'Now, now, Harriet! It's all right! There's no need to cry!'*

b   An expression used as a warning or mild rebuke: ▷ *'Now, now, you two; don't start fighting again!'* Also **Now then:** ▷ *'Now then, stop teasing baby!'*

3   **Now or never**   This is the moment to act; if we don't act now, we never will: ▷ *'If we don't buy that car now, we never will—it's now or never!'* Also **Now for it:** ▷ *I went into the interview room with my knees shaking—'Now for it!' I thought.*

4   **Now then**   Used to arouse someone's attention to what is about to be said or to the next point in the argument: ▷ *'Now then, what's all this about?'* ▷ *'Now then, why did you want to see me?'* ▷ *'There we were, we'd climbed halfway up. Now then, it started to snow—so what do you think we did?'* Also **Right then.**

Nowhere

Nowhere near *see* **Anything 3.**

Number

Number one   A way of referring to oneself: ▷ *'I can certainly assure you I'm looking after number one all right.'*

O

Oblige

(I'm) much obliged (to you) A polite way of thanking someone for doing something: ▷ *'I'm much obliged to you for all your help!'*

Odd

Oddly enough *see* **Enough 5.**

Odds

1 **It makes no (or little) odds** It makes no (or only a little) difference: ▷ *'It makes little odds which party we vote for—nothing ever seems to change much!'* ▷ *'It makes no odds which road we take, we'll come to the same place in the end.'*

2 **What's the odds?** What does it matter?: ▷ *'What's the odds? Whatever we do, we're bound to lose money!'*

Off

1 **It's (or that's) a bit off** It's most unsatisfactory: said as a complaint: ▷ *'It's a bit off not letting us know you'd be coming on a later coach—we've been waiting around for two hours!'*

2 **Off with . . .** A request to remove something: ▷ *'Off with your coats—they're soaking wet!'*

3 **Off with his (or her) head!** *see* **Head 3.**

4 **Off with you (him, etc.)!** Go away!: ▷ *'Off with you! What are you doing here, anyway?'* Also **Be off with you!**

5 **They're off!** The horses, runners, etc., have set off!: ▷ *'They're under starter's orders . . . and they're off!'*

Oh

1 **Oh for . . .!** *see* **For.**

2 **Oh, yeah!** *see* **Yeah.**

OK

OK *see* **All 6.**

Old

Any old how Any way, especially in a careless way: ▷ *'We can paint the back of this cupboard any old how, as no one will ever see it.'*

On

1 **It's (just) not on!** This is unacceptable or unsatisfactory: often used of someone's behaviour: ▷ *'It's just not on, son, coming home so late without even ringing—your mother was worried stiff about you.'*

2 **On, on!** Go on; come on: ▷ *'On, on! The fight is not yet over!'* Sometimes used with a name: ▷ *'On, Henry, on!'*

3 **On with . . .** Let's continue (something): ▷ *'On with the show!'*

4 **You're on!** I'll accept your offer: used in making a bet or coming to an agreement: ▷ *'I bet I can get to the windmill before you!' 'Right, you're on!'* ▷ *'OK, so let's say £1000 for the car then.' 'All right, you're on!'*

Once

1 **At once** Immediately: ▷ *'Can you come and see me at once?'*

2 **Once again!** Please repeat this: ▷ *'That was fine; now, once again, "The rain in Spain falls mainly on the plain." '*

One

1 **A good one** *see* **Good 1.**

2 **. . . for one** As far as (someone) is concerned: ▷ *'I, for one, don't think it's a good idea.'* ▷ *'Who's for going to the park? Audrey, for one—anyone else?'*

3 **It's all one to me** I don't mind: used to express agreement with any of the choices offered, and often also a lack of interest in all of them: ▷ *'It's all one to me where we go—round the shops, to the museum again; I'm getting rather bored with all this sightseeing anyway.'*

4 **One for . . .** Take one spoonful for (a particular person): used to encourage children to eat their food: ▷ *'One for Auntie Julie—there, that's right! Good!'*

5 **One for the road** One more drink before going home or going on a journey: ▷ *'I think I'll be going home in a minute.' 'What about having one for the road?' 'No, thanks, I'm driving.'*

6 **One to (for,** etc.) ... The kind of person (to do something): ▷ *'He's not usually one to talk about people behind their backs, but I did hear him being rather nasty about Peter, you know.'* ▷ *'I'm not really one for eating lots of cakes, but since you insist, I think I will have another one.'*

7 **The one and only** Used in announcing or presenting an actor, singer, etc.: ▷ *'And now, ladies and gentlemen, the star of tonight's show, the one and only Rob Robertson!'*

8 **We've got a right one 'ere** *see* **Mother 3.**

Only
1 **If only** . . . *see* **If 3.**
2 **The one and only** *see* **One 7.**

Oops
Oops a daisy! *Becoming old-fashioned*
a An expression used when helping someone into or out of a car, climb over something, etc.: ▷ *'Oops a daisy . . . Are you all right? Now you're in OK; are you comfortable enough?'*
b An expression used when someone falls down, drops something, or makes a mistake: ▷ *'Oops a daisy! That was a silly thing to do, wasn't it!'*

Open
Open sesame! *Often humorous* A supposedly magical or mysterious formula used to gain entrance to something inaccessible: ▷ *He cried out, 'Open sesame!' and the rock moved aside to show a cave full of riches.* From the words used by Ali Baba in the *Arabian Nights* to open the door of the treasure cave.

Order
Order! Order! An expression called out at a formal meeting when someone has broken the rules of the running of that meeting: ▷ *'Order! Order!' the chairman shouted, trying to make himself heard above the unruly noise.*

Ought
You ought to . . . *see* **Want 2.**

Out
1 **. . ., out!** A slogan used to show disapproval of (someone)

and often seeking the removal of a leader from an official position: ▷ *'Smithson, out! Smithson, out!' the crowd all chanted as the minister drove past.*

2   **Out with it**   Say what you've got to say or what's on your mind: ▷ *'Don't just stand there! Out with it! Who won?'* ▷ *'Out with it, John! What's troubling you?'*

3   **Out you go!**   Go out!: ▷ *'Out you go, Rover!' Jim said to his dog, as he shut the door.*

Over

1   **Over and out**   The expression used at the end of a conversation on a radio transmission, etc.: ▷ *'Alice two. Will go to scene of accident. Over and out.'*

2   **Over (to you)**   You speak now; I await your reply: used in radio transmissions, etc.: ▷ *'Come in, please, over.'* Also used in wider contexts: ▷ *'We've done all we can, boys—it's now over to you to see if you can put into practice what we've been trying to teach you.'*

Owe

How much do I owe you?   How much do all these things, this service, etc., that I am buying, cost?: ▷ *'That's it—I'll take all these, please. Now how much do I owe you?'* ▷ *'Thanks for doing the roof and guttering. How much do I owe you for it all?'*

p

Pack

Pack it in (or up)! Stop what you're doing: often used when something foolish is being done: ▷ *'Pack it up, will you! You're so noisy I can't hear myself think!'* ▷ *'It's so hot in here! Let's pack it in and go home!'*

Pair

I've only one pair of hands You are asking me to do too much work: a complaint: ▷ *'Rob, could you do the washing-up, and then make a start on the housework, please?' 'Wait a minute, I've only one pair of hands, you know!'*

Pardon

(1) beg your pardon

a *Formal* I did not hear what you said exactly; I did not understand what you said: could you repeat it please: ▷ *'I beg your pardon: what did you say? I didn't catch it properly.'* Also *(informal)* **(Beg) pardon**; *(American)* **Pardon me?**

b I am sorry: ▷ *I accidentally pushed Jo as I passed her, so I said to her, 'I beg your pardon.'* Also *(informal)* **(Beg) pardon**: ▷ *Harry belched rather too loudly. 'Pardon!' he exclaimed.*

c I disagree with what you said; I think you're wrong: ▷ *'I beg your pardon, but what you're saying is really the opposite of the truth.'* Also **Pardon me.**

Part

It's all part of the service! *see* **Service 2.**

Pay

1 I wouldn't have it if you paid me! *see* **Have 5.**
2 You pays your money and you takes your choice *see* **Money.**

Pecker

Keep your pecker up! *see* **Chin.**

Peg

Bring (or take) down a peg (or two) To make someone

think they are less important: ▷ *'I'm glad Petra told him off—it's about time someone brought him down a peg or two.'*

Penny

1 **A penny for your thoughts!** What are you thinking about: said to a person who has been quiet for a long time and looking deep in thought: ▷ *'A penny for your thoughts, Martin! You've not said a word all evening!'*

2 **The penny dropped** *British* The meaning of what is being said is finally understood: ▷ *We tried to suggest that she might give us a lift home, but she didn't seem to understand. Then suddenly the penny dropped and she said, 'Can I take you home now?'*

3 **Two a penny** Very cheap or common: ▷ *'University degrees are two a penny these days.'*

People

Some people have all the luck! A saying used when someone else is fortunate, and often when the speaker has been unlucky; said in a resigned tone: ▷ *'I see Perry's got himself a new girlfriend—some people have all the luck!'*

Perish

Perish the thought! *see* **Thought 2.**

Person

1 **I'd be the first (person) to . . .** I am willing to (support some statement, decision, etc.) wholeheartedly: ▷ *'Minister, what are your views on the economy?' 'Well, I'd be the first person to admit that things aren't exactly right.'* ▷ *'I'd be the first to say we must decide on our priorities immediately.'*

2 **I'd be the last (person) to . . .** I am unwilling to (do something): ▷ *'I'd be the last person to criticise someone else for their failures.'*

Pete

For Pete's sake! *see* **Goodness 1.**

Phrase

To coin a phrase To make up an expression: but often really used with a very common or trite expression: ▷ *'To coin a phrase, we could kill two birds with one stone, by visiting friends and doing the shopping when we go there.'*

Pick

1 I've a bone to pick with you *see* **Bone 1.**

2 **Pick and choose** To choose very carefully: ▷ *'He likes to pick and choose before buying a new shirt.'*

Piece

. . . **is a piece of cake** (Something) is very easy: ▷ *'I think swimming is a piece of cake.'*

Pig

Pigs might fly A saying showing that the speaker thinks that it is highly unlikely that something will happen: ▷ *'I might get a job one day soon!' 'And pigs might fly!'* Also **If pigs could fly.**

Pile

Pile it on (thick) *see* **Lay 1.**

Pin

1 Not care (or give) two pins *see* **Damn 4.**

2 **You could hear** (or **have heard**) **a pin drop** It is (or was) extremely quiet: ▷ *'When he started to tell us about how his son died, there was a sudden hush—you could have heard a pin drop.'*

Pink

Strike me pink! *see* **Strike.**

Pip

Pip, pip! *British, old-fashioned* A cheerful greeting or expression used when saying goodbye: ▷ *'Pip, pip, old fellow!'* Perhaps originally from an imitation of the sound of a motor-car horn.

Pipe

1 **Pipe down!** Shut up; be quiet: ▷ *'Pipe down, will you, I've got my work to do!'*

2 **Put that in your pipe and smoke it!** Think about what I've said!; you'll have to accept it even though you don't like it: used after a statement that the speaker knows will be found unpleasant and said in a defiant tone: ▷ *'You can't spend any more money, as we simply haven't got any more! So you can put that in your pipe and smoke it!'*

Pity

1 For pity's sake! *see* **Goodness 1.**

2 **More's the pity** Unfortunately; that is indeed something to be sorry about: ▷ *'There's a rumour going round that they're getting divorced, and it's true, more's the pity.'*

Place

In the first place *Formal* The first reason is . . .: ▷ *'What do you think were the reasons for the war starting?' 'Well, in the first place, the people were oppressed for a long time.'*

Plague

(A) plague on you (him, etc.)! *Old-fashioned* Used to express anger or disgust at someone or something: ▷ *'A plague on you! Why do you always turn up so late?'*

Play

1 Play it by ear *see* **Ear 3.**

2 Two can play at that game *see* **Game 4.**

Please

1 If you please

a Used in making a polite request: ▷ *'Step this way, ladies and gentlemen, if you please.'*

b Used with something unreasonable or unbelievable: said with an indignant or angry tone: ▷ *'He crashed my car, and now, if you please, he expects me to pay the repair bill!'* ▷ *'I want you to do it now, not tomorrow, if you please!'*

2 Please God *see* **God 18.**

3 **Please yourself** Do what you like; it doesn't matter to me: ▷ *'Please yourself when you start—eight or nine o'clock, as long as you do your eight hours' work, I don't mind.'*

4 Pleased to meet you! *see* **Meet 1.**

5 We aim to please *see* **Aim.**

Pleasure

1 **(It's) a pleasure!** *Polite* I was pleased to help, etc., you; there is no need to thank me: ▷ *'Thank you, Marjorie, for all the help you've given us since we moved in!' 'It's a pleasure!'* Also My (or **our**) pleasure!

2 May I have the pleasure (of the next dance)? *Formal* May I ask you to dance with me?: ▷ *Robin plucked up courage and eventually asked, 'May I have the pleasure?' 'Certainly!' Sally replied.*

3 **With pleasure** *Polite* Yes, certainly: ▷ *'Could you post these letters on your way home, please?' 'With pleasure!' answered John, eager to please as ever.*

Point

1 In point of fact *see* **Fact b, c.**

2 **Not to put too fine a point on it** To speak frankly and honestly: ▷ *'Not to put too fine a point on it, your work has been unsatisfactory recently.'* ▷ *'We're most unhappy about the lack of clear religious teaching in our schools, not to put too fine a point on it.'*

3 **Point taken** I accept what you are telling me: often used when acknowledging a correction: ▷ *'When was the last time we beat them—the late 1970s, wasn't it?' 'Surely not, what about 1982?' 'Point taken, yes, I'd forgotten about that!'* Also **I take your point.**

4 **That's not the point** What you are saying is not important or not really relevant to what is being talked about: ▷ *'Since the early 1970s, since the price of oil went up so much . . .' 'That's not the point; we've always had economic difficulties; we don't put enough money into building new factories.'*

5 **That's the (whole) point** That is the essence or the main thing in what I am trying to tell you: often used when the hearer is only slowly understanding an explanation: ▷ *'That's the whole point, with the tax going down, the goods will cost less, don't you see?'*

6 **The point is . . .** Used to direct the hearer's attention or to introduce a statement with emphasis: ▷ *'The point is do you want to go or not, not whether we can make all the necessary arrangements.'*

7 **You've (got) a point there** What you've said is true, I think; I'd not thought of that before: ▷ *'Do you know, you've got a point there—I think I might just try washing my hair with beer—I'd never even thought of that.'*

8 **You've made your point** You have told us your argument and so we know it already: often also implying a request to be quiet: ▷ *'Yes, Henry, you've made your point, so now let's hear what other people have got to say about it!'*

Poison

What's your poison?   *Often humorous* What would you like to drink?: ▷ *'Let me get you one—what's your poison?'* Also **Name your poison.**

Possess

What(ever) possessed you (him, etc.) **. . .?**   Why did you (do something): often used of strange, unusual, or foolish actions: ▷ *'Whatever possessed her to do that? She must have been mad!'* ▷ *'What possessed you to behave in such a stupid way?'*

Power

More power to your elbow!   *Becoming old-fashioned* An expression of encouragement: ▷ *'More power to your elbow! Keep on revising and you'll soon know it all!'*

Praise

1   Praise be   *Old-fashioned*

a   An expression of true thankfulness to God: ▷ *'Praise be! God has saved His people!'* Also **Praise be to God!** *(old-fashioned)*; **Praise the Lord!**

b   An expression of thanks, relief, etc.: ▷ *'I've finished my work at last, praise be!'*

2   (That's) praise indeed!   That is a true compliment: but also often used when the opposite is intended: ▷ *'She's the best student I've ever had!' 'That's praise indeed!'* ▷ *'Jo's not a very good actor, is he?' 'Praise indeed, eh! After all, you're no great Laurence Olivier yourself, are you?'*

Preserve

Saints preserve us!   *Becoming old-fashioned* An expression of surprise, annoyance, impatience, fear, etc.: ▷ *'You say you want some more money? Saints preserve us, woman, you'll be asking for every penny I ever earned next!'* Also **God preserve us!**; **Heaven preserve us!**

Presto

Hey presto! *see* **Hey.**

Presume

. . . , I presume   Am I right in thinking that you are (a

particular person)?: ▷ *'Mr Smith, I presume?' 'Yes.' 'Then
come in!'* Probably patterned on the words *Doctor
Livingstone, I presume* spoken by Henry Stanley when he
met David Livingstone in central Africa in 1871.

Price
What price . . .? *Chiefly British* What are the chances of
(something) happening now?: ▷ *'What price freedom of
speech if we can't say what we want about the
government?'* ▷ *'What price success if it gives you a nervous
breakdown?'*

Problem
No problem! That will present no difficulties!: ▷ *'One
double room with shower? No problem! Let me see—ah yes,
room thirty-six is free.'*

Promise
1   **I promise you** I assure you: used to emphasise a statement,
threat, or warning: ▷ *'I didn't mean to do it, I promise you!'*
2   **Promises, promises!** All you do is make promises, you
never keep them!; I don't believe the promise you're making
this time, because you've always broken them before: ▷
*'We'll go abroad for our holiday this year!' 'Promises,
promises!'*

Proud
I hope you feel proud of yourself! *see* **Hope 1.**

Pull
Pull the other one (it's got bells on)! I cannot believe what
you're saying: used humorously to express ridicule or
scorn: ▷ *'I hear Mark's putting his car in for the London to
Brighton race!' 'Pull the other one! I don't believe it would get
as far as the end of his drive!'* The phrase is a development of
pull someone's leg, to make fun of someone.

Purpose
Accidentally on purpose *see* **Accidental.**

Push
1   **At a push** Just about; with difficulty: ▷ *'I'll be able to get
the work done by five for you at a push.'*

2 **Push off!**   Go away: ▷ *'Push off, will you—can't you leave us alone?'*

Put
1 **Put 'em up!** *see* **Hand 4b.**
2 **Put it there!**   Let's shake hands on this!: said by a person as he puts out his hand for the other person to shake it: used when coming to an agreement or reconciliation, or as an expression of admiration: ▷ *'OK, so £500 it is, put it there!'* ▷ *'I think that's settled all our differences, hasn't it? Put it there, then, John!'* Also **Stick it there!**
3 **To put it mildly**   Without exaggerating: ▷ *'These books are very, very expensive, to put it mildly!'* Also **To say the least.**

q

Question

Ask a silly question (and you get a silly answer)! An expression said in reply to a question whose answer is obvious: ▷ *'What are you doing up that ladder?' 'Ask a silly question! What does it look like I'm doing? I'm painting the house, of course!'* Also used in the proverb *Ask no questions and (you'll) be told no lies.*

Quite

1 **Quite a . . .** A (person or thing) of a special or unusual type: sometimes used to hurt someone's feelings: ▷ *'Your wife's quite a girl, isn't she?'* ▷ *'It really was quite a shock to get the news.'* ▷ *'Quite a little man about town, aren't we, going to all these clubs every day!'* Also *(chiefly American)* **Quite some**: ▷ *'That's quite some library!'*

2 **Quite (so)** *see* **Just 4.**

3 **When you've quite finished!** An expression used to stop someone continuing doing something: ▷ *'When you've quite finished, children . . . thank you, we'll now start again!'* Also **When you're quite ready!**

r

Race
It's anyone's race *see* **Anyone 2.**

Rain
Come rain or shine   Whatever the weather; whatever happens: ▷ *'I'll see you again on Tuesday, come rain or shine.'*

Rate
At any rate   Anyway: said before the main point is mentioned, to bring out a contrast with something just said: ▷ *'What a terrible thing to have to go through! At any rate you're all right, now; that's the most important thing.'*

Rather
. . . would rather . . . *see* **Would 3.**

Ready
1   **Ready, steady, go!**   The words the starter says before a race, to get the competitors to start: ▷ *'Now come on everybody, up to the line—ready, steady, go!'* Also **On your mark(s), (get) set, go!**

2   **When you're quite ready!** *see* **Quite 3.**

Really
1   **Not really**   An expression of doubt or surprise: ▷ *'Are you happy to be here?' 'Well, no, not really.'*

2   **(Oh) really**   An expression of surprise, doubt, interest, etc.: ▷ *'I've been promoted!' 'Oh really? That's good!'* ▷ *'He's away at the moment.' 'Oh really!' 'Yes, he's been away about a month.'* ▷ *'I collect old model cars.' 'Oh really, how interesting!'*

3   **(Well) really!**   An expression showing slight disapproval or annoyance: ▷ *'Well really! Who'd have thought he'd end up in prison?'* ▷ *'Really! I'm surprised at you. I find your attitude wholly objectionable!'*

Reason
1   **It stands to reason (that)**   It is reasonable and obvious from

what is stated (that): ▷ *'It stands to reason that if the government lowers taxes, then its income will be less.'* ▷ *'I won't do the work unless you pay me promptly— it stands to reason—I've got a wife and two children to support, you know.'*

2 Ours (is) not to reason why We have no right to ask questions; our only responsibility is to continue doing what we have been asked to do: ▷ *'Why on earth are they getting rid of this new metric size and going back to the old ones?'* *'Ours is not to reason why!'* Also **Ours is not to reason why, Ours but to do or die,** adapted from *The Charge of the Light Brigade,* by Alfred, Lord Tennyson.

Reckon

I reckon Used to make an opinion sound less strong: ▷ *'It's time to go now, I reckon.'* ▷ *'I reckon they'll be here soon.'*

Red

Was my face red! *see* **Face 4.**

Remember

Here's something to remember me by An expression said when giving someone something such as a present, but also a punch or blow: ▷ *'Here's something to remember me by!'* *'Oh—a book on the English countryside! How lovely!'* ▷ *'Here's something to remember me by,'* he shouted as he hit the man in the chest.

Remote

Not have the remotest idea *see* **Foggiest.**

Repeat

No, repeat, no Definitely no: ▷ *'No, repeat, no, I can't come to your concert. We've got to go to a parents' evening at school.'*

Respect

With (all due) respect Used when politely disagreeing with what has been said: sometimes used in formal situations: ▷ *'I'm sure I could drive better than you.'* *'H'm, with respect, how many times did you have to take your driving test?'* ▷

'With all due respect to the last speaker, I must point out that the lessons we can learn from history are rather different from those that he gave us.'

Rest

1 A change is as good as a rest *see* **Change 1.**

2 **Give it a rest!** Stop it; stop talking!: ▷ *'Give it a rest, Ron, we all know you can play the piano, but we'd like some peace and quiet, too!'*

3 (May God) rest his soul *see* **Soul 2.**

4 **(You can) rest assured** You can be certain: ▷ *'Rest assured, we are doing all we can to find your son.'* ▷ *'You can rest assured that no efforts are being spared to provide you with the finest accommodation in town.'*

Return

Many happy returns (of the day)! An expression of greeting on someone's birthday, to wish happiness: ▷ *'Many happy returns, darling! May you have a lovely birthday!'* ▷ *'Let me wish you many happy returns of the day!'*

Rhubarb

Rhubarb, rhubarb The noise made by performers in a play, etc., to make, rather humorously, the sounds of a normal conversation.

Rich

That's rich! That's ridiculous: said about something that is contrary to what is expected: ▷ *'An Englishman teaching a Scotsman how to make kilts—that's rich!'*

Riddance

Good riddance! An expression used to show pleasure at being rid of someone or something: ▷ *'David's leaving next week!' 'Good riddance!'* ▷ *'Thank heavens we've finally sold that car—good riddance to it!'* Sometimes in the phrase *Good riddance to bad rubbish!*

Ridiculous

From the sublime to the ridiculous *see* **Sublime.**

Right

1 All right *see* **All 6.**

2 I'm all right, Jack *see* **Jack 2.**

3 Right enough *see* **Sure 8.**

4 **Right on!** *Slang* An expression of agreement or approval: ▷ *At the rally the speaker asked the crowd, 'We all want cheap fares, don't we?' The whole crowd shouted back, 'Right on!'* ▷ *'You played real bad,' said Dad. 'You're right on there, father,' she replied.* This phrase is American in origin.

5 Right then *see* **Now 4.**

6 **Right you are!** All right, OK: used to show agreement with an order or suggestion and a willingness to do what is asked: ▷ *'Two coffees, please.' 'Right you are!'* ▷ *'You can come on Tuesday, if you want.' 'Right you are, then—see you next week!'* Also **Right oh!**

7 That's (or it's) all right *see* **All 23.**

8 **(That's) right!** Yes; what you say is correct: an expression of agreement or approval: ▷ *'So your first book was published last year?' 'That's right!'* ▷ *'You're filming a new series of the programme, I gather.' 'Right; we've just started the third episode.'*

9 **Too right!** Used to express strong agreement: ▷ *'I'm a bit of a fool, aren't I, coming out here and forgetting my map!' 'Too right you are!'* Also **Too true!**

Ring

1 Don't ring us, we'll ring you *see* **Call 1.**

2 That rings a bell *see* **Bell 2.**

3 **You rang, sir?** *Formal* What may I do for you?: said by a butler, etc., in answer to the ringing of the bell: ▷ *'You rang, sir?' 'Yes, Smithy, may we have some port?'*

Rip

Let her rip Let the car, boat, etc., go at full speed: ▷ *'Let her rip, Joe, we're out in the country now!'*

Rise

Rise and shine *Often humorous* Get out of bed quickly and look fresh!: ▷ *I was lying in bed asleep and suddenly I heard Dad shout, 'Rise and shine!'*

Road

One for the road *see* **One 5.**

Robinson

Before you can (or could) say Jack Robinson *Becoming old-fashioned* Very quickly: ▷ *'I'll be downstairs before you can say Jack Robinson.'* ▷ *'Before you could say Jack Robinson, he'd taken my wallet and dashed out of the room.'* It is not known who Jack Robinson actually was. Also (*rare*) **Before you can say knife.**

Roll

Roll on . . . Used to express a wish for the quick approach of (a time or occasion): ▷ *'Roll on spring! The winter's so long!'* ▷ *'Roll on the year that I retire!'* ▷ *'Roll on the weekend!'*

Roundabout

Swings and roundabouts *see* **Swing.**

Rub

There's the rub *Becoming old-fashioned* That is the central point of the matter, the one on which the difficulty or problem comes: ▷ *'Yes, I think we've agreed on how long it will take to build. Now what about the cost?' 'Ah, there's the rub—our figures don't seem to tally on this.'* From *Hamlet,* by William Shakespeare, Act 3, Scene 1: *To sleep! perchance to dream; ay, there's the rub.*

Run

Run for it! Move as fast as you can to escape from the danger: ▷ *'The house is on fire! Don't go and collect your things! Just run for it!'* ▷ *'Run for it! They're after us!'* Also **Run for your life!**

S

Saint
1   Saints alive! *see* **Aunt.**
2   Saints preserve us! *see* **Preserve.**

Salt
The salt of the earth   An expression used to describe people who are very kind or reliable, or have other very good features: ▷ *The newspaper described the youth group who helped in the local old people's home as the salt of the earth.* From the Bible, Matthew, chapter 5, verse 13.

Same
1   **All the same**
a   Not making any difference at all: ▷ *'If it's all the same to you, I think I'll go now!'* ▷ *'It's all the same whether we go by train or coach.'*
b   Even so; nevertheless; in any case: ▷ *'I know he's rich, but all the same, it doesn't mean he's got an endless supply of money, you know!'* ▷ *'Despite his unfaithfulness, I shall go on loving him all the same.'*
2   **(And) the same to you**
a   I wish you the same thing: said in reply to a greeting or wish: ▷ *'Happy Christmas!' 'The same to you!'*
b   I wish you the same thing: said in reply to an unkind wish or insult: ▷ *'I wish you'd go and jump in a lake!' 'The same to you!'* To strengthen this expression *(And) the same to you with (brass) knobs on* is used: ▷ *'You're the biggest idiot I've ever met! Why don't you go and put your head in a bucket!' 'The same to you with brass knobs on!'*
3   **Same here**   The same applies to me; and the same for me: ▷ *'I'm fed up with revising!' 'Same here! Let's go and watch television.'* ▷ *'Can I have pie and chips, please?' 'Same here!' 'OK, two pie and chips coming up!'*
4   **(The) same again**   An order for another drink, dish, etc., of the same kind as the previous one: ▷ *'The same again, please, Jan!'*

Save

To save his (her, etc.) life *see* **Life 8.**

Say

1 **And so say all of us** *Sometimes humorous, becoming old-fashioned* An expression of agreement or approval by everyone present: ▷ *'I'm sure we'll want to express our deepest gratitude to our guest speaker tonight!' 'Yes! And so say all of us!'* ▷ *'For he's a jolly good fellow, and so say all of us!'*

2 **As you say** You are right; I'll do what you ask: often used when the speaker is really not willing to do something: ▷ *'That's absolute nonsense!' 'As you say, sir!'* ▷ *'We must leave at once. Come on; pack your bags!' 'As you say!'*

3 **Confucius, he say . . .** *see* **Confucius.**

4 **(Do) you mean to say?** Used to express surprise, disbelief, etc.: ▷ *'You mean to say you're leaving us?'* ▷ *'Do you mean to say I've come all this way for nothing?'*

5 **Don't say . . .** An expression of impatient surprise or annoyance: ▷ *'Don't say I've gone and locked my keys in the car!'* ▷ *'Don't say you can't help me now after you promised you would!'*

6 **How say you?** *British* The formula spoken by the clerk of the court to the defendant, when the charge is read out at the start of the trial: ▷ *'How say you? Are you guilty or not guilty?'*

7 **I can't say** A way of making a negative expression seem less strong: sometimes said in a rather reluctant tone: ▷ *'To tell you the truth, I can't say I like your choice of wallpaper!'*

8 **I couldn't say** I don't know: ▷ *'How many people came to the party?' 'I couldn't say—perhaps twenty, perhaps forty—it's difficult to tell.'*

9 **I dare say** *Chiefly British* It is quite likely, I think; probably: ▷ *'We've run out of sugar, but I dare say there's some in the cupboard.'* ▷ *'I dare say you're hungry after your long walk!'* Sometimes written *I daresay.*

10 **I (he, etc.) said** Used in reporting a conversation: ▷ *'I said to the lady downstairs, "What about your bunions?" and so she told me about all the illnesses she'd ever had.'* Also used by the speaker to make a quotation of one's own words, to show that the quotation applies to oneself: ▷ *'All of us have bad days, she said!'* remarked the presenter at the end of the programme, when so many things had gone wrong. Also **Said I (he, etc.); Says I (he, etc.)** (*nonstandard*); **I (he, etc.) says**

(*nonstandard*): ▷ '*I spoke to the fellow who knows the boss and I says to him, "When am I getting my pay rise, then?"* '

11 I mean to say

a An expression of surprise, disbelief, disgust, etc.: ▷ '*Well, I mean to say! Who does she think she is? Coming in here and telling us how to run the kitchen!*'

b An expression used to clarify or expand on a previous statement: ▷ '*I was standing by the pond, that's all. I mean to say, I was just looking at the ducks, when suddenly this man came up and pushed me in!*' Often shortened to *I mean*.

12 I must say An expression used to add force to an often critical opinion or statement: ▷ '*It's not the most exciting novel I've ever read, I must say, but it wasn't too bad.*' ▷ '*You've been a great help, I must say! You might as well not have come for all the support you've given!*'

13 I say *British, rather old-fashioned*

a An expression of surprise: ▷ '*I say, look at the time—it's nearly midnight; we must be going home!*'

b An expression used to attract someone's attention: ▷ '*I say, Colonel, just look at that Rolls-Royce, it's like the one we had before the war!*'

14 I say, I say, I say! Used to introduce a joke: especially in theatrical contexts: ▷ '*I say, I say, I say! Can you sing Faust?*' '*Yes—and I can sing slow, as well!*' Made more current by the variety duo Harry Murray and Harry Mooney in the 1930s.

15 I wouldn't say Used to introduce a statement or opinion that is then further qualified: ▷ '*I wouldn't say we're not happily married—it's just that we do seem to have more than our fair share of quarrels.*'

16 I wouldn't say no A polite way of saying yes: ▷ '*Would you like another piece of cake?*' '*I wouldn't say no!*'

17 I wouldn't say that A polite way of disagreeing with someone: ▷ '*So you think £100 will be enough?*' '*I wouldn't say that—I was thinking of nearer £500!*' ▷ '*Pete's helped you quite a bit since you moved in, hasn't he?*' '*I wouldn't say that—I think he's come in only once, that's all!*' Also **I'm not saying that.**

18 If I may (or **might**) **say so** A polite expression used to make an opinion or statement sound less strong: ▷ '*If I may say so, that jacket doesn't quite fit you.*' ▷ '*I'm not sure he's the right person to ask, if I might say so.*'

19 I'll say!   Yes indeed: a strong form of agreement: ▷ *'Do you want to go to the seaside?' 'I'll say!'* ▷ *'Were they happy at the thought of going away on holiday?' 'I'll say they were!'*

20 I'll say this much   I will say only this, and no more: used to state the positive side of a person or thing: ▷ *'I'll say this much for him—he's always honest, even if he is poorly dressed.'*

21 I'm not just saying this   I really mean what I'm saying: ▷ *'We've appreciated your help enormously, and I'm not just saying this.'*

22 (Let's) say   Let us suppose: ▷ *'We'll meet, say, at six o'clock.'* ▷ *'What if I were to offer you, let's say, £1000 for the whole lot?'*

23 Never say die!   *Becoming old-fashioned* Do not despair!; do not give up hope!: ▷ *She spoke to me gently, 'Never say die! It won't last forever!'*

24 Say again? *see* **Come 2.**

25 Say no more   Your intended meaning is clear just from what you've said: ▷ *'I saw her going into his room at ten o'clock last night.' 'Say no more!'* Also (*rather more formal*) **Enough said.** This phrase is sometimes written *'nuff said.*

26 Say something   Say a few words; make a short speech: ▷ *'Go on, say something—we can't just sit here with everyone looking at us expectantly!'*

27 Say what you like   Even though you may not agree with what is being said: ▷ *'Say what you like, it won't make me change my mind!'*

28 Say when   Please tell me when to stop or start something: used especially when a host is pouring a drink for someone: ▷ *'Say when!'* . . . *'Right, that's enough, thanks!'* ▷ *'Say when!'* . . . *'When!'* ▷ *'As soon as you're ready, say when, and I'll switch on!'*

29 Says (or sez) you (he, etc.)!   I don't believe that; I strongly disagree with what you (he, etc.) have just said: said in a rude, sneering, or scornful tone: ▷ *'Our team'll win today!' 'Says you! We'll beat yours easily!'* Also **Says (or sez) who?:** ▷ *'I'm taking Jo to the party.' 'Sez who? She's my girlfriend, not yours!'* The spelling *sez* is nonstandard.

30 That is (to say)   An expression used to clarify or expand on something that has just been said: ▷ *'He didn't sign the register, that is to say, I've no record that he ever did.'* ▷ *'We're leaving on 2 March, that is, Friday.'* Abbreviated to *i.e.*, Latin *id est.*

31 That's what you say! I think there might be other opinions as well as yours: used to express doubt about the truth of a statement: ▷ *'That's what you say, but I'm sure your sister wouldn't agree with you!'*

32 They say People in general say; it is an opinion that is widely held: ▷ *'They say, "Nothing succeeds like success" and I'm certainly proving it in my business!'* ▷ *'They say that if it rains on St Swithin's Day, the rain will continue for the next forty days.'*

33 Though I say it (or so) **myself** An expression used with a statement of boasting, to make this seem less strong, but also to give self-assurance: ▷ *'I think I've made a good job of decorating this room, though I say so myself.'* Also **Though I says it as shouldn't.**

34 To say the least *see* **Put 3.**

35 What can I say? I am lost for words; I can't think how to express my thoughts: ▷ *'Well, what can I say? I'm overwhelmed by all the kindness you've shown me! However can I say thank you?'*

36 What did I say! What I say has now come true!: ▷ *'There you are! What did I say! I said they'd been meeting secretly, and now it's come out that they have! It's just as I thought!'* Also **What did I tell you!**

37 What do you say?

a Do you like it?; do you agree with my suggestion?: ▷ *'How about each putting in £100? What do you say?' 'OK, it's a deal!'* Also **What would you say?:** ▷ *'What would you say to going to Brighton for the afternoon?' 'Yes, that's fine by me!'* ▷ *'What would you say to another cup of tea?'*

b Said to encourage a child to say please or thank you: ▷ *'Can I take another banana?' 'What do you say?' 'Please!' 'Right, OK, then—help yourself!'*

38 You can say that again! I agree very much with what you've said: ▷ *'I don't think he looks after his wife.' 'You can say that again: he goes out drinking with his friends every night.'* Also **You said it!:** ▷ *'That exam was very hard, wasn't it?' 'You said it!'*

39 You could say that I agree with you partly: ▷ *'He's plump, isn't he?' 'You could say that, but he's not too fat, really.'* The stress falls on *could*.

40 You don't say? Used to show surprise at what has just been said: ▷ *'We're thinking of emigrating to Australia next year.'*

'You don't say? I thought you were very happy here.' The stress falls on *don't*.

Saying

As the saying goes An expression used with a fixed phrase such as a proverb or idiom: ▷ *'There were ten of us working there, but everything seemed to go wrong, and the project was abandoned—too many cooks spoiling the broth, as the saying goes.'*

Scott

Great Scott! *Old-fashioned* An expression showing great surprise or astonishment: ▷ *'Great Scott! That car's going very fast!'* The origin of this phrase is uncertain but it seems likely that Scott was General Winfield Scott (1786-1866), soldier and nominee in a US presidential election.

Scout

Scout's honour! *see* **Honour 2.**

Seal

My lips are sealed *see* **Lip.**

Search

Search me! I do not know the answer; I do not know what to do: ▷ *'Where's Barry got to?' 'Search me! I've no idea!'* ▷ *'What shall we do next?' 'Search me! Haven't you got any bright ideas?'*

Second

1 Just a second *see* **Just 2.**
2 Wait a second *see* **Wait 4 b, c.**

See

1 **As far as I can see** To the best of my understanding or judgement: ▷ *'As far as I can see, the only honourable course of action open to you is to resign immediately.'*
2 **As I see it** In my opinion: ▷ *'As I see it, you can either invest the money or spend it!'* ▷ *'As I see it, the best thing to do is to take half an hour's exercise every day, and then you'll feel a lot better.'*
3 **Do you see (what I mean)?** Also **Don't you see?**

a Do you understand what I'm trying to explain?: ▷ *'If we extend the shelves this way, then that'll give us a lot more room—do you see what I mean?'*

b It is as I said; didn't I tell you that this was so?: ▷ *'Do you see what I mean, whenever these two get together, they always start to fight. Just look at them now!'*

4 I see I understand your explanation: ▷ *'If the government lowers taxes . . .' 'Oh, I see—you mean then the price will come down.' 'Exactly!'*

5 I see what you mean

a I understand what you're trying to explain: ▷ *'This cog wheel turns this bigger one.' . . . 'And the whole thing moves round—I see what you mean.'*

b It is as you said; you are quite right: ▷ *'I see what you mean—Peter's ears do stick out a little, don't they? I'd not noticed that before.'*

6 I'd like to see . . . *see* **Like 2.**

7 I'll (or **we'll**) **be seeing you!** Goodbye: used between friends: ▷ *'I'll be seeing you then, Jackie!' 'Right oh, Mark!'* Also shortened to **Be seeing you!**: ▷ *'Be seeing you, Alf!' 'OK, be seeing you!'*

8 I'll (or **we'll**) **see (about that)** I (or we) may do something, but are unable to make a decision or commitment at the moment; it depends on various things: ▷ *'We may come round tonight. We'll see.'* Also **I'll** (or **we'll**) **have to see (about that).** This phrase is used to show near-refusal: ▷ *'Do you think I could borrow some money?' 'I'll have to see about that.'*

9 Let me (or **let's**) **see** An expression used to give the speaker time to think what to say next: ▷ *'Let me see, when would he have been born? It must have been about 1900.'* ▷ *'Do you know that smell?' 'Ah! Let me see . . . Yes, it's rotten eggs!'* ▷ *'Let's see, there must be a way out of here somewhere!'* Also **Let me think:** ▷ *'Let me think; I may be able to see you on Friday.'*

10 Long time no see *see* **Time 4.**

11 See here! *see* **Look 4.**

12 See you later! Goodbye: used between friends: ▷ *'See you later, Peter!' 'Yes, goodbye!'* Also (*slang, becoming old-fashioned*) **See you later, alligator!** *Alligator* is rhyming slang for *later.* Also **See you!; See you around!**

13 So I see What you say is obvious: used in reply to an apology or an excuse that may be rejected: ▷ *'I'm sorry. I'm late.' 'So I see!'* ▷ *'I'm afraid I've brought in all this mud onto your carpet!' 'So I see!'*

14 We'll (soon) see about that! I will put an end to that!: ▷ *'You say the kids are playing behind the sheds again—we'll soon see about that!'*

15 (You) see An expression used in an explanation, reminding the hearer of something that has just been said or that the hearer already knows, sometimes making what is said sound less strong: ▷ *'I was coming down the road, see, and then this car suddenly came towards me.'* ▷ *'I had to go and talk to Mr Smith—that's why I'm five minutes late, you see.'* ▷ *'You see, I know this town very well.'*

16 You see if . . . An expression stating that the speaker will be proved right by (events to come): ▷ *'He'll quietly forget about all that money he owes you, you see if he won't.'*

Serious

You can't be serious! You don't really mean that, do you?: used to try to dissuade someone from a course of action: ▷ *'Climb that ladder? You can't be serious! You know I don't like heights!'*

Serve

1 If my memory serves me right . . . *see* **Memory.**

2 It (or that) serves you (him, etc.) right! That is a just punishment for what you have (he has, etc.) done: ▷ *'I've just heard Rod failed his exams—I think it serves him right as he didn't do any work for them!'* Also **Serves you (him, etc.) right!**: ▷ *'I've got such a pain in my stomach!' 'Serves you right for eating so many cakes!'*

Service

1 At your service *Formal* I am (or we are) waiting for your instructions and will do exactly as you ask: used in polite or pompous contexts: ▷ *'Should you require any assistance, all my staff are at your service.'* ▷ *'At your service, sir!'*

2 It's all part of the service! A response made to someone saying thank you: used by shopkeepers, etc., or humorously in a wider context: ▷ *'I want to thank you very much for seeing that I have all my shopping!' 'It's all part of the service, madam!'* ▷ *'Thanks for looking after me so well during my*

stay here, son.' 'Ah, Mother! It's all part of the service!' Also
(in public contexts) **It's what we're here for!**

Sez

Sez you! *see* **Say 29.**

Shake

1 He's (it's, etc.) **no great shakes** He (it, etc.) has no skill,
value, merit, or importance: ▷ *'Ethel is no great shakes at
speaking French but she can write it quite well.'*

2 Shake a leg! *see* **Leg 2.**

3 Shake hands *see* **Hand 7.**

Shall

Shall we (I, etc.) . . .? *Formal* Used in asking questions in a
polite way: ▷ *'Shall we have dinner now?'* ▷ *'Shall I take
you to the station?'*

Shame

1 **Shame on you!** You should be ashamed: ▷ *'Shame on you,
Peter, for behaving like that—I'd have thought you'd know
better!'*

2 **Shame, shame!** You should be ashamed of such behaviour:
called out to a speaker at a public meeting or, usually
humorously, by a theatre audience: ▷ *The spokesman con-
tinued, 'I have to admit that we have made some administra-
tive mistakes . . .' and this brought cries of 'Shame, shame!'
from the audience.*

Sharp

1 **Look sharp!**

a Be quick; hurry up: ▷ *'Don't walk so slowly! Look sharp!'*
Also **Be sharp about it!**

b Be careful: ▷ *'Look sharp! There's a lot of traffic about!'*

2 Sharp's the word! *see* **Word 12.**

Shine

1 Come rain or shine *see* **Rain.**

2 Rise and shine! *see* **Rise.**

Shirt

1 **Keep your shirt on!** There is no need to get so annoyed!;

calm down!: ▷ *'Keep your shirt on, Rod! I only asked if I could borrow the car for this evening, not for you to give it to me for ever!'* Also (*British*) **Keep your hair on!**: ▷ *'What are you doing with my radio?' 'Keep your hair on! I'm just putting a new battery in it for you!'*

2 You (can) bet your shirt *see* **Bet 4.**

Shiver

Shiver me timbers! *see* **Timber.**

Shoot

1 Nosey got shot! *see* **Nosey.**

2 **The whole bang shoot** *Slang* Everything: ▷ *'I want all your furniture and books—the whole bang shoot—out of there by ten o'clock tomorrow.'*

Shot

1 **A shot in the dark** A very rough guess or random action, made without any real thought: ▷ *Because of pressure of time, the company's advertisements for their new ballpoint pen were just a shot in the dark.*

2 Not by a long shot *see* **Chalk.**

Should

1 **I should . . .** An expression used in giving advice: ▷ *'I should get rid of that old car, if I were you, and buy yourself a newer one.'*

2 **Who (how, why, etc.) should . . .?** An expression of surprise: ▷ *'Who should come to see me but Pedro?'* ▷ *'Why should she want to do that?'* ▷ *'What should he suggest, but that we get married!'*

3 You should . . . *see* **Want 2.**

Show

1 **Bad (or poor) show!** *Old-fashioned* Used to express sympathy with someone for something unfortunate that has happened: ▷ *'Bad show, Milton! A pity Joe was a bit faster than you in the end!'*

2 **Good show!** *Old-fashioned* Used to express approval: ▷ *'I hear Jack's coming back from India!' 'Oh, good show! I've not seen him for ages!'* ▷ *'Jolly good show you turned up—I was just giving up all hope of ever seeing you again!'*

3 Show a leg! *see* **Leg 2.**

Shut

Shut up! Stop talking!; be quiet!: ▷ *'Shut up, Ian, do you have to go on and on all the time?'* Also (*slang*) **Shut your face!; Shut your mouth!; Shut your trap!**

Sight

Out of my sight! Go immediately: ▷ *'Out of my sight! I never want to see you again!'*

Sin

. . . for my sins! *Humorous* Used when the speaker considers what is being talked about as slightly disagreeable or as a gentle form of punishment: ▷ *'He's left all the holiday arrangements to me, for my sins!'* ▷ *'Is that pile of books all yours?' 'Yes, for my sins! I've got to mark them all for tomorrow!'*

Sink

Now we're sunk! All our efforts, hopes, etc., have failed us; we're in a desperate situation!: ▷ *'Now we're sunk! We've run out of food and it's getting dark!'*

Six

Six of one and half a dozen of the other *see* **Dozen.**

Size

That's about the size of it! That's a fair account of the matter, situation, etc.: ▷ *'That's about the size of it—the roof will have to be repaired within a month or two, I'm afraid.'*

Skin

It's (or that's) no skin off your (his, etc.) nose It doesn't bother or affect you (him, etc.): ▷ *'Why shouldn't I come in late if I want to? After all, it's no skin off your nose, is it?'*

Skip

Skip it! There is no need to bother about something, such as an apology or thanks; also used for dropping a subject of conversation: ▷ *'Let me pay you back what I owe you—how* *much was it?' 'Oh, skip it—it doesn't matter!'* ▷ *'Skip it! Can't you two talk about anything but politics?'*

Smart

Look smart! *see* **Look 5.**

Smile

1 Keep smiling! *see* **Keep 3.**
2 Take (or wipe) that smile off your face *see* **Grin 2.**

Smoke

Holy smoke! *see* **Holy.**

Snappy

Make it snappy! *see* **Make 4.**

So

1 Ever so *see* **Ever 2.**
2 How so? *see* **How 13.**
3 **Is that so?** Is it really as you say: an expression of surprise: ▷ *'Brian's coming to see us tonight, you know.' 'Is that so? I thought it was tomorrow!'*
4 **It is so!** Used to contradict a negative statement: ▷ *'It's not raining, is it?' 'It is so!'*
5 Just so *see* **Just 4.**
6 **So be it!** *Formal* Let it be as you say: used in accepting something, sometimes in a resigned manner: ▷ *'If that's what you want, so be it, though it's not what we'd have chosen for you!'* ▷ *'So be it—the dead are now departed from among us and we must face the future with boldness.'*
7 So there! *see* **There 1.**
8 So what? *see* **What 6.**

Sock

1 Bless his (little) cotton socks *see* **Bless 4.**
2 **Pull your (his, etc.) socks up** To make a definite effort to improve one's work: ▷ *The teacher told John to pull his socks up or he would have to leave.*
3 **Put a sock in it!** *Becoming old-fashioned* Be quiet!; stop what you're doing!: ▷ *'Put a sock in it! Why don't you two shut up? It's two o'clock in the morning, and I've got to be up at six!'*

Some

Some . . .

a   You are (or it is) no kind of a . . . at all: said in an indignant or angry tone: ▷ *'Some help you've been, I must say— you've just sat there and done nothing all afternoon!'* ▷ *'Some people! You know you make me sick, Peter, the way you've treated me recently.'*

b   A (person or thing) of a special or unusual type: ▷ *'That was some storm!'* ▷ *'That was some game you played!'*

Something

1   **Or something**

a   Used when the speaker disagrees with or does not fully believe the meaning of a particular word: ▷ *'I thought jobs here were supposed to be well-paid or something!'*

b   Or something very like it: used when the speaker is unsure of what is said: ▷ *'I think he's studying sociology or something at university.'* ▷ *'Are you trying to kill me or something, with all this work you keep on giving me?'*

2   **Say something** *see* **Say 26.**

3   **Something tells me**   I think that: used when the speaker suspects something: ▷ *'Something tells me those two are getting married soon.'* Also used in the past tense: ▷ *'Something told me it wasn't safe to go into the room, so I stayed outside.'*

4   **You know something?** *see* **Know 26.**

Son

1   **My son**   A way of addressing a man, used by an older man when speaking to a much younger man or by a priest to a person confessing his sin: ▷ *'My son, I remember years ago when all this was just fields, and how we used to go for long walks in the summer.'* ▷ *'My son, you may go in peace, knowing that God has forgiven your sins.'*

2   **Son of a gun**   *Old-fashioned* A way of addressing a man in a friendly way: used by other men: ▷ *'Come on, you old son of a gun, what have you been up to these last few years?'* The phrase was originally a term of abuse and meant 'the bastard son of a soldier or sailor'.

Sorry

(I'm) sorry!

a   An expression used as an apology after the speaker has done or said something that may have annoyed someone else: ▷ *'I'm sorry, I hope you've not been waiting long.'* ▷ *'Sorry! Did I step on your toe?'* Also **So sorry!**

b Used to express polite disagreement, excusing of oneself, etc.: ▷ *'I'm sorry, but it's getting late, and I think we'd better be going now.'*

Sort
1 A sort of . . . *see* **Kind 1.**
2 Sort of . . . *see* **Kind 3.**
3 Sort of thing *see* **Thing 9.**

Soul
1 God bless my soul! *see* **Bless 2.**
2 (May God) rest his (or her) soul A wish that God would give a dead person's soul peace: ▷ *'He's been dead twenty years, now, God rest his soul.'*
3 Upon my soul! *see* **Bless 2.**

Speak
1 So to speak If it may be described in this way: sometimes used to make an opinion sound less strong: ▷ *'This machine's, so to speak, the Rolls-Royce of computers.'*
2 Speak for yourself! Do not imagine that other people agree with you!: ▷ *'I think Catherine Cookson's books are the best I've ever read!' 'Speak for yourself—I'm sticking to Rudyard Kipling!'*
3 Speak of the devil! *see* **Devil 4.**

Speech
Speech, speech! We want you to give a speech!: ▷ *They gave me my leaving present and there were cries of 'Speech, speech!' so I had to say a few words.*

Speed
Full speed (or steam) ahead! Let's work or go as fast as we can!: ▷ *'I've got to finish writing this in a few days, so it's full steam ahead!'* ▷ *'Now we're out on the open seas—full speed ahead!'* Originally, *Full steam ahead!* was used of a steam engine on the railway, and *Full speed ahead!* of a ship.

Spender
The last of the big spenders! I see you are spending a lot of

money: but only used ironically when a person is really spending very little: ▷ *'This coat cost me all of £5!' 'Ah—the last of the big spenders!'*

Spit

Spit it out!   Say what you've got to say or what's on your mind: ▷ *'Come on, spit it out, old chap—we're all friends here; feel free to say what's troubling you.'*

Spoil

Be spoiling for a fight *see* **Look 1.**

Square

Back to square one   We must go back to the beginning: ▷ *'I've spent years writing this book, and now I've been told to write it all differently, so it's back to square one, I'm afraid.'* The phrase comes from games with squares on the playing-surface of the board.

Stand

1   **It stands to reason (that)** *see* **Reason 1.**
2   **Stand and deliver!** · Stop and hand over your valuable belongings to us: said in former times by highwaymen to travellers in carriages.

Star

(You can) thank your lucky stars!   Be very thankful; consider yourself very fortunate: ▷ *'Thank your lucky stars that that car didn't run you down just then—it only just missed you!'* ▷ *'You can thank your lucky stars your job's a lot easier than mine!'*

Station

Action stations! *see* **Action.**

Steady

Steady on   *British* Stop what you're doing; slow down; be more moderate: ▷ *'Steady on! I can't keep up with you fast walkers!'* ▷ *'Steady on with the milk—it's the last carton we've got!'* ▷ *'Steady on, old chap, there's no need to tell her everything about my past all at once!'*

Steam
> Full steam ahead! *see* **Speed.**

Step
1　**Mind** (or **watch**) **your step!**　Be very careful: used as a warning: ▷ *'Mind your step, young Michael! There are plenty of people looking at your job enviously!'*
2　**Step on it!**　Go faster: ▷ *I got into the taxi quickly. 'Euston station, please, and step on it! My train goes in ten minutes!'* The phrase refers to pushing the accelerator on a car further down to make the car go faster.
3　**Step outside**　Come outside and we can settle our differences: said as a challenge to a fight: ▷ *Big Max was getting angry. 'Would you care to step outside and repeat that?' he called out to Dave, who looked absolutely terrified.*
4　**Step this way** *see* **Way 4.**

Stick
1　**Jolly hockey sticks!**　*Old-fashioned* An expression showing pleasure or delight at something traditional or conventional: used to mock mildly the hearty atmosphere of British girls' public schools: ▷ *'Term finishes in two weeks' time!' 'Ooh, jolly hockey sticks!'* Originally, coined by Beryl Reid in the radio programme *Educating Archie*.
2　**Stick 'em up!** *see* **Hand 4b.**
3　**Stick it there!** *see* **Put 2.**

Stir
> **Stir, stir!**　An expression used when someone is trying to cause an argument or trouble between other people: often said with a movement of one's arms, as if stirring a large pot: ▷ *'Michael, what about you and Jane, then?' 'Stir, stir! There he goes again!'*

Stone
> **Stone the crows!**　*British slang, old-fashioned* An expression of surprise, shock, disbelief, etc.: ▷ *'Stone the crows! Do you really expect me to believe that story?'* Also **Stone me!:** ▷ *'Stone me! I've not seen one of those cars for years!'*

Stool
> **Fall between two stools**　To be neither totally one thing nor

another but partly both and therefore unsatisfactory: ▷ *The book fell between two stools—the author tried to make it suitable for both students and lay people.*

Stop

1 **. . . full stop** That is the end of the matter: said at the end of a statement, to add force to it: ▷ *'I'm not going to the party, full stop.'*

2 **Stop, thief!** *see* **Thief.**

Story

1 **A likely story!** I don't believe what has just been said: ▷ *'He says he was at church on Sunday!' 'A likely story—I bet he was playing football as usual!'*

2 **But that's (quite) another story**

a That is very different from what has just been said: ▷ *'He can write French well, but speak it—that's quite another story—he's hopeless at that!'* Also **That's a different kettle of fish.**

b An expression used when the speaker reaches a very interesting point in a story but he does not describe further details at that time: ▷ *'Do you see that barn over there? It's been there many years now. Of course, there once was another one, which was burnt down in a mysterious fire, but that's another story.'*

3 **The story of my life!** This continually happens to me; used to comment on unfortunate events: ▷ *'That's the third time this year a girl has chucked me—it's the story of my life!'*

4 **To cut a long story short** I'll miss out the less important details to come to the main point in my description of the events: ▷ *'Stephen met Claire one night at a party. They saw each other the next Saturday at the club dance, and, to cut a long story short, they got married last week!'*

Strain

Don't strain yourself! An expression used when someone is very slow at doing something: ▷ *'It's taken you three hours to write ten lines. Don't strain yourself, will you?'*

Strange

Strangely enough *see* **Enough 5.**

Stranger

Hello stranger!   An expression said to someone whom the speaker knows quite well but has not seen for some time: ▷ *'Hello, stranger! Where have you been these past few weeks?'*

Strength

Give me strength!   I need help and courage to bear what is going on: used when the speaker is annoyed or impatient: ▷ *'You stupid boy! Can't you even tell me what twelve twelves are? Give me strength!'* Short for *God, give me strength.*

Strike

Strike me pink!   *Old-fashioned* An expression of surprise, disbelief, etc.: ▷ *'Strike me pink! So Andrew's finally passed his exam after all those attempts!'* Also **Strike a light!; Strike me dead!**

Stuff

1   **Get stuffed!**   *Slang* A rude expression of strong contempt, used to show that the speaker disapproves of something or does not want to do something: ▷ *'Can I borrow your pen again?' 'Get stuffed! You borrow my pens, pencils, rubbers, and dictionaries, and you never give any of them back to me!'* Also **Stuff it!; Stuff you!:** ▷ *'I got up at six o'clock, travelled for three hours to get here, and now you tell me I needn't have come! Stuff you! Don't think I'm coming next week!'*

2   **Stuff and nonsense!**   That's stupid, foolish, untrue, etc.!: ▷ *'They say he's the best wrestler in the area!' 'Stuff and nonsense! Our Harold could beat him any day!'* The stress falls on *nonsense.*

3   **That's the stuff!**   That's the way to do it!; you're doing the right thing!: ▷ *'That's the stuff! Some more good hits like that and we'll beat them hollow!'* The stress falls on *that's.* Also **Great stuff!**

Subject

Change the subject   To talk about a new topic, in order to avoid discussing something embarrassing: ▷ *'Talking of school, Jenny, you never did tell us how you did in your history test.' 'Er, well, let's change the subject! It's a nice day, isn't it?'*

Sublime

From the sublime to the ridiculous From something very good, or noble, to something of much poorer quality or silly: used when contrasting two very different things: ▷ *'You had a Rolls-Royce, and now you've bought that old crock— that's going from the sublime to the ridiculous!'* ▷ *'A talk on the merits of various educational methods, followed by two hours of rock music—that's going from the sublime to the ridiculous!'*

Suck

Yah boo sucks to you! *Becoming old-fashioned* An expression of defiance, disgust, or ridicule: ▷ *'I told Auntie you didn't like the colour of my dress, but she said it was the nicest she'd ever seen, so yah boo sucks to you!'* Also shortened to *Sucks (to you)!*

Suffice

Suffice it to say I will just say: ▷ *'Suffice it to say, she discovered she was pregnant, but had the baby and all is now well.'*

Suit

Suit yourself! Do what you like; it doesn't matter to me: sometimes said in a rude tone: ▷ *'Suit yourself—if you want to hang the picture upside-down, I don't mind!'* ▷ *'Shall I have another cake, then?' 'Suit yourself!'*

Suppose

1 I don't suppose A polite way of making a request: used when the speaker hopes for a positive answer: ▷ *'I don't suppose you could drive us into town, could you? We've got some shopping to do.' 'Yes, I think I could.'* ▷ *'I don't suppose you could lend me £5?'*

2 I suppose

a A polite way of enquiring about something: ▷ *'I suppose you'll not be staying to dinner, then, if you've got to be back soon?'*

b Used to make an opinion, statement, etc., sound less strong: ▷ *'Being ill is just one of those things you have to put up with, I suppose.'*

3 I suppose so Used to express reluctant agreement: ▷ *'We ought to be going now.' 'Yes, I suppose so.'*

4 **Suppose we** Used to make a suggestion: ▷ *'Suppose we had enough money to buy a car, could we afford to run it?'*

Sure

1 **(And) that's for sure** That is certain: ▷ *'He won't live much longer, and that's for sure.'*

2 **As sure as . . .** Used to add strength to a statement: ▷ *'As sure as I'm standing here talking to you, I tell you I did see a flying-saucer last night!'*

3 **I don't know, I'm sure** *see* **Know 12.**

4 **I'm not (so) sure** A way of expressing doubt or disagreement in a hesitant way: ▷ *'I'm not so sure you've got your facts right there.'* ▷ *'I thought that film was great!' 'I'm not so sure—parts of it were OK, I suppose.'* ▷ *'Do you understand what I've said?' 'I'm not sure I do.'*

5 **. . . I'm sure**

a I am certain (of something): ▷ *'I shut the door, I'm sure.'* ▷ *'It'll rain soon, I'm sure.'*

b *Humorous* I am sure it was not (as described): ▷ *'We then had a lecture on his approach to sociolinguistics!' 'Fascinating, I'm sure!'*

6 **I'm sure . . .** I am certain (of something): ▷ *'I'm sure I shut the door.'* ▷ *'I'm sure she'll be here any minute now.'*

7 **Sure do!** *see* **Do 15.**

8 **Sure enough** As was expected: ▷ *'She said she'd come at ten o'clock, and sure enough, she arrived on time.'* Also **Right enough.**

9 **Sure thing!** *see* **Thing 11.**

10 **To be sure**

a Certainly; it must be acknowledged that: ▷ *'It's not the most beautiful car in the world, to be sure, but it's very economical, you know.'*

b *Irish or old-fashioned* An expression of surprise or delight: ▷ *'And there he was, to be sure!'* ▷ *'It's Aunt Freda after all, to be sure!'*

Surprise

Surprise, surprise!

a This is a surprise: ▷ *'Surprise, surprise! It's me! I'm back!'* ▷ *'Close your eyes for a moment. . . . Now open them! Surprise, surprise! It's a present for you!'*

b An expression used when fears of something poor or disappointing are confirmed: ▷ *'When we set up a stall in our local market to sell my wife's pottery, we didn't think we'd do very well, and—surprise, surprise!—we didn't sell a thing!'*

Sweat

No sweat   It will be done easily; it will be no problem: ▷ *'Will you fix my television by tonight?' 'Yes, no sweat—you can pick it up any time after three!'* ▷ *'Build that house for you in two months?' 'No sweat, man!'*

Swing

Swings and roundabouts   A saying that there are disadvantages, if one thing is done, that are equal to the advantages gained, if another is done. Also **What you lose on the swings you gain on the roundabouts.**

System

All systems go!   Everything is ready to start; you can start now: ▷ *'The royal couple have just arrived—so it's all systems go for the celebrations!'* Used originally in the launching of space vehicles, when everything was ready for take-off.

t

Tablet

Keep taking the tablets!   An expression used in response to someone's supposedly mad or crazy action: ▷ *'I've just walked on the headmaster's ceiling!' 'Don't worry, Martha, just keep taking the tablets!'*

Take

1   **. . ., I take it**   *Formal* Am I right in thinking . . .: used especially when the speaker assumes that someone is a particular person: ▷ *'Mr Jones, I take it?' 'Yes.' 'Then come this way, please, sir.'* ▷ *'May I take it that you'll be staying to dinner?'*

2   **It takes one to know one**   You are as bad as the person you are complaining about: ▷ *'Perry really is a fool.' 'It takes one to know one.'* Probably from the proverb *It takes a thief to catch a thief.*

3   **Point taken** *see* **Point 3.**

4   **Take a running jump!** *see* **Jump 3.**

5   **Take care!** *see* **Care 8.**

6   **Take it away!**   An instruction to start playing or singing music: ▷ *'From the thirteenth bar, take it away!'* ▷ *'Take it away, Sam!'*

7   **Take it easy!**

a   There is no need to worry!: ▷ *'Take it easy, Mary—Ruth is only a little late. I'm sure nothing's happened to her.'*

b   Don't rush!; don't get excited!: ▷ *'Take it easy, Mark—the taxi won't be here for half an hour yet—there's no need to panic!'*

8   **Take it or leave it**   It does not matter whether you accept something; it is only available on these terms: ▷ *'I'll give you £100 for that desk!' 'No! £200 is the price. Take it or leave it—I'm not bargaining with you!'*

9   **Take that!**   An expression said at the same time as hitting someone: ▷ *'Take that, you stupid boy! Will you never learn to respect your elders?'*

10   **Take that grin (or smile) off your face** *see* **Grin 2.**

11   **Take your (my, etc.) name in vain** *see* **Name 4.**

12 We can't take you anywhere! *see* **Anywhere 2**.

13 **(You can) take it from me**   You can believe me when I say this: ▷ *'You can take it from me; they're up to no good, I tell you—I've met their sort before!'* Also **(You can) take my word (for it)**: ▷ *'Take my word for it, if he says he'll do something, then he won't break his promise.'*

Tale

Thereby hangs a tale   There is an interesting or unusual story connected with what has just been talked about: often used only to suggest something further without actually saying anything more: ▷ *'When they built the new library in less than three months, not everyone was happy about the building methods they used, and thereby hangs a tale.'*

Talk

1 **Now you're talking**   At last what you're suggesting appeals to me: ▷ *'How much will you sell that car to me for?' '£600?' 'No!' '£500?' 'No!' '£400?' 'No!' '£250?' 'Now you're talking—it's a deal!'*

2 **Talk about**   This is a very good (or bad) example of something: ▷ *'Talk about a wonderful holiday! All our money was stolen!'* ▷ *'Talk about pride—he's the most big-headed man I've ever met!'*

3 **Talk of the devil!** *see* **Devil 4**.

4 **You can talk**

a You are much more comfortably off than I am, not having to do the particular thing yourself: ▷ *'I'm going to stay in bed late tomorrow.' 'You can talk—I've got to be up at six to go to work.'* The stress falls on *you*.

b You yourself are as guilty in the very matter you are complaining about in someone else: ▷ *'Johnny's eaten all the cakes, Mummy.' 'You can talk, Peter—you've eaten all the bread and butter!'* The stress falls on *you*. Also **Look who's talking!**; **You can't talk!**

Taste

There's no accounting for tastes   A saying that people all have different likes and dislikes; often said by a speaker who disapproves of what has just been mentioned: ▷ *'I've just bought their latest record.' 'Well, there's no accounting for tastes!'*

Teach

That (or I) will teach you to (do something) That (or I) will make you regret doing something, so that you will not do it again: ▷ *'So you were sick after eating all that chocolate—that'll teach you to spend all your pocket money on sweets!'* ▷ *'I'll teach you to interfere in my business—you can pay me back for those useless machines you made me buy.'*

Tear

That's torn it! That has spoiled our plans, etc.!; that has dashed our hopes!: ▷ *'It's raining! That's torn it! We were hoping for good weather for the fête!'* ▷ *'That's really torn it now! We'll never beat the other side now they know our secret!'*

Tell

1 **A little bird told me** *see* **Bird 1.**

2 **Do tell** Tell me about it: used to show interest and some surprise at what has just been said: ▷ *'Have you heard about Ralph and Pauline?'* *'No, do tell!'* The stress falls on *do*.

3 **Don't tell me!** An expression of disbelief, surprise, etc.: ▷ *'Don't tell me you've heard the news already! Yes, Marcia's expecting a baby!'* ▷ *'Don't tell me you can't make the party after all the preparations we've made?'* *'No, I'm sorry, but I'm busy tonight—I've got to work late!'* The stress falls on *don't*.

4 **I can tell you** Used to emphasise a statement: ▷ *'It's boiling hot outside, I can tell you!'* The stress falls on *tell*.

5 **I can't tell you . . .** I'm overwhelmed by (something, usually something pleasant): ▷ *'I can't tell you what it means to have company; I get so lonely here all by myself, you see.'* The stress falls on *tell*.

6 **I tell you** Used to add force to a statement: ▷ *'I tell you I really did see a flying-saucer last night!'* The stress falls on *tell*.

7 **(I) tell you what** *see* **Know 16.**

8 **I told you so** I warned you that this would happen, you didn't listen, and now you see that I was right: ▷ *'Jack's gone and broken a window!'* *'There you are—I told you so—I said we shouldn't let him play near the greenhouse.'* ▷ *'Daddy, my teddy bear won't squeak any more!'* *'I told you so—you shouldn't keep on hitting him!'* The stress falls on *told*.

9 **I'll tell you what** *see* **Know 16.**

10 I'm not telling! I won't answer your question: ▷ *'Where were you last night?' 'I'm not telling!'* Also **I'm not saying!**

11 I'm telling you Used to strengthen a previous statement that the speaker has made and that the other person is unsure of: ▷ *'They needn't pay us any money if we're made redundant, you know.' 'But surely we'd get something?' 'No, I'm telling you—we could be unemployed and get no money at all—there's no way round it.'*

12 Something tells me *see* **Something 3.**

13 Tell it like it is Just give us the straight facts in an honest way: ▷ *'Tell it like it is, Dick, we want to hear it all, however bad it is.'*

14 Tell it to the marines! *see* **Marine.**

15 Tell me another! *Rather old-fashioned* I simply can't believe you: ▷ *'Did you know that Jim's just got engaged to Sarah?' 'What? Tell me another! I thought he was going out with Judy last week!'*

16 That would be telling I am not telling you; used when the speaker wants to keep something secret: ▷ *'Who were you with last night?' 'Ah! That would be telling!'* The stress falls on *telling*.

17 There's no telling *see* **Know 22.**

18 To tell (you) the truth *see* **Truth.**

19 What did I tell you! *see* **Say 36.**

20 You can't tell him (her, etc.) anything

a He (she, etc.) can't keep a secret: ▷ *'You can't tell him anything. The moment he hears some bit of gossip, it's all round the town!'*

b He (she, etc.) knows everything: ▷ *'You can't tell her anything! She's been to college and thinks she knows it all!'*

21 You never can tell *see* **Know 28.**

22 You tell 'em! An expression used to encourage someone in what they are saying: ▷ *'You tell 'em, Barnie!' the man shouted out to the speaker at the election meeting.* The stress falls on *tell*.

23 You tell me I don't know; I've no idea: ▷ *'How can we possibly get through this week with just this amount of money?' 'You tell me.'* The stress falls on *you* and *me*.

24 You're telling me! I know what you're saying very well already: ▷ *'It's raining outside.' 'You're telling me—I've been out to get the paper and I'm absolutely soaked!'* ▷ *'I* *don't think I've done this very well, have I?' 'You're telling me you've not—it's awful!'* The stress falls on *me*.

Temper

Temper, temper! There's no need to get so angry!: used mainly to children; but usually having the effect of making matters worse: ▷ *Sarah was slowly getting more and more annoyed. 'Temper, temper, Sarah!' Patrick called out, but she flew more into a rage.*

Test

1 Just testing A reply to an answer given that corrects an error in the speaker's original statement or behaviour: often used humorously in an attempt to hide the speaker's ignorance or stupidity: ▷ *'The Battle of Hastings was 1166, wasn't it?' 'No, 1066.' 'Oh, yes, just testing!'*

2 Testing, testing An expression used in testing a microphone or other broadcasting equipment: ▷ *'Testing, testing, one, two, three; can you hear me at the back there?'*

Thank

1 I thank you . . . *Formal* Please (do something): ▷ *'I thank you not to walk on the grass.'*

2 I'll thank you to . . . Used to strengthen a command, request, etc., implying criticism: ▷ *'I'll thank you to mind your own business!'* ▷ *'I'll thank you to shut the door behind you!'*

3 Thank God! Also **Thank heavens!**

a An expression of gratitude to God: ▷ *'Thank God for life, and breath, and everything!'*

b An expression of gratitude: used especially to show delight or relief after some trouble has passed: ▷ *'Thank God you're back—we were getting worried about you!'* ▷ *'Thank heavens the weather stayed fine!'* ▷ *'Thank God it's Friday!'* Also **Thank goodness!**

4 Thank you Also *(stronger)* **Thank you very much**

a A polite expression of gratitude when accepting a present or service, or acknowledging praise: ▷ *'Thank you for the flowers—they were lovely!'* ▷ *'Thank you for coming!' 'Don't mention it; thanks for having us!'* Also **Many thanks**; **Thanking you.**

b A polite way of accepting or refusing an offer: ▷ *'Would* *you like some more tea?' 'No, thank you!'* ▷ *'Can I get your coat?' 'Thank you—it's lucky I brought one as it's so cold!'*

c Used as a polite expression at the end of an announcement: ▷ *'Please make sure you have all your belongings with you when you leave the train. Thank you.'*

d Used to stop something or to ask someone to leave: ▷ *Patrick was playing the piano in the music competition. 'Thank you!' the judge called out, 'I've heard enough now!'* ▷ *'Thank you, Bertram, that will be all! You may go now!'*

e Used after a statement to show delight, pleasure, or criticism: ▷ *'Last year our sales of maps did very nicely, thank you very much.'* ▷ *'Our football team is doing very well this season, thank you very much!'* ▷ *'Leave my private life alone, thank you!'*

f Used to show displeasure at something: ▷ *'I'll have my meal now and you can wait for yours!' 'Thank you, pal!'*

5 **Thank you for nothing** *see* **Nothing 5**.

6 **Thank your lucky stars!** *see* **Star**.

7 **Thanks (or thank you) for having me (us,** etc.**)** Thank you for your hospitality: said as you say goodbye to someone: ▷ *'Thanks for having us, Jo—we've had a lovely time!' 'That's OK—see you again sometime!'*

That

1 **Be that as it may** *see* **Be 3**.

2 **How's that?** *see* **How 15**.

3 **How's that for . . .** *see* **How 16**.

4 **Is that so?** *see* **So 3**.

5 **It is (or was) that** Used to confirm and strengthen something that someone else has just said: ▷ *'It's cold out, isn't it?' 'It is that!'* Also **That it is (or was)**: ▷ *'It was a bright, crisp winter last year, wasn't it?' 'Yes, that it was!'*

6 **That . . .!** *Formal or literary* Used in exclamations to express a wish: ▷ *'That things should have come to this!'* ▷ *'Oh, that I could be near my beloved!'*

7 **That does it!** *see* **Do 16**.

8 **That is (to say)** *see* **Say 30**.

9 **That will do** *see* **Do 17**.

10 **That's a . . .** *see* **There 9**.

11 **That's about it** That is more or less everything: ▷ *'Well, that's about it for tonight, folks. We'll see you same channel, same time, next week!'*

12 That's all

a No more need be said or done; there is no alternative: ▷ *'If we've not got any money, we won't be able to afford a holiday, that's all.'* Also **That's all there is to it:** ▷ *'I saw you taking the money from the drawer. You can't say you didn't, because I caught you in the act, and that's all there is to it!'*

b Only: used at the end of a sentence for emphasis: ▷ *'Can't we have a new car?' 'Sorry, but there just isn't the money!' 'I was just thinking, that's all.'*

13 That's as maybe! It is not yet definite that it is true: ▷ *'When I'm at college next year . . . !' 'That's as maybe, my girl! You've not passed your exams yet!'*

14 That's done it! *see* **Do 18.**

15 That's . . . for you *see* **There 10.**

16 That's how it is This is the position; these are the facts: said after an explanation: ▷ *'My job's in Birmingham, and I have to travel up there every day—that's how it is at the moment.'*

17 That's it

a That is the real problem: ▷ *'That's it—I just don't seem to have enough time these days to do all I want to do!'* The stress falls on *it*.

b That is the end; it is finished: ▷ *'That's it—it's all over, and a remarkable victory for England in this competition at last!'* ▷ *'That's tomorrow's weather forecast. And that's it from me until later.'*

c That is the right way to do it: used to show approval or encouragement: ▷ *'That's it! Now keep on like that and you won't lose your balance!'* Sometimes also used to mean the opposite: ▷ *'That's it! Go on—show us up in front of all our friends—that's typical of you!'* The stress falls on *that's*.

d Used to express annoyance at something: ▷ *'That's it! I'm fed up with you children breaking things! You can go straight to bed!'*

e Used to express disappointment: ▷ *'Well, that's it, then! If we're beaten as badly as that in every match this season, we'll never get promoted in the league!'* The stress falls on *it*.

f That is what is wanted: ▷ *'Yes, that's it—a little screwdriver—just what I need for my jobs around the house!'*

g What you say is right: ▷ *'You mean he stole all that money?' 'Yes, that's it!'*

18 That's more like it! *see* **Like 4.**

19 That's that

a That is the end of the matter: said at the end of a statement; and often implying regret at a state of affairs: ▷ *'Harry, you're not going to play football, and that's that!'* ▷ *'The post has just gone!' 'Oh well, that's that, then—this letter will never get there in time!'*

b That is the end of the discussion: ▷ *'Well, that's that for this week. We'll be back next Monday with another edition of World Vision.'*

c That is the end: said at the end of doing some work: ▷ *'Phew! That's that! I'm glad I've finished that essay at last!'*

20 That's what it is (or **was**)   That is (or was) the reason or explanation: ▷ *'That cab driver didn't look very happy!' 'You drove straight out in front of him at the last set of traffic lights, that's what it was.'*

21 You do that *see* **Do 26.**

There

1 So there!   Note what I'm saying or what has happened: said in a defiant tone: ▷ *'You can stop boasting—I've beaten you now, so there!'*

2 There again   Used to introduce a further explanation or reason: ▷ *'How could I get to Basingstoke?' 'Well, you could drive down, or, there again, you could come by train and I'll meet you at the station.'*

3 There are . . . and . . .   There are good and bad kinds of (things): ▷ *'There are cars and cars.'*

4 There it is   This is the problem; this is the state of affairs: ▷ *'There it is, I'm afraid, the firm's run out of money, so we've got no choice but to make some of the workers redundant.'*

5 There, there!   An expression of comfort or sympathy, as to a child: ▷ *'There, there, dear! Don't worry!'* Also **There now!**

6 There you are

a An expression used when giving something to someone; this is what you wanted: ▷ *'There you are, sir, your shoes, mended as you asked.'*

b An expression of triumph: used when one's opinion has been shown to be correct: ▷ *'There you are—I said we'd win first prize this year!' she called out, smiling excitedly.* ▷ *'Well, there you are, then! I knew all along he'd refuse.'*

c An expression used when finishing a presentation: ▷ *'I hope* *you liked my choice of records on this week's programme. There you are—and now, till next Tuesday, goodbye.'*

d An expression used at the end of an explanation: ▷ *'Turn right at the traffic lights, then second left, and there you are, the library will be opposite you.'*

e An expression used to make clear that something cannot be changed: ▷ *'That roof will have to be repaired within a month or two, I'm afraid—but there you are, you asked me what was wrong.'* Also **There we are.**

7 There you go again *see* **Go 18.**

8 There's . . . Used in making a suggestion: ▷ *'Who could we ask to be chairman next year?' 'Well, there's Mr Smith for a start—he's shown signs of interest.'* The phrase *There's always . . .* is used to introduce a suggestion that is a last resort but is known to be reliable: ▷ *'Where else could we go?' 'There's always London—I'd quite like to go round some of the museums again.'*

9 There's a . . . An expression of praise or encouragement to (a person or animal): ▷ *'You eat all your cabbage now, there's a good boy!'* ▷ *'Fetch it, there's a good dog!'* Also **That's a . . .:** ▷ *'Could you pass me that book, that's a good chap!'* ▷ *'Now that's a good girl! Don't pull your sister's hair!'*

10 There's (or **that's**) **. . . for you** An expression used to emphasise (a particular quality): used to show enthusiasm, but also sometimes annoyance or resignation: ▷ *'I arrived at the hotel, and a porter took my cases upstairs, someone ran my bath, and dinner was brought to my room—now, there's service for you!'* ▷ *'That's gratitude for you—I've been working hard all day, and she's not said a word of thanks the whole time!'*

Thick

Through thick and thin In the good times and the bad times; always, whatever happens: ▷ *'I'll stick by you, Sandra, through thick and thin.'*

Thief

Stop, thief! The cry of a person who has been robbed when chasing the thief: ▷ *'Stop, thief! Stop, thief!' the manager shouted, running out of his shop and going after the men who had stolen the jewels.*

Thing

1 (And a) good thing too *see* **Good 2.**

2 **First things first** Things must be done in order of the most important first: sometimes used as a reminder of something obvious: ▷ *'You must go and finish off your work, before you can go out to play. First things first!'* ▷ *'I'd like to build a new boat!' 'First things first—have you got the time and the money?'*

3 **For one thing** Here's a reason: used to introduce a reason or explanation: ▷ *'Why can't I get a motorbike?' 'For one thing, you're too young, and for another, you're not sensible enough yet.'*

4 **How are things?** *see* **How 6.**

5 **How are things going?** *see* **Go 13.**

6 **It's a good thing** It is fortunate: ▷ *'It's a good thing these walls are thick, or our neighbours might hear what we're saying!'*

7 **(Just) one of those things** Something that is liable to happen and cannot be avoided: used of unpleasant things: ▷ *'Being made redundant is just one of those things these days, I suppose.'*

8 **Just the thing!** That is exactly what was wanted: ▷ *'Here's a screwdriver!' 'Ah, just the thing!'*

9 **Kind (or sort) of thing** Used to make something sound less certain or definite: ▷ *'How long did it go on, kind of thing?'* ▷ *'It was a big car, sort of thing, a Cadillac, perhaps.'*

10 **Old thing** *Old-fashioned* A way of addressing someone in a friendly way: ▷ *'I say, old thing, what a funny hat you're wearing today!'*

11 **Sure (thing)!** Yes; of course: ▷ *'Can you come round tonight?' 'Sure thing! I'll be with you at six!'* This phrase is American in origin.

12 **That's the thing** *see* **This 2c.**

13 **The thing is . . .** The real, most important, point, or idea is . . .: ▷ *'The thing is, I love him.'* ▷ *'He said they'd come, but his brother said they wouldn't—the thing is, who am I to believe?'*

Think

1 **Good thinking!** What a good idea!: ▷ *'Why don't we go to Milton Keynes to do our Christmas shopping?' 'Good thinking! They've one of the best shopping-centres in the country!'*

▷ *'As she's not here, she could have gone home earlier.'* *'That's good thinking—let's go and see!'* The phrase was made more popular by *Good thinking, Batman* in the *Batman* strip cartoons.

2 **I don't think** *Humorous* An expression of disbelief in what has just been said: used to contradict the previous statement, often to criticise a person or thing: ▷ *'She's good-looking, I don't think!'* ▷ *'I thought the film was great!'* *'Great, I don't think!'* The stress falls on *don't*.

3 **I should have thought . . .** Used to express surprise (at something): ▷*'Isn't he here yet? I should have thought he'd be on time for his own wedding!'*

4 **I should think . . .** Of course: used to support a previous statement strongly: ▷ *'He's very proud of his first book!'* *'I should think so, the years it's taken for him to write it!'* ▷ *'Hot—I should jolly well think it was—it was baking in there!'*

5 **I think** Used to make an opinion sound less strong: ▷ *'It's usual, I think, to decide how big a dictionary should be before you start to write it.'* ▷ *'She's wrong, I think.'* ▷ *'I think I'll go and have a wash.'*

6 **I thought as much** It is just as I expected: often used about something bad: ▷ *'I thought as much—you've been out with that boy down the road again, haven't you? I can see it on your face!'* ▷ *'Did you have difficulty finding our house? I thought as much, since you were so late.'*

7 **I thought I told you . . .** Used as a criticism when someone has failed (to do something): ▷ *'I thought I told you to shut the door behind you!'* Also used with other verbs: ▷ *'I thought I asked you to come early this week!'*

8 **If you think (he thinks, etc.) that, you've (he's, etc.) got another think coming** If you (or he) think(s) like that, then you're (he's) very much mistaken: used to express strong disagreement or disapproval of a suggestion, statement, etc., in an angry way: ▷ *'If he thinks I'm going to work for that miserable wage, he's got another think coming.'* Sometimes shortened to **You've (he's, etc.) got another think coming.**

9 **Let me think** *see* **See 9.**

10 **(Now I) come to think of it** *see* **Come 12.**

11 **That's what you think** That is your opinion, but you are probably wrong: often said with a tone of contempt: ▷ *'When I get my extra money back from the tax people, I'm going to spend it on a new dress!'* *'That's what you think—I'm*

keeping it to pay for the repairs to the car!' The stress falls on
you.

12 **Think nothing of it!** *see* **Nothing 9.**

13 **To think . . .** Just imagine; just consider (this): ▷ *'To
think that the Queen stayed in my hotel! What an honour!'* ▷
'To think I once was a millionaire, and now look at my rags!'
Also **Just to think of it!**

14 **What do you think?** Used to introduce something surprising: ▷ *'What do you think? I've been promoted!'*

15 **Who do you (does he, etc.) think you are (he is, etc.)?** A
response to someone who has a high opinion of themselves: ▷ *'Just look at her, dressed like that! Who does she
think she is?'* Originally from the catch phrase *Who do you
think you are—Clark Gable?*

This

1 **This is how it is** This is the position; these are the facts: said
before an explanation is given: ▷ *'This is how it is: we can
lend you the money, provided you pay it back in two years.'*

2 **This is it**

a This is what you've been waiting for: used when introducing
or showing something: ▷ *'And now, ladies and gentlemen,
this is it, the most successful one-man act in the world—the
Owen Opie show!'* ▷ *'This is it, the finest vase of its kind in
the country!'*

b This is the crucial point: ▷ *'Well, this is it, then Robby!' 'Yes,
my love, it's time to say goodbye!'* ▷ *'Well, this is it! It's now
or never!'* I thought as I went into the interview room.

c That is indeed the reason: used as a reply when the speaker
agrees with the statement made by the previous speaker: ▷
*'We've not got enough money to buy a house.' 'This is it—they
cost such a lot of money, don't they?'* Also **That's the thing.**

3 **What's all this?** *see* **What 20.**

Thought

1 **A penny for your thoughts!** *see* **Penny 1.**

2 **Perish the thought!** *Becoming old-fashioned* I very much
hope this is not so: used about something unpleasant or
undesirable: ▷ *'Sally's not back yet. If something should
have happened to her, and perish the thought, you'll be to
blame for not looking after her properly, you know.'*

Thousand

I believe you, thousands wouldn't! *see* **Believe 4.**

Thrill

Big thrill! How exciting!: but usually used when the opposite is true: ▷ *'What's the next lecture, then?' 'Dr Stephens speaking to us on butterflies!' 'Oh, big thrill!'*

Thumb

1 **Thumbs down!** An expression showing disapproval of something: ▷ *'It's thumbs down for the cuts in fares on public transport, as it's against the law.'* The thumb is held out and pushed down slightly.

2 **Thumbs up!** An expression showing satisfaction, agreement, or victory: ▷ *'Thumbs up! We've got the go-ahead to make another film!'* The thumb is held out and stuck up slightly. The phrases in **1** and **2** come from the practice in ancient Rome, when the crowd would decide whether a defeated gladiator would be killed, in which case they would point their thumbs down, or be allowed to live, in which case they would point their thumbs up.

3 **Twiddle your (my,** etc.**) thumbs** To do nothing; wait for something to happen: ▷ *'What do you expect me to do all day—just sit around, twiddling my thumbs?'*

Thunder

By thunder! *see* **Jove.**

Tick

Half (or just) a tick *see* **Just 2a.**

Ticket

That's (just) the ticket *see* **Job 2.**

Timber

Shiver me (or my) timbers! *Old-fashioned* Used to express great surprise: used in rather humorous contexts: ▷ *'Shiver me timbers! It's Captain Cook!'* Originally, this phrase was used by sailors to mean 'shatter the sides of my ship!'

Time

1 **All in good time!** It will happen at the right time: said implying that the speaker does not want to be rushed and the person being spoken to should be patient: ▷ *'Can you give me back the money and the books I lent you?' Jo asked hurriedly. 'All in good time!' Geraldine replied calmly.*

2 **(And) about time, too!** An expression used when someone or something that has been delayed actually comes, happens, etc.: ▷ *'Good—I can see the bus coming—and about time, too!'* ▷ *'Here's Peter! About time, too! We've been waiting ages for you!'* Also used after *it's*: ▷ *'It's about time you started taking your studies more seriously, isn't it?'*

3 **Any time!** There is no need to say thank you; do what you have done any time: ▷ *'Thanks for a lovely evening!' 'Any time! It was very nice to see you again and have a good chat!'*

4 **Long time no see** It's nice to see you again after such a long time: ▷ *'Hello there! Long time no see!' 'Yes, it is a while, isn't it?'* A translation of the Chinese *háo jiǔ bù jiàn.*

5 **Time, gentlemen, please!** An expression used by the landlord in a public house when it is time to stop selling alcoholic drinks, and close: ▷ *'Time, gentlemen, please!' Jack called out at 10.30.*

6 **Time's up!** There is no more time allowed: ▷ *'Time's up! Put your pens down please and leave the examination hall quietly.'*

7 **Until the next time!** *see* **Meet 2.**

Tip

It's on the tip of my tongue I can't exactly remember it at the moment, although I'm thinking hard: ▷ *'His name's on the tip of my tongue—ah, yes, Pressworth, that was it.'* Also used when the speaker is about to say something: ▷ *'The words are on the tip of my tongue, but I don't quite know how to put what I want to say.'*

Toffee

. . . can't . . . for toffee (A person) just can't (do something) at all: ▷ *'He can't dance for toffee!'*

Together

All together now! *see* **All 9.**

Tongue

1 **Has the cat got your tongue?** *see* **Cat 1.**

2 It's on the tip of my tongue *see* **Tip.**

Tooth

1 **Fight tooth and nail** To make the strongest possible effort in a confrontation: ▷ *'We'll fight tooth and nail to make sure the motorway is not built through the countryside.'*

2 Hell's teeth! *see* **Hell 2.**

Top

1 **On top of that** Additionally; often used to introduce a further reason after having given one already: ▷ *'The firm went bankrupt as it ran out of money, and on top of that, there were just no more orders for its goods.'* ▷ *'He broke his leg, and on top of that, caught smallpox.'*

2 **The top of the morning (to you)!** *Irish* An expression used when greeting people in the morning.

Torn

That's torn it! *see* **Tear.**

Touch

Touch wood *see* **Wood 2.**

Trap

Shut your trap! *see* **Shut.**

Trick

1 **For my next trick . . .** *Humorous* An expression used, followed by a pause, after the speaker has failed to do something, dropped something, or missed a catch, etc.: ▷ *The box fell heavily to the ground. 'Oops! For my next trick . . . I'll balance it on my head!'* Originally from the language of the entertainer, to announce the next trick.

2 **How's tricks?** A greeting; how are you?: used between friends who have not seen each other for some time: ▷ *'Hello, Bill! How's tricks? It's ages since we had a chat, isn't it?'*

Trouble

1 **A trouble shared is a trouble halved** A saying that talking about your worries with someone will make them seem smaller.

2 Be looking for trouble *see* **Look 1.**

True

1 It just isn't true An expression used to emphasise and add strength to a statement: ▷ *'I'm so happy, it just isn't true!'* ▷ *'It just isn't true how much work I've got to do this weekend!'*

2 Too true! *see* **Right 9.**

Truly

Yours truly *see* **Yours 3.**

Trust

Trust you (him, etc.) to . . . You have (he has, etc.) as expected managed to (do something): used with things that have turned out badly: ▷ *'Trust you to open your big mouth and let out the secret!'* ▷ *'Trust Sarah to go and lose the keys!'*

Truth

To tell (you) the truth

a An expression used to make an apology for not fulfilling the other person's expectations in some way: ▷ *'What did you think of the book I lent you?' 'To tell you the truth, I've not had a chance to look at it yet.'*

b Used to introduce a personal comment on something that has just been said: ▷ *'Sue pretended that she knew Paris well, but to tell the truth, it was the first time she had been there.'*

c A way of expressing something negative, making the whole statement seem less strong: ▷ *'To tell you the truth, I don't really go for your choice of wallpaper somehow.'*

Turn

1 That's a turn-up for the book! That's very surprising: ▷ *'Well, Jim's here early for a change—that's a turn-up for the book!'*

2 Whatever turns you on! *Slang* I don't find this interesting in the least, even if you do: ▷ *'I think that that new record by the* Louts *is fantastic!' 'Whatever turns you on!'*

Tut

Tut, tut! An expression of disapproval or criticism: ▷

'Tut, tut, Perry! I'm surprised at your behaving like that! I'd have thought you'd have known better!'

Twenty-one

Twenty-one today!   *Humorous* A birthday greeting said to a woman who is obviously over twenty-one.

Two

Two can play at that game. *see* **Game 4.**

u

Unaccustomed

Unaccustomed as I am to public speaking . . . I am not experienced at speaking in public, but . . .: often used at the start of a speech as a mild apology: ▷ *'Unaccustomed as I am to public speaking,' the best man began, and the guests at the wedding all cheered, 'it gives me great pleasure as a close friend of the groom to be part of this happy event.'*

Uncle

(And) Bob's your uncle *see* **Bob.**

Up

1 **Up with . . .!** A slogan used to show the speaker's approval of something or someone: ▷ *'Up with the revolution!'* ▷ *'Up with the workers!'*

2 **Up with you!** Get up!: ▷ *'Up with you!' Mum shouted, as she pulled back the sheets, 'school begins in half an hour and you're not yet out of bed!'*

3 **Up yours!** *Slang* A rude expression used as a reply to express contempt, disagreement, or refusal and showing a disregard of the other person: ▷ *The car-park attendant told Andrew, 'You can't park here!' but he called back, 'Up yours!' and drove in.*

4 **What's up?** *see* **What 21.**

Use

Use your loaf! *see* **Loaf.**

Usual

The (or my) usual A request for the drink, food, etc., that the speaker usually has: ▷ *'The usual please, love.' 'Right, beans and chips coming up!'*

W

Wait

1   **I can hardly wait**   Used to show that the speaker is not really looking forward to something: used as a reply: ▷ *'Mother's coming down from Glasgow next week to stay with us.' 'I can hardly wait!'*

2   **I can't wait**   Used to show impatience and excitement in looking forward to something: ▷ *'I can't wait to see her face when she opens her present!'* ▷ *'I can't wait for the holidays to come!'*

3   **(Just) you wait**   Used as a threat of punishment: ▷ *'Just you wait—I'll get you back for this!'* ▷ *'Just you wait till your father comes home!'*

4   **Wait a minute** (or **moment**)

a   I shall not keep you waiting for a long time: ▷ *'Wait a minute, while I just find your record card.'* ▷ *'Wait a moment and I'll ask someone for you.'*

b   I wish to make a comment or objection: ▷ *'Wait a minute! Didn't we try that plan a few months ago and found it didn't work?'* ▷ *'Wait a moment! I've got an idea!'* Also **Wait a second.**

c   An expression of surprise or amazement: ▷ *'Wait a moment! Haven't we met before? Ah yes, didn't we meet at that training camp in Hampshire?'* Also **Wait a second.**

5   **Wait for it!**

a   Don't move, speak, etc., before the proper moment: ▷ *'Right, class, go when I blow the whistle, wait for it . . . now, go!'*

b   Used to introduce something exciting: ▷ *'He may be about to get the highest score in the whole history of the game—wait for it—yes, McDonald's done it!'*

6   **Wait for me!**   Don't go so fast or go away so that I'm left behind!: ▷ *'Wait for me, everyone! I'm just coming!'*

Wakey

Wakey, wakey!   *Often humorous* Wake up!: ▷ *I was sound asleep in bed when suddenly my dreams were shattered by mother crying out, 'Wakey, wakey, Peter!'* The phrase was

made more current by the radio and television programme,
Billy Cotton's Band Show, first broadcast in 1949.

Want

1 **He (she, etc.) didn't want to know** He (she, etc.) took no
interest or notice in what was being said or happening: ▷
*'There I was talking to her, but she just looked at me blankly—
she didn't want to know.'* ▷ *'The crowds just walked past the
injured man—they just didn't want to know.'*

2 **You want to . . .** Also **You ought to . . .; You should . . .**

a A wish that the person the speaker is talking to would (do
something): used to describe something that is special or
unusual in some way: ▷ *'You want to see the way she plays
tennis!'* ▷ *'He might think he's got a very good mark, but you
ought to wait till you hear mine!'*

b A wish that the person the speaker is talking to would (do
something): used as a warning or criticism: ▷ *'You want to
look where you're going, young man!'* ▷ *'You should be
more careful!'*

Wart

Warts and all *see* **All 11a.**

Watch

1 **Watch it!** Be careful!: ▷ *'Watch it! The bottom of that box
looks as if it might fall out!'* ▷ *'You'd better watch it! Unless
your marks improve, you'll be moved down a class!'*

2 **Watch out!** Be careful!: used as a warning: ▷ *'Watch out!
There's a car coming!'* ▷ *'Watch out! There's a thief about!'*

3 **Watch your step!** *see* **Step 1.**

Way

1 **(Be) on your way!** Go!: ▷ *'On your way!' the teacher
shouted angrily to the boys playing around after school had
finished.*

2 **By the way** Used to introduce a new subject or something
that the speaker has just thought of into a conversation: ▷
'By the way, how did you get on at the doctor's?' ▷ *'By the
way, when you saw Ruth, did she say anything about coming
round?'* The stress falls on *way*.

3 **No way** No; under no circumstances; what you're suggesting is impossible: ▷ *'Will you lend me £50?' 'No way—
you didn't pay me back the last time I lent you some, so I'm not*

giving you any more now!' This phrase is American in origin.

4   **Step this way**   *Formal* Please come this way; follow me: ▷ *'Step this way, ladies and gentlemen, to see the world's biggest man-eating spider!'*

5   **That's the way it goes** *see* **Cookie.**

6   **That's the way the cookie crumbles** *see* **Cookie.**

7   **There's (or there are) no two ways about it**   There is no alternative; it is definite; there is no other opinion: ▷ *'There's no two ways about it—I'm afraid we shall have to follow the rules.'* ▷ *'There are no two ways about it—as manager of our export section, you've been a dismal failure, and we must ask you to leave.'*

8   **Way out**   *Slang* Very unusual, because it is very modern or even ahead of its time: ▷ *'Wow! That dress is a bit way out, isn't it?'*

Weather

1   **Lovely weather for ducks!**   *Humorous* Aren't we having rainy weather at the moment!: ▷ *Geoff passed Jill in the street. 'Lovely weather for ducks!' he called out from under his umbrella.*

2   **Under the weather**   Not very well or not very happy: ▷ *Robert was feeling a bit under the weather as he'd not had much sleep for several nights.*

Weave

Get weaving! *see* **Crack.**

Week

Any day of the week *see* **Day 1.**

Weight

Worth its (his, etc.) weight in gold   Very valuable: ▷ *'He's worth his weight in gold—I don't know anyone who's more reliable.'*

Welcome

You're welcome!   *American* There is no need to thank me: ▷ *'Thanks for your help!' 'You're welcome!'*

Well

1   **(All) well and good**   Used to express detached acceptance of a suggestion or decision: ▷ *'If he offers me some more work, all well and good, if not I don't mind too much.'* ▷ *'If you refuse to take my advice, well and good, but don't come crying to me in six months, saying it didn't work out.'* Also used to show dissatisfaction at the subject being discussed: ▷ *'It's all well and good for you to just sit there and expect me to keep the house clean, when I've got my own job to do and I look after the children as well.'*

2 **It's all very well** An expression showing discontent, dissatisfaction, or sometimes envy, at a reply or at someone's advice: ▷ *'Why don't you work it out the way I've just shown you?' 'It's all very well for you to make suggestions, you don't have to sit down and do it!'* Also **It's all right**: ▷ *'When do you go back to work?' 'Next week.' 'It's all right for some, isn't it—I'm going back tomorrow!'* Also used with a noun as subject: ▷ *'These clothes are all very well for wearing in the summer, but they're not heavy or warm enough for the winter.'*

3 **Just as well** An expression used as a reply to show that something, such as an event or circumstance, was indeed fortunate: ▷ *'We were too late for the concert!' 'Just as well—it wasn't very good anyway.'* ▷ *'It's just as well you came—we needed someone with your experience.'*

4 **Oh well** Used to show a resigned acceptance of something bad: ▷ *'Oh well, I shouldn't grumble, I suppose, this is the first time something like this has happened.'* ▷ *'Oh well, it can't be helped.'*

5 **Very well** An expression showing acceptance of or agreement to something that has just been said, but often showing unwillingness also: ▷ *'Please be home early tonight—I want to wash your hair.' 'Very well, mother!'* ▷ *'I'm not sure I really want to take your advice.' 'Very well, then, if you don't want to, I don't mind, but don't say I didn't warn you!'*

6 **Well done!** *see* **Do 19.**

7 **Well I never did!** *see* **Do 20.**

8 **Well then** An expression showing expectation of something: ▷ *'Well then, what's your answer?'* ▷ *'Well then, what do we do now?'*

9 **Well, well** An expression of surprise: ▷ *'Well, well, who'd have thought those two would end up getting married?'* Also **Well, well, well.**

Well-off

You don't know when you're well-off *see* **Know 24.**

What

1   And I don't know what *see* **Know 1.**

2   And what's more *see* **More 1.**

3   For what it's worth *see* **Worth.**

4   I know what *see* **Know 16.**

5   **Or what**   Used when the speaker is unsure of what is said: often used when there are a number of alternatives and there may be more: ▷ *'I've not seen her recently—I don't know whether she's moved away, whether I've upset her, or what.'* Also **Or whatever.**

6   **So what?**   What importance or relevance does that have?: used to show a lack of interest and often said in an impolite, unfriendly way: ▷ *'I'm going to New York on business next week.' 'So what—we've still got to stay here and work all the same!'* ▷ *'He can have his suspicions if he wants—so what? We don't care!'* Also *(more formal)* **What of** (or **about**) **it?**

7   That's what it is *see* **That 20.**

8   Well, what do you know (about that)! *see* **Know 23.**

9   **What . . .!**   Used to introduce an exclamation: ▷ *'What a fool I've been!'* ▷ *'What awful weather we're having at the moment!'* ▷ *'What lovely flowers!'*

10   What about . . .? *see* **About 1.**

11   What about that! *see* **About 2.**

12   What can I do for you? *see* **Help 1.**

13   What do you do (for a living)? *see* **Do 22.**

14   **What ho!**   *Old-fashioned* An expression of greeting or used to attract attention: ▷ *'What ho, old chap!'*

15   **What if . . .?**   What would or will happen if (something were to happen)?: ▷ *'What if we bought a new carpet— would it make any difference to the room?'* ▷ *'What if the President were shot?'*

16   **What is it?**   What do you want?: ▷ *'Herby, are you in there?' 'What is it? I'm busy!'* Note also **What is it now?** Why are you bothering me again?: ▷ *'Herby, are you still there?' 'What is it now? You've seen me once already today!'* The stress falls on *now.*

17   **What is it to you?**   Why are you interested in this?: ▷ *'How old are you?' 'Why do you want to know? What is it to you?'*

18   **What next?**   What further surprising or cheeky thing will come now?: ▷ *'What next? You'll be asking us to pay you to take these books away, instead of you paying us!'*

19 **What with** Used to introduce a number of reasons for something, usually something bad: ▷ *'What with one thing and another, over the last few weeks, I've not got round to ringing her up, I'm afraid.'* ▷ *'We've had awful weather this year, what with all the snow and heavy frosts.'*

20 **What's all this?** What's going on?; what's the matter?: ▷ *'What's all this, boys? Why aren't you paying attention and listening?'*

21 **What's up?** What is happening?; what's the matter?: ▷ *'What's up? What's everyone looking at?'* ▷ *'What's up with Rachel today?'* ▷ *'What's up, Rolf? You look as if you've seen a ghost!'*

22 **What's yours?** What would you like to drink?: ▷ *'What's yours, Nick?' 'Gin and tonic, please.'*

23 **You know what?** *see* **Know 26.**

24 **You know what you can do with . . .** *see* **Know 27.**

25 **You what?** *Slang*

a Please repeat what you said as I didn't hear it properly: ▷ *'The postman's at the door.' 'You what?' 'I said the postman's come.'*

b An expression of dismay, surprise, etc.: ▷ *'You remember you still owe me £500?' 'You what! I paid that back to you, didn't I?'*

Whatever

Or whatever *see* **What 5.**

When

Say when *see* **Say 28.**

Where

1 Where do we go from here? *see* **Go 19.**

2 **Where were we?** What were we talking about before our thoughts were interrupted?: ▷ *'Where were we? Oh yes, we were discussing the arrangements for the party next month.'*

Who

1 And I don't know who *see* **Know 1.**

2 Who goes there? *see* **Go 20.**

3 Who is it? *see* **It 4.**

4   Who's . . . when he's at home? *see* **Home 4.**

Whole

On the whole   Generally speaking: taking everything into consideration: ▷ *'On the whole, I'm inclined to agree with you, but we do see things differently in one or two places.'* ▷ *'Britain is still an industrialised country on the whole.'* Also **By and large.**

Why

Why not . . .?   Used to introduce a suggestion: ▷ *'Why not take a chance on it?'* ▷ *'Why not ask him for yourself?'*

Wife

The wife *see* **Missis.**

Will

1   God willing *see* **God 13.**
2   Have . . ., will . . . *see* **Have 2.**
3   Will do! *see* **Do 25.**

Win

1   May the best man win! *see* **Man 5.**
2   You can't win (them all)   An expression of resignation after a failure or series of failures: ▷ *'We spent years campaigning for a by-pass. Now it's been built, you hear the heavy lorries driving by so fast that it's as noisy as ever. You can't win, can you?'* *Them* is often shortened to *'em.*

Wipe

Wipe that grin off your face *see* **Grin 2.**

Woe

1   Woe betide   *Rather old-fashioned* Punishment, misfortune, etc., will come: often used as a threat: ▷ *'Woe betide if you arrive late!'* ▷ *'Woe betide the man who fails to keep the rules!'*
2   Woe (is me)!   *Archaic* An exclamation of sorrow or grief.

Woman

My good woman   An offensive expression used to show the speaker thinks that he or she is more important than the woman he is speaking to: ▷ *'Look here, my good woman! No one has ever been so rude to me before in all my life!'*

Wonder

1 **I shouldn't wonder** I wouldn't be surprised; I'm fairly confident (that): ▷ *'He'll have left that job by now, I shouldn't wonder.'* ▷ *'I shouldn't wonder if he's at university—he was very clever, you know.'*

2 **I wonder if . . .** A polite way of asking (something): ▷ *'I wonder if you'd mind opening the window.'* ▷ *'I wonder if I could see the doctor this evening.'* Also **I was wondering if . . .**: ▷ *'I was wondering if I might have another glass of wine.'*

3 **It's a wonder (that)** It's surprising that: ▷ *'It's a wonder you're still living here after all these years!'*

4 **(It's) no wonder** (I am) not very surprised that . . .; of course: ▷ *'No wonder Jack couldn't come dancing with us; he has broken his leg, after all.'* Alternatives to *no* are *little* and *small*: ▷ *'It's little wonder you're so thin—you never seem to eat much.'* ▷ *'We've not had a new car for years. Small wonder, as we've hardly any money.'*

5 **The wonder is** What is surprising: ▷ *'The wonder is that she remembered my name!'*

6 **Wonders will never cease** I am most surprised by what you have done, what has happened, etc.: ▷ *'I've done the washing-up, Mum!' 'Wonders will never cease!'*

Wood

1 **Not see the wood for the trees** To be so occupied with details that you do not look at what you are doing more generally: ▷ *Many leaders get absorbed in small matters and so don't see the wood for the trees.*

2 **Touch wood** An expression used when the speaker hopes that things will be or continue as has just been said: used to bring good luck; often said touching something near made of wood: ▷ *'We've had no expensive repair bills on the car so far, touch wood!'* American equivalent *Knock on wood.*

Word

1 **(Could I have) a word in your ear?** May I speak to you in private?: ▷ *'A word in your ear, John? It's about those new contracts we mentioned.'* ▷ *'Could I have a word in your ear,* *if you can bear to leave everyone here for a moment? It's rather urgent.'*

2 Famous last words!   An expression used as a reply to a boasting, self-assured, or optimistic statement: often said as a warning or in a mocking, disbelieving tone: ▷ *'Playing with matches is a good game!' 'Famous last words! You'll set fire to yourself if you're not careful.'* ▷ *'I'll be back in half an hour!' 'Famous last words—you've said that before and you've been gone all morning!'*

3 In other words   An expression used to clarify or expand on something that has just been said: ▷ *'Patrick works hard; in other words, he's an excellent student.'* ▷ *'The first verse in the Bible begins, "In the beginning God created . . ."; in other words, it states firmly that God exists and that He acts.'* Also used as a reply: ▷ *'I'm not very happy about what you're doing.' 'In other words, you don't trust me?' 'I wouldn't quite say that.'*

4 . . . isn't the word for it   An expression used to show that something is not put in an extreme enough way: ▷ *'It's rather cold today, isn't it?' 'Cold isn't the word for it—it's absolutely freezing!'*

5 Mark my words!   Take note of what I'm saying: often used as a warning or threat: ▷ *'Mark my words, he'll let you down. He's worked for me in the past, so I know he's not very reliable.'* ▷ *'He'll be back soon, mark my words—he never stays away for long.'* ▷ *'Mark my words, never come near this house again!'*

6 Mum's the word *see* **Mum.**

7 My word!   An expression showing surprise, annoyance, etc.: ▷ *'My word! How nice to see you again!'* ▷ *'My word, you've got a lot of explaining to do, you know!'* Also *(old-fashioned)* **Upon my word!**

8 Not a word   Don't say anything (about something): ▷ *'Here comes Mum, so remember, not a word about her birthday present!'* ▷ *'Not a word to the others, OK?'*

9 Not another word   Don't say anything more (about something): ▷ *'So that's settled then, is it? Now, not another word about it!'* ▷ *'Now goodnight, children, and I don't want another word out of you tonight.'*

10 Not in so many words   Not quite the right or exact way of expressing something: ▷ *'Would you say the talk was a success?' 'Well, not in so many words . . . but it was quite* *useful, nevertheless.'* ▷ *'We weren't invited in so many words; but she certainly told us she was having a party.'*

11 **One more word out of . . .** Be quiet; a threat or warning to (someone) that punishment will follow if there is not silence: ▷ *'One more word out of you, and I won't let you go on the trip.'*

12 **Sharp's the word!** Be quick!: ▷ *'Sharp's the word! We've got to go in a minute—come on and get ready!'*

13 **Words fail me** I am too surprised, shocked, angry, happy, etc., to express my thoughts adequately: ▷ *'You say you spent £1000 on that car! Words fail me! What a fool you are!'* ▷ *'Words fail me! You come in here and expect me to give you all my attention for a whole hour. You know I'm busy, so just go!'*

14 **(You can) take my word (for it)** *see* **Take 13.**

Work
(It's) all in a day's work *see* **Day 4.**

World
1 **It's a small world!** An expression used when one meets in an unexpected place a person whom one knows: ▷ *'Janet— how nice to see you! What are you doing here in Germany?' 'I'm on holiday, too! It's a small world, isn't it!'*

2 **On top of the world** Very happy; very well: ▷ *'I'm feeling on top of the world today—I've just heard I've passed all my exams!'*

3 **The world and his wife** Everyone: ▷ *'It seemed that the world and his wife were at the reception!'*

Worry
1 **Don't worry** There is no need for you to worry: ▷ *'I can't quite reach the tin on the top shelf.' 'Don't worry, I'll get it for you.'* ▷ *'I'll be fine, don't worry!'*

2 **Not to worry** There is no need to worry: ▷ *'I've lost my ticket.' 'Well, not to worry, we can pay when we get to London.'* Also **No worry.**

3 **You should worry!** *Humorous* You certainly need not worry: ▷ *'You should worry with a salary like that coming in every month! You don't know how lucky you are!'*

Worse
(Things) could be worse A reply to a greeting such as 'How

are you?', saying that one's health and well-being are really not too bad: ▷ *'How are you, Jim?' 'Things could be worse—we're not managing too badly at the moment, thanks.'* Also **It could be worse.**

Worst

If the worst comes to the worst   If all the better alternatives are impossible or if the worst possible thing happens: ▷ *'If the worst comes to the worst, and all the hotels are full, you could always stay with us, I suppose.'* ▷ *'We'll have to close the whole business down, if the worst comes to the worst, and if there are no more orders.'*

Worth

For what it's worth   An expression used when the speaker is not sure of the importance of a statement, opinion, etc.: ▷ *'For what it's worth, I don't really think she's the right girl for the job.'*

Would

1   If you would *see* **If 4.**

2   Would . . .   *Becoming old-fashioned* I wish: ▷ *'Would that he were alive to see our new baby daughter!'* ▷ *'Would that things were different!'*

3   . . . would rather . . .   (Someone) would prefer to (do something): used to show a choice: ▷ *'Would you rather go by train or coach?'* ▷ *'I'd rather you came a bit earlier, really, if you can.'* ▷ *'May I smoke?' 'I'd rather you didn't.'*

4   Would you . . .? *see* **Mind 1.**

5   You (he, etc.) would . . .   An expression used to show annoyance at what someone has done because they often do it or is just the kind of thing they do: ▷ *'You would go and spoil our plans again by telling us now that you can't come!'* ▷ *'That's just like Jackie—she would forget to bring the tickets!'*

Wrap

Wrap up!   *Becoming old-fashioned* Be quiet!: ▷ *'Wrap up, Pete! Can't you stop moaning?'*

Writing

Could I have that in writing!   An expression used when

someone has made a compliment or said something flattering about the speaker: used humorously: ▷ *'We've always found you to be a man of most remarkable abilities!' 'Could I have that in writing!'*

Wrong

Don't get me wrong *see* **Get 1**.

y

Yah

Yah boo sucks to you! *see* **Suck.**

Yeah

Oh, yeah! An expression of rude disbelief: ▷ *'If you don't shut up, I'll come and hit you!' 'Oh, yeah—really?'*

Year

Happy new year! An expression of greeting around the time of the beginning of a new year: ▷ *'Happy New Year!' 'Happy New Year, everyone!' they all cried, raising their glasses, as the clock struck midnight.* ▷ *'We wish all our friends a happy new year!'*

Yes

Yes and no An ambiguous answer to a question, showing that the speaker wants to reply 'yes' to some aspects and 'no' to other aspects of the matter: ▷ *'Would you like a job in London?' 'Yes and no—the salaries are high, and there's lots to do, but it's so noisy and busy.'* ▷ *'Have you made up your mind whether to go?' 'Yes and no.'*

Yesterday

I wasn't born yesterday *see* **Born 2.**

You

1 There's . . . for you *see* **There 10.**
2 **You and your . . .** Used to express disapproval of what someone has said or done: ▷ *'You and your idea of coming early to the exhibition—just look at the queue!'* ▷ *'You and your statistics! Why don't you shut up about the gross national product and come down to earth?'*
3 **You there!** An expression used to call someone's attention: ▷ *'Hey, you there! What are you doing with that picture?'*
4 **You're another!** An expression used as a reply to show that the accusation just made of someone else applies to them

also: ▷ *'I think Jim's rather a fool!' 'Yes, and you're another!'*

Young
You're not as young as you used to be A polite way of saying that someone is getting older: ▷ *'You shouldn't spend the whole day rushing round town like that—remember, you're not as young as you used to be!'* Also **You're not getting any younger.**

Your
1 You and your . . . *see* **You 2.**
2 Your actual . . . *see* **Actual.**

Yours
1 Up yours! *see* **Up 3.**
2 What's yours? *see* **What 22.**
3 Yours truly *Humorous* A way of referring to oneself: ▷ *'Who was it that was left behind to clear up the mess? Yours truly!'*

Yourself
How's yourself? *see* **How 6.**

Index

How to use the index

In the index the idioms in the dictionary are listed under subjects. If you are looking for a suitable idiom to express a particular topic or function of the language, you can consult this list. You will then be referred to the keyword in the dictionary where the idiom is listed. Note that the index does not include any style markers on levels of formality, etc.: guidance on this is given at the entries in the dictionary itself.

I beg your pardon **Pardon c**
I'm not so sure **Sure 4**
I'm sorry! **Sorry b**
Just a moment **Just 2b**
Not if I can help it **Help 3**
Not if I know it **Help 3**
Not so fast **Fast**
Pardon me **Pardon c**
That does it! **Do 16**
That's done it! **Do 18**
Up yours! **Up 3**
Wait a minute **Wait 4b**
Wait a moment **Wait 4b**

Agreement *see under* **Actions;
    Explanations;
    Statements; Suggestions.**

Anger *see* **Annoyance or
    anger.**

Angry, requests not to get
Cool it! **Cool**
Count to ten before you lose your
    temper! **Count**
Keep your hair on! **Shirt 1**
Keep your shirt on! **Shirt 1**
Temper, temper! **Temper**

Annoyance or anger
A plague on you! **Plague**
All right **All 6d**
As if . . . **As 2**
Blast it! **Blast 1**
Blast you! **Blast 1**
Blow it! **Blow 1**
By Gad! **Gad**
By George! **George**
By golly! **Golly**
By heaven! **Good 7**
Come, come! **Come 5**
Confound it! **Confound**
Confound you! **Confound**
Curse it! **Curse 1**
Curse you! **Curse 1**
Damn it! **Damn 2**

Damn me! **Damn 3**
Damn you! **Damn 2**
Darn it! **Darn 1**
Dash it! **Dash**
Don't . . . me! **Do 6**
Don't mind me **Mind 3b**
Don't say . . . **Say 5**
Don't strain yourself! **Strain**
Drat it! **Drat**
Drat you! **Drat**
Excuse me **Excuse 2c**
For crying out loud! **Cry 2**
For God's sake! **Goodness 1**
For goodness' sake! **Goodness 1**
For heaven's sake! **Goodness 1**
For mercy's sake! **Goodness 1**
For Pete's sake! **Goodness 1**
For pity's sake! **Goodness 1**
Get along with you! **Get 4**
Get away! **Get 4**
Get away with you! **Get 4**
Get on! **Get 4**
Get stuffed! **Stuff 1**
Give me strength! **Strength**
Go along with you! **Get 4**
Go to the devil! **Devil 3**
God almighty! **God 17**
God preserve us! **Preserve**
Good God! **Good 7**
Good gracious! **Good 7**
Good heavens! **Good 7**
Good Lord! **Good 7**
Goodness gracious me! **Good 7**
Goodness me! **Good 7**
Hang it! **Hang 2**
Heaven preserve us! **Preserve**
Heavens above! **Heaven 8**
Heavens to Murgatroyd!
    Heaven 8
Hell's bells! **Hell 2**
Hell's teeth! **Hell 2**
Holy smoke! **Holy**
I ask you! **Ask 4**
I don't know **Know 10a**
I thought I told you . . . **Think 7**
If you please **Please 1b**

If you think that, you've got another think coming **Think 8**
I'll be damned! **Damn 3**
I'll be darned **Darn 2**
I'll thank you to . . . **Thank 2**
I'm damned! **Damn 3**
I'm jiggered! **Jigger**
. . . in a minute! **Minute 1**
Mind your own business! **Business 2**
My God! **God 17**
My goodness! **Good 7**
My word! **Word 7**
Naughty, naughty! **Naughty**
Of all the . . . **All 21**
Oh brother! **Brother**
Oh God! **God 17**
Oh Lord! **God 17**
Oh my! **My 2**
Saints preserve us! **Preserve**
Some . . . **Some a**
Stuff it! **Stuff 1**
Stuff you! **Stuff 1**
Thank you **Thank 4e, f**
That does it! **Do 16**
That's . . . for you **There 10**
That's it **That 17d**
The devil you do! **Devil 6**
There's . . . for you **There 10**
Well I do declare! **Declare**
Well I like that! **Like 5**
Well I'll be! **Blow 3**
Well I'll be blowed! **Blow 3**
Well really! **Really 3**
What do you mean by . . .? **Mean 7**
What on earth? **Earth 2**
What the blazes? **Blaze 3**
What the deuce? **Deuce**
What the devil? **Devil 9**
What the dickens? **Dickens**
What the heck? **Hell 5**
What the hell? **Hell 5**
. . . will be the death of me **Death**
Words fail me **Word 13**

You can keep . . . **Keep 5**
You what? **What 25b**
You would . . . **Would 5**

Apologies
Beg pardon **Pardon b**
Excuse me **Excuse 2b**
How could I have . . .? **How 8**
I beg your pardon **Pardon b**
I'm sorry! **Sorry a**
Oops a daisy! **Oops b**
Pardon **Pardon b**
Pardon my French **French**
So sorry! **Sorry a**
To tell you the truth **Truth a**
Unaccustomed as I am to public speaking . . . **Unaccustomed**

Apologies, acknowledging
Don't mention it! **Mention 1**
Forget it! **Forget**
It's all right **All 23**
No matter! **Matter 3**
Not at all! **Not 1**
Skip it! **Skip**
So I see **See 13**
That's all right **All 23**
Think nothing of it! **Nothing 9**

Appearances
And about time, too! **Time 2**
It's a small world! **World 1**
Lo and behold! **Lo**
Speak of the devil! **Devil 4**
Talk of the devil! **Devil 4**

Approval, slogans expressing
. . . for ever! **Ever 3**
Thumbs up! **Thumb 2**
Up with . . .! **Up 1**

Approval and praise
And a good job too **Good 2**
And a good thing too **Good 2**

Could I have that in writing!
 Writing
Good show! **Show 2**
Great stuff! **Stuff 3**
Hear! hear! **Hear 1**
Hip, hip, hurrah! **Hip**
How about that, then! **About 2**
How's that for . . . **How 16**
I'd be the first to . . . **Person 1**
If you like **Like 3a**
Just the thing! **Thing 8**
Now that's what I call . . . **Call 3**
Put it there! **Put 2**
Quite a . . . **Quite 1**
Right on! **Right 4**
Stick it there! **Put 2**
That can't be bad! **Bad 4**
That's a . . . **There 9**
That's it **That 17c**
That's just the job **Job 2**
That's my boy! **Boy 3**
That's praise indeed! **Praise 2**
That's the stuff! **Stuff 3**
There's a . . . **There 9**
There's my boy! **Boy 3**
Three cheers! **Cheer 2**
Thumbs up! **Thumb 2**
Too right! **Right 9**
Too true! **Right 9**
Up with . . .! **Up 1**
Well done! **Do 19**
What about that! **About 2**

Asking *see* **Enquiries and asking for information; Requests, making.**

Attention, attracting
Excuse me **Excuse 2a**
Get a load of this! **Load 1**
Hello there! **Hello 3**
Here you are **Here 3b**
I hate to mention it, but . . .
 Mention 2
I say **Say 13b**
If you don't mind my mentioning
 it **Mention 2**

Look here! **Look 4**
Look you! **Look 10**
Now then **Now 4**
Right then **Now 4**
See here! **Look 4**
Would you believe **Believe 6**
You there! **You 3**

Belief, inviting
Believe me **Believe 2**
Believe you me **Believe 2**
Do you see what I mean? **See 3a**
Take it from me **Take 13**
Take my word for it **Take 13**
You see if . . . **See 16**

Boasting
As a matter of fact **Fact a**
So there! **There 1**
Though I say it myself **Say 33**
Yah boo sucks to you! **Suck**

Boasting, replies to
Big deal! **Deal**
Big thrill! **Thrill**
Famous last words! **Word 2**
Get you! **Get 13**
Look who's talking! **Talk 4b**
So there! **There 1**
Who do you think you are?
 Think 15
You can talk **Talk 4a**
You can't talk! **Talk 4b**
You flatter yourself **Flatter**

Caution or care
Easy does it **Do 7**
Go easy **Go 5**
Have a care! **Care 4**
Hold your horses! **Horse**
Look after yourself! **Look 3**
Look out! **Look 6**
Look sharp! **Sharp 1b**
Mind how you go! **Mind 10**
Mind out! **Mind 11**

Mind your head(s)! **Head 2**
Mind your step! **Step 1**
Steady on **Steady**
Take care! **Care 8**
Watch it! **Watch 1**
Watch out! **Watch 2**
Watch your step! **Step 1**

Certainty
And I don't mean maybe **Mean 1**
And no mistake **Mistake 1**
And that's for sure **Sure 1**
Depend on it **Depend 2**
I bet **Bet 1a**
I knew it **Know 14**
I should think . . . **Think 4**
I tell you **Tell 6**
I wouldn't dream of it **Dream 1**
If I know you **Know 19**
I'll be bound **Bound**
I'm sure . . . **Sure 6**
It's no wonder **Wonder 4**
Knowing you **Know 19**
Make no bones about it! **Make 5**
Make no mistake about it!
    Make 5
No doubt **Doubt**
Not a hope! **Hope 2**
Not have an earthly **Earthly**
Not on your life! **Life 4**
. . . or my name's not . . .
    Name 3
Rest assured **Rest 4**
Some hope! **Hope 2**
That figures! **Figure**
There's no mistake about it!
    Mistake 3
There's no two ways about it
    Way 7
To be sure **Sure 10a**
You bet **Bet 3**
You can bet your bottom dollar
    Bet 4
You can depend on it **Depend 2**
You can rest assured **Rest 4**
You know what he is **Know 19**

Children, adults'
    expressions to
Act your age! **Age 1**
All together now! **All 9**
Be your age! **Age 1**
Bless his (little) cotton socks
    Bless 4
Has the cat got your tongue?
    Cat 1
Naughty, naughty! **Naughty**
Night, night **Night 2**
One for . . . **One 4**
Sweet dreams! **Dream 2**
Take that! **Take 10**
That's a . . . **There 9**
There, there! **There 5**
There's a . . . **There 9**
What do you say? **Say 37b**
Who's she? The cat's mother?
    Cat 3

Children, typical
    expressions of
Bags I . . . **Bag 1**
Can I be excused? **Excuse 1**
Cross my heart and hope to die
    Cross 2
Cross one's fingers **Finger 1**
Finders keepers **Finder**
Jolly hockey sticks! **Stick 1**
Nosey got shot! **Nosey**
Temper, temper! **Temper**

Comfort or sympathy
Bad luck! **Luck 1**
Bad show! **Show 1**
Dear, dear **Dear 2**
Dear me! **Dear 2**
Dear, oh dear! **Dear 2**
Deary me! **Dear 2**
Hard cheese! **Cheese 1**
Hard lines! **Luck 1**
Hard luck! **Luck 1**
Have a heart **Heart 3**
I know the feeling **Feeling 1**

It's not the end of the world
  End 1
Join the club! **Club**
My heart bleeds for you **Heart 4**
Never mind **Mind 17**
Now, now! **Now 2a**
Oh dear! **Dear 2**
Oh no! **No 2**
That's the way it goes **Cookie**
That's the way the cookie
  crumbles **Cookie**
There, there! **There 5**
Tough luck! **Luck 1**
You're breaking my heart
  Heart 4

Complaints and criticism
. . . for my sins! **Sin**
He must have been born in a barn
  Barn
I thought I told you . . . **Think 7**
It's a bit off **Off 1**
It's just not on! **On 1**
I've a bone to pick with you **Bone**
I've only one pair of hands **Pair**
Look here! **Look 4**
Look what you've done! **Look 8**
See here! **Look 4**
What is . . . coming to?
  Come 13
. . . who shall be nameless
  Nameless

Concern only for oneself
I'm all right, Jack **Jack 2**
It's no skin off your nose **Skin**
Number one **Number**

Confidence
And that's for sure **Sure 1**
Depend on it **Depend 2**
I bet **Bet 1a**
I knew it **Know 14**
I shouldn't wonder **Wonder 1**
I'm sure . . . **Sure 6**
Make no bones about it! **Make 5**

Make no mistake about it!
  Make 5
No doubt **Doubt**
To be sure **Sure 10a**
You can depend on it **Depend 2**

Congratulations
Good for you! **Good 6**
Good on you! **Good 6**
Hip, hip, hurrah! **Hip**
Put it there! **Put 2**
Stick it there! **Put 2**
That can't be bad! **Bad 4**
That's great! **Great**

Contact between people
After you **After 1**
Age before beauty! **Age 2**
Ladies first **Lady 2**
Mind your back(s)! **Back 4**
Next please! **Next 1**
Step this way **Way 4**
What name shall I say? **Name 6**
Who is it? **It 4**
Who's next? **Next 2**

Conversation topics
Change the subject **Subject**
Where were we? **Where 2**

Conversations or talks,
  beginning
A word in your ear? **Word 1**
Could I have a word in your ear?
  Word 1
Full of the joys of spring **Joy 1**
Look here! **Look 4**
See here! **Look 4**
Unaccustomed as I am to public
  speaking . . . **Unaccustomed**
What do you do (for a living)?
  Do 22

Conversations or talks,
  ending
But that's quite another story
  Story 2b

Leave it at that **Leave 1**
Over and out **Over 1**
That's about it **That 11**
That's it **That 17b**
That's that **That 19b, c**
That's your lot **Lot 3**
There you are **There 6c**
Thereby hangs a tale **Tale**
To cut a long story short **Story 4**

Corrections
As you were **As 5**
I tell a lie **Lie**
Just testing **Test 1**

Criticism *see* **Complaints and criticism.**

Deceived, showing one will not be
Come off it! **Come 6**
I wasn't born yesterday **Born 2**
There are no flies on him **Fly 3**

Decisions, asking for
How about . . .? **About 1d**
Take it or leave it **Take 8**
What about . . .? **About 1d**
What do you say? **Say 37a**

Defiance
Oh, yeah! **Yeah**
So there! **There 1**
That's what you think **Think 11**
Up yours! **Up 3**
Yah boo sucks to you! **Suck**

Difficulty and misfortune
Bad show! **Show 1**
Be the very devil **Devil 2**
If the worst comes to the worst **Worst**
It's a dog's life **Life 3**
It's no go **Go 14**
Just my luck! **Luck 6**

Just one of those things **Thing 7**
No go **Go 14**
No such luck **Luck 7**
Not likely **Likely 2**
Pigs might fly **Pig**
Some people have all the luck! **People**
The devil of a . . . **Devil 5**
The story of my life! **Story 3**
There's the rub **Rub**
To save his life **Life 8**
What a life! **Life 10**
Worse luck **Luck 10**
You have me there **Get 16a**
You've got me there **Get 16a**

Disagreement *see under* **Actions; Explanations; Statements; Suggestions.**

Disappointment and resignation
Back to square one **Square**
Back to the drawing board **Board**
Hang it! **Hang 2**
It's too bad **Bad 1**
Oh well **Well 4**
So be it! **So 6**
So much for . . . **Much 2**
Some people have all the luck! **People**
That's it **That 17e**
That's that **That 19a**
There's nothing for it **Nothing 6**
Too bad **Bad 1**
You can't win them all **Win 2**

Disapproval
As if . . . **As 2**
Away with . . .! **Away 1**
Down with . . .! **Down**
Get knotted! **Knot**
. . . go home! **Home 1**
Groan, groan! **Groan**
He's been and . . . **Be 5**
He's been and gone and . . . **Be 5**

He's gone and . . . **Be 5**
I thought I told you . . . **Think 7**
I'd be the last to . . . **Person 2**
. . . is a dead loss **Loss**
Look what you've done! **Look 8**
More fool you! **Fool**
. . ., out! **Out 1**
Over my dead body **Body**
That's a fine kettle of fish
   Kettle 2
That's praise indeed! **Praise 2**
There's no accounting for tastes
   Taste
Thumbs down! **Thumb 1**
To hell with . . . **Hell 4**
Tut, tut! **Tut**
Two cheers! **Cheer 3**
We can't take you anywhere!
   Anywhere 2
Well I never did! **Do 20b**
Well really! **Really 3**
What the heck! **Hell 6**
What the hell! **Hell 6**
What's . . . doing? **Do 23**
You and your . . . **You 2**
You ought to . . . **Want 2b**
You should . . . **Want 2b**
You want to . . . **Want 2b**

Disapproval, slogans
  expressing
Away with . . .! **Away 1**
Down with . . .! **Down**
. . . go home! **Home 1**
Off with his head! **Head 3**
. . ., out! **Out 1**
Thumbs down! **Thumb 1**

Disbelief
A good one **Good 1a**
A likely story! **Story 1**
By Gad! **Gad**
By George! **George**
By golly! **Golly**
By heaven! **Good 7**
By Jove! **Jove**

Come, come! **Come 5**
Do me a favour! **Favour b**
Do you mean to say? **Say 4**
Don't give me that **Give 1**
Don't make me laugh! **Laugh 1**
Don't tell me! **Tell 3**
Excuses, excuses! **Excuse 3**
Fancy that! **Fancy**
Get along with you! **Get 4**
Get away! **Get 4**
Get away with you! **Get 4**
Get on! **Get 4**
Get you! **Get 13**
Go along with you! **Get 4**
Go on **Go 8a**
Go on with you **Go 8a**
God almighty! **God 17**
Good God! **Good 7**
Good gracious! **Good 7**
Good heavens! **Good 7**
Good Lord! **Good 7**
Goodness gracious me! **Good 7**
Goodness me! **Good 7**
Heavens above! **Heaven 8**
Heavens to Murgatroyd!
   Heaven 8
I bet **Bet 1b**
I don't think **Think 2**
I mean to say **Say 11a**
If you believe that, you'd believe
   anything! **Believe 5**
If you please **Please 1b**
I'll eat my hat **Hat 1**
I've heard that one before!
   Hear 2
Just fancy! **Fancy**
My eye! **Eye 3**
My foot! **Foot**
My God! **God 17**
My goodness! **Good 7**
My hat! **Hat 2a**
Oh God! **God 17**
Oh Lord! **God 17**
Oh my! **My 2**
Oh, yeah! **Yeah**
Or something **Something 1a**

Promises, promises! **Promise 2**
Pull the other one, it's got bells on! **Pull**
Says who? **Say 29**
Says you! **Say 29**
Sez you! **Say 29**
Stone me! **Stone**
Stone the crows! **Stone**
Strike a light! **Strike**
Strike me dead! **Strike**
Strike me pink! **Strike**
Stuff and nonsense! **Stuff 2**
Tell it to the marines! **Marine**
Tell me another! **Tell 15**
That's news to me! **News**
That's rich! **Rich**
The devil you do! **Devil 6**
Well I do declare! **Declare**
What a load of cobblers! **Load 2**
You can't be serious! **Serious**
You must be joking! **Joke 3**
You what? **What 25b**
You'll be lucky! **Lucky 2**
You're kidding! **Kid 3**

Discouragements
Don't you dare! **Dare 3**
Just you dare! **Dare 3**
That's torn it! **Tear**

Discovery
Hello, hello, hello! **Hello 1**
I have it **Get 15**
I'm your man **Man 3**
I've got it **Get 15**
So that's your little game **Game 2**
The game is up **Game 3**

Disgust
A plague on you! **Plague**
Get stuffed! **Stuff 1**
How dare you! **Dare 1**
I ask you! **Ask 4**
I mean to say **Say 11a**
Some . . . **Some a**
Stuff it! **Stuff 1**

Stuff you! **Stuff 1**
Yah boo sucks to you! **Suck**
You can keep . . . **Keep 5**

Dislike
All well and good **Well 1**
Bully for you **Bully**
Don't I know it **Know 3a**
Get stuffed! **Stuff 1**
Good grief! **Grief**
Here we go again **Go 12**
He's been and gone and done it **Be 6**
He's gone and done it **Be 6**
I can hardly wait **Wait 1**
It's all in a day's work **Day 4**
It's all right **Well 2**
It's all very well **Well 2**
It's not my day **Day 5**
One of those days **Day 7**
Stuff it! **Stuff 1**
Stuff you! **Stuff 1**
There's no accounting for tastes **Taste**
To hell with . . . **Hell 4**
Well I like that! **Like 5**
What the heck! **Hell 6**
What the hell! **Hell 6**
You know what you can do with . . . **Know 27**
see also **Disapproval.**

Doubt
I'm not so sure **Sure 4**
Not really **Really 1**
Oh really **Really 2**
That's what you say! **Say 31**
That's what you think **Think 11**

Drinking *see* **Eating and drinking; Toasts.**

Ease
No problem! **Problem**
No sweat **Sweat**
There's nothing to it **Nothing 8**

Eating and drinking
After you with . . . **After 2**
Be mother **Mother 1**
Come and get it! **Come 3**
. . . coming up **Come 9**
Do the honours **Honour 1**
Here you are **Here 3a**
My compliments to the chef
   Compliment 1
One for the road **One 5**
Say when **Say 28**
The same again **Same 4**
The usual **Usual**
Time, gentlemen, please! **Time 5**
Time's up! **Time 6**
What's your poison? **Poison**
What's yours? **What 22**

Embarrassment
It was nothing **Nothing 1**
Was my face red! **Face 4**
We can't take you anywhere!
   Anywhere 2

Emphasis
All of **All 4**
And all **All 11d**
And I don't mean maybe **Mean 1**
And no kidding! **Kid 1**
And no mistake **Mistake 1**
And that's flat **Flat**
As a matter of fact **Fact b**
As sure as . . . **Sure 2**
By Jiminy! **Jiminy**
By Jove! **Jove**
Cross my heart **Heart 2**
Cross my heart and hope to die
   Cross 2
Do you know **Know 25c**
For dear life **Life 1**
For that matter **Fact b**
For the life of me **Life 2**
For the love of God **Love 1**
For the love of Mike **Love 1**
. . . full stop **Stop 1**

God knows **Know 8b**
Goodness knows **Know 8b**
Heaven knows **Know 8b**
Honest to God **God 15**
I can tell you **Tell 4**
I must say **Say 12**
I promise you **Promise 1**
I tell you **Tell 6**
I'd have you know **Know 18**
If you like **Like 3b**
I'll say this much **Say 20**
I'll thank you to . . . **Thank 2**
I'm telling you **Tell 11**
In actual fact **Fact b**
In all my born days **Day 3**
In fact **Fact b**
In heaven's name **Heaven 9**
In point of fact **Fact b**
It just isn't true **True 1**
Lord knows **Know 8b**
Mark you **Mind 12**
Mind you **Mind 12**
No, repeat, no **Repeat**
Not to put too fine a point on it
   Point 2
Rest assured **Rest 4**
So help me **Help 4**
So help me God **Help 5b**
Suffice it to say **Suffice**
Surely to goodness **Goodness 7**
That's all **That 12b**
That's . . . for you **There 10**
There's . . . for you **There 10**
. . . to goodness **Goodness 7**
To put it mildly **Put 3**
To say the least **Put 3**
Upon my life! **Life 9**
What on earth? **Earth 2**
What the blazes? **Blaze 3**
What the deuce? **Deuce**
What the devil? **Devil 9**
What the dickens? **Dickens**
What the heck? **Hell 5**
What the hell? **Hell 5**
You can rest assured **Rest 4**
You heard! **Hear 3**

You know **Know 25c**
You ought to . . . **Want 2a**
You should . . . **Want 2a**
You want to . . . **Want 2a**
Your actual . . . **Actual**

Encouragements
Be a devil! **Devil 1**
Be a man! **Man 1**
Cheer up! **Cheer 1**
Chin up! **Chin**
Come along **Come 7a**
Come on **Come 7a**
Gee up! **Gee 1**
Go man, go! **Man 2**
Go to it **Go 9**
Great stuff! **Stuff 3**
Hang in there! **Hang 1**
It's not the end of the world
 End 1
Keep smiling! **Keep 3**
Keep your chin up! **Chin**
More power to your elbow!
 Power
Never say die! **Say 23**
On, on! **On 2**
On with . . . **On 3**
That's a . . . **There 9**
That's it **That 17c**
That's my boy! **Boy 3**
That's the idea **Idea 4**
That's the stuff! **Stuff 3**
There's a . . . **There 9**
There's my boy! **Boy 3**
You don't know when you're
 well-off **Know 24**
You don't know you're alive
 Know 24
You tell 'em **Tell 22**

Endearment
Bless his (little) cotton socks
 Bless 4
Bless you **Bless 4**
Bless your heart **Bless 4**
God bless you **Bless 4**

My dear **Dear 1**

Endurance, limit of personal
Enough is enough! **Enough 1**
Enough of . . . **Enough 2**
It's a bit much **Much 1**
That does it! **Do 16**
That's all I needed! **Need**
That's torn it! **Tear**
The end **End 2**
The limit **End 2**

**Enquiries and asking for
 information**
Anything doing? **Anything 2a**
How about . . .? **About 1c**
How come . . .? **Come 10**
How do you do it? **Do 12**
How is it? **How 10**
How is it for . . .? **How 11**
How much do I owe you? **Owe**
How so? **How 13**
How's that? **How 15b**
I suppose **Suppose 2a**
What about . . .? **About 1c**
What do you mean by . . .?
 Mean 7
What gives? **Give 10**
What is it? **What 16**
What is it now? **What 16**
What price . . .? **Price**
Whatever possessed you?
 Possess
What's cooking? **Cook**
What's . . . doing? **Do 23**
What's . . . in aid of? **Aid**
What's the damage? **Damage**
What's the game? **Game 5**
What's the matter **Matter 6**
What's up? **What 21**
What's your little game? **Game 6**
Who's . . . when he's at home?
 Home 4

Envy see **Jealousy and envy.**

Exaggeration
Lay it on thick **Lay 1**
Pile it on thick **Lay 1**

Excitement
By Jiminy! **Jiminy**
By jingo! **Jingo**
By Jove! **Jove**
Far out! **Far 3**
Gee whiz! **Gee 2**
Good egg! **Egg**
I can't tell you . . . **Tell 5**
I can't wait **Wait 2**
Just to think of it! **Think 13**
Oh boy! **Boy 1**
Oh man! **Man 7**
Over the moon **Moon**
Thank you **Thank 4e**
That's . . . for you **There 10**
That's my boy! **Boy 3**
There's . . . for you **There 10**
There's my boy! **Boy 3**
To think . . . **Think 13**
Too much! **Much 3**
Top hole! **Hole**
Wait for it! **Wait 5b**

Excusing someone else
May you be forgiven! **Forgive 2**
Oops a daisy! **Oops b**

Explanations, agreement with
I believe you, thousands wouldn't **Believe 4**
I couldn't agree more **Agree 2**
I suppose so **Suppose 3**
Just so **Just 4**
Quite so **Just 4**
So I see **See 13**
That's the thing **This 2c**
The hell you will **Hell 3b**
This is it **This 2c**
You can say that again! **Say 38**
You could say that **Say 39**
You said it! **Say 38**

You've got a point there **Point 7**

Explanations, asking for
How about . . .? **About 1d**
What about . . .? **About 1d**
What's . . . in aid of? **Aid**
see also **Enquiries and asking for information.**

Explanations, disagreement with
Hang about **Hang 3b**
Hang on **Hang 3b**
I beg your pardon **Pardon c**
I couldn't agree less **Agree 1**
I don't know about that **Know 11**
If you think that, you've got another think coming **Think 8**
I'm not so sure **Sure 4**
I'm sorry! **Sorry b**
Just a moment **Just 2b**
Like hell **Hell 3b**
My eye! **Eye 3**
My foot! **Foot**
Pardon me **Pardon c**
Say what you like **Say 27**
That's not the point **Point 4**
That's what you say! **Say 31**
Wait a minute **Wait 4b**
Wait a moment **Wait 4b**

Explanations, giving
After all **All 1b**
And Bob's your uncle **Bob**
As a matter of fact **Fact b**
Elementary, my dear Watson! **Elementary**
First off **First 1**
For that matter **Fact b**
In fact **Fact b**
In the first place **Place**
On the one hand . . . and on the other **Hand 6**
On top of that **Top 1**

There again **There 2**
This is how it is **This 1**
You know **Know 25f**

Expressions, intensifying
A . . . and a half **Half 1**
As . . . as anything **Anything 4**
As . . . as they come **Make 1**
As . . . as they make 'em **Make 1**
Ever so **Ever 2**
For dear life **Life 1**
. . . isn't the word for it **Word 4**
Like anything **Anything 7**
Like blazes **Blaze 2**
Like hell **Hell 3a**
Like mad **Mad**
Not half **Half 5a, b**
Talk about **Talk 2**
Too . . . by half **Half 8**

Expressions, less strong
And all that **All 12**
As it were **As 4**
For what it's worth **Worth**
Forgive me, but . . . **Forgive 1**
I can't say **Say 7**
I feel **Feel 2**
I reckon **Reckon**
I suppose **Suppose 2b**
I think **Think 5**
If I may say so **Say 18**
If you like **Like 3c**
I'm inclined to . . . **Incline**
Kind of . . . **Kind 3**
Kind of thing **Thing 9**
Mind you **Mind 12**
More or less **More 2**
Or what **What 5**
So to speak **Speak 1**
Sort of . . . **Kind 3**
Sort of thing **Thing 9**
Though I say it myself **Say 33**
To tell you the truth **Truth c**
You know **Know 25b, d**
You see **See 15**

Expressions, linking
After all **All 1b**
And what's more **More 1**
As you know **Know 2**
Come to that **Come 8**
Curiously enough **Enough 5**
First off **First 1**
Funnily enough **Enough 5**
I mean to say **Say 11b**
If it comes to that **Come 8**
Oddly enough **Enough 5**
On the one hand . . . and on the other **Hand 6**
On top of that **Top 1**
Strangely enough **Enough 5**
That is **Say 30**
That is to say **Say 30**
There again **There 2**
Well then **Well 8**

Expressions, modifying
Above all **Above 1**
Above and beyond **Above 2**
All right **All 6c**
As a matter of fact **Fact b**
As it were **As 4**
Come to that **Come 8**
For that matter **Fact b**
Give or take **Give 5**
I mean **Mean 4**
If it comes to that **Come 8**
If you like **Like 3c**
In actual fact **Fact b**
In fact **Fact b**
In other words **Word 3**
In point of fact **Fact b**
Of course **Course b**
So to speak **Speak 1**

Failure
A fat chance! **Hope 2**
Back to square one **Square**
Back to the drawing board **Board**
For my next trick . . . **Trick 1**
No dice **Dice**
No joy **Joy 2**

Not a hope! **Hope 2**
Nothing doing **Do 14c**
Now we're sunk! **Sink**
Some hope! **Hope 2**
That's a fine kettle of fish
    Kettle 2
You can't win them all **Win 2**

Fairness
Fair do's **Do 8**
Fair's fair **Fair 2**
No hard feelings **Feeling 2**

Farewells
All the best! **Best 1**
Be seeing you! **See 7**
Don't do anything I wouldn't do!
    Anything 5
Expect me when you see me
    Expect
God bless (you) **Bless 3**
Good afternoon **Good 3**
Good day **Good 4**
Good evening **Good 5**
Good morning **Good 9**
Good night **Good 10**
I must love you and leave you
    Love 3
I'll be seeing you! **See 7**
Look after yourself! **Look 3**
Mind how you go! **Mind 10**
See you! **See 12**
See you around! **See 12**
See you later! **See 12**
So long **Long 2**
Take care! **Care 8**
Thanks for having me **Thank 7**
Till the next time! **Meet 2**
Till we meet again! **Meet 2**
Until we meet again! **Meet 2**

Friendship
Come back . . ., all is forgiven
    Come 4
I didn't know you cared! **Know 9**
No hard feelings **Feeling 2**

Old thing **Thing 10**
Son of a gun **Son 2**
We're just good friends! **Friend 3**
What's . . . between friends?
    Friend 4

Games and races
It's anyone's game **Anyone 2**
On your marks, get set, go!
    Ready 1
Ready, steady, go! **Ready 1**
They're away! **Away 3**
They're off! **Off 5**

Generosity
Here's something to remember
    me by **Remember**
That's big of you **Big**

**Getting someone to say
    something**
A penny for your thoughts!
    Penny 1
Do tell **Tell 2**
Fire away! **Fire**
Has the cat got your tongue?
    Cat 1
Next please! **Next 1**
Out with it **Out 2**
Over to you **Over 2**
Say something **Say 26**
Speech, speech! **Speech**
Spit it out! **Spit**
Tell it like it is **Tell 13**
Who's next **Next 2**
You tell 'em! **Tell 22**

**Giving something to
    someone**
Here you are **Here 3a**
Here's something to remember
    me by **Remember**
There you are **There 6a**

Go away, requests to
Beat it! **Beat 1**

Buzz off! **Buzz**
Clear off! **Clear 2**
Do me a favour! **Favour a**
Drop dead! **Drop 1**
Get lost! **Lost**
Get off my back! **Back 3**
Go and jump in the lake! **Lake**
Go fly a kite! **Kite**
Go on **Go 8b**
Go to blazes! **Blaze 1**
Go to hell! **Hell 1**
Go to the devil! **Devil 3**
Hop it! **Hop**
Let's be having you **Have 6**
Never darken my door again!
  Door
Off with you! **Off 4**
On your way! **Way 1**
Out of my sight! **Sight**
Out you go! **Out 3**
Push off! **Push**
Take a running jump! **Jump 3**
Two's company, three's a crowd
  Company 2

Good quality
Not bad **Bad 2**
Not half bad **Bad 3**
Not so bad **Bad 2**
Not too bad **Bad 2**

Greetings
Evening all! **All 14**
Good afternoon **Good 3**
Good day **Good 4**
Good evening **Good 5**
Good morning **Good 9**
Hello stranger! **Stranger**
How are things going? **Go 13**
How do you do **Do 11**
How goes it? **Go 13**
How's it going? **Go 13**
How's tricks? **Trick 2**
Long time no see **Time 4**
Morning all! **All 14**
The top of the morning to you!
  Top 2

Greetings, seasonal
And the same to you **Same 2a**
Happy birthday! **Birthday**
Happy Christmas! **Christmas**
Happy new year! **Year**
Many happy returns of the day!
  Return
Merry Christmas **Christmas**
The compliments of the season
  Compliment 2

Happiness *see* **Pleasure and happiness.**

Health, enquiries about
How are things? **How 6**
How are you? **How 6**
How are you doing? **How 6**
How are you keeping? **How 6**
How's yourself? **How 6**

Health, replies to enquiries about
All right **All 6a**
Can't complain **Complain**
Mustn't grumble **Complain**
Not bad **Bad 2**
Not so bad **Bad 2**
Not too bad **Bad 2**
Things could be worse **Worse**

Help, asking for
Anything doing? **Anything 2b**
God help me **Help 2**
Heaven help me **Help 2**

Help, offering
At your service **Service 1**
Can I help you? **Help 1**
What can I do for you? **Help 1**

Hopes or wishes
And the same to you **Same 2**
Better luck next time **Luck 2**

God forbid **Forbid**
God grant **God 7**
God save . . . **God 11**
God willing **God 13**
Heaven forbid **Forbid**
How . . .! **How 3**
I should like to **Like 1**
I would like to **Like 1**
If only . . .! **If 3**
Keep one's fingers crossed for
 Finger 2
Long live . . . **Live 2**
May God rest his soul **Soul 2**
Oh for . . .! **For**
Perish the thought! **Thought 2**
Please God **God 18**
Roll on . . . **Roll**
So help me God **Help 5b**
That . . .! **That 6**
Touch wood **Wood 2**
What . . .! **What 9**
With any luck **Luck 9**
Would . . .! **Would 2**

Humour

Age before beauty! **Age 2**
. . . and have done with it **Do 1**
Aye, aye **Aye b**
Come back . . ., all is forgiven!
 Come 4
Confucius, he say . . .
 Confucius
Could I have that in writing!
 Writing
Don't call us, we'll call you **Call 1**
Don't do anything I wouldn't do!
 Anything 5
For my next trick . . . **Trick 1**
. . . for my sins! **Sin**
Free, gratis, and for nothing
 Free 2
God help me **Help 2**
Great minds think alike **Mind 4**
Groan, groan! **Groan**
Heaven help me **Help 2**

Hello, hello, hello! **Hello 1**
Home, James! **Home 2**
I believe you, thousands wouldn't
 Believe 4
I didn't know you cared! **Know 9**
. . . in your old age **Age 3**
. . . is my middle name **Name 2**
It makes you go blind **Make 3**
It's as clear as mud **Mud 2**
Just testing **Test 1**
Keep taking the tablets! **Tablet**
Lovely weather for ducks!
 Weather 1
My better half **Half 4**
Naughty, naughty! **Naughty**
Not just a pretty face **Face 2**
Pull the other one, it's got bells
 on! **Pull**
Rhubarb, rhubarb **Rhubarb**
Shame, shame! **Shame 2**
Some of my best friends are . . .
 Friend 1
That's the way it goes **Cookie**
That's the way the cookie
 crumbles **Cookie**
Three bags full, sir! **Bag 2**
Twenty-one today! **Twenty-one**
We can't take you anywhere!
 Anywhere 2
. . . will be the death of you
 Death
You pays your money and you
 takes your choice **Money**
You should be so lucky! **Lucky 2**
Yours truly **Yours 3**

Ignorance

Ask me another! **Ask 3**
God knows **Know 8a**
Goodness knows **Know 8a**
Heaven knows **Know 8a**
I couldn't say **Say 8**
I don't know, I'm sure **Know 12**
I give up **Give 7**
I wouldn't know **Know 17**
It's all Greek to me **Greek**

It's anybody's guess **Guess 3**
It's on the tip of my tongue **Tip**
Lord knows **Know 8a**
Not have the faintest idea
  Foggiest
Not have the foggiest idea
  Foggiest
Search me! **Search**
That's all you know about it
  Know 21
There's no knowing **Know 22**
There's no telling **Know 22**
What can I say? **Say 35**
You have me there **Get 16b**
You tell me **Tell 23**
Your guess is as good as mine
  Guess 4
You've got me there **Get 16b**

Impatience
All right **All 6d**
Come, come! **Come 5**
Damn it! **Damn 2**
Damn you! **Damn 2**
Darn it! **Darn 1**
Dash it! **Dash**
Don't say . . . **Say 5**
For God's sake! **Goodness 1**
For goodness' sake! **Goodness 1**
For heaven's sake! **Goodness 1**
For mercy's sake! **Goodness 1**
For Pete's sake! **Goodness 1**
For pity's sake! **Goodness 1**
Get along with you! **Get 4**
Get away! **Get 4**
Get away with you! **Get 4**
Get on! **Get 4**
Give me a chance! **Chance 2**
Give me strength! **Strength**
Go along with you! **Get 4**
God preserve us! **Preserve**
Heaven preserve us! **Preserve**
Heavens above! **Heaven 8**
Heavens to Murgatroyd!
  Heaven 8
Hell's bells! **Hell 2**

Hell's teeth! **Hell 2**
Holy smoke! **Holy**
I can't wait **Wait 2**
I don't know, I'm sure **Know 12**
I'd like to see . . . **Like 2**
Oh brother! **Brother**
Saints preserve us! **Preserve**
What do you mean by . . .?
  Mean 7
You heard! **Hear 3**

Important things see
  **Summarising and
  expressing important
  things.**

Indifference
All the same **Same 1a**
Be that as it may **Be 3**
Don't call us, we'll call you **Call 1**
For all I care **All 16**
For all I know **All 16**
For aught I care **Aught**
For aught I know **Aught**
Go back to sleep **Go 4**
He didn't want to know **Want 1**
I couldn't care less **Care 5**
I don't care a damn **Damn 4**
I'm easy **Easy 3**
It makes no odds **Odds 1**
It's all one to me **One 3**
It's no skin off your nose **Skin**
No matter how **Matter 4**
So what? **What 6**
Suit yourself! **Suit**
To the devil with you! **Devil 8**
What about it? **What 6**
What matter? **Matter 5**
What of it? **What 6**
What the heck! **Hell 6**
What the hell! **Hell 6**
What's the odds? **Odds 2**
Who cares? **Care 9**

Information, asking for see
  **Enquiries and asking for
  information.**

Information, refusal to give
I'm not saying! **Tell 10**
I'm not telling! **Tell 10**
No comment **Comment**
That would be telling **Tell 16**

Interfere, requests not to
Curiosity killed the cat **Curiosity**
God save me from . . . **God 12**
Hands off! **Hand 3**
Mind your own business!
  Business 2
Never you mind **Mind 18**
Nosey got shot! **Nosey**
What is it to you? **What 17**

Introductions
A big hand for . . . **Hand 1**
Glad to meet you! **Meet 1**
How do you do **Do 11**
. . ., I believe? **Believe 3**
. . ., I presume **Presume**
. . ., I take it **Take 1**
Pleased to meet you! **Meet 1**
The one and only **One 7**
This is it **This 2a**
Your friend and mine **Friend 5**

Irony and sarcasm
Ask a silly question . . . !
  Question
That's big of you **Big**
That's great! **Great**
The last of the big spenders!
  Spender
You and whose army? **Army**

Jealousy and envy
Bully for you **Bully**
It's all right **Well 2**
It's all very well **Well 2**
Sour grapes **Grape**

Jokes
A good one **Good 1b**
I get it **Get 14**

I say, I say! **Say 14**
Knock, knock **Knock 2**

Language, comments on
As it were **As 4**
As the saying goes **Saying**
Funny peculiar or funny ha-ha?
  Funny 2
I said **Say 10**
Pardon my French **French**
So to speak **Speak 1**
To coin a phrase **Phrase**

Lavatory, going to the
Answer the call of nature **Nature**
Can I be excused? **Excuse 1**
Little Jimmy's had an accident
  Accident
Nature calls **Nature**
Obey the call of nature **Nature**

Like
Bless his (little) cotton socks
  Bless 4
Bless you **Bless 4**
Bless your heart **Bless 4**
Far out! **Far 3**
Give me . . . **Give 3**
God bless you **Bless 4**
Oh for . . . ! **For**
see also **Approval and praise.**

Misfortune see **Difficulty and
  misfortune.**

Mottoes and sayings
A change is as good as a rest
  Change 1
A trouble shared is a trouble
  halved **Trouble 1**
Age before beauty! **Age 2**
An apple a day keeps the doctor
  away **Apple**
Business is business **Business 1**
Confucius, he say . . . .
  Confucius

Crime docsn't pay **Crime**
Curiosity killed the cat **Curiosity**
Everything in the garden is lovely
   Everything 1
Finders keepers **Finder**
First things first **Thing 2**
Great minds think alike **Mind 4**
If you can't beat 'em, join 'em
   Beat 3
It makes a change **Change 4**
It's all in a day's work **Day 4**
It's all in the mind **Mind 9**
Kill two birds with one stone
   Bird 2
Like father, like son **Father**
Nothing ventured, nothing gained
   Nothing 4
Open sesame! **Open**
Ours is not to reason why
   Reason 2
Pigs might fly **Pig**
So far, so good **Far 4**
Some mothers do 'ave 'em!
   Mother 3
Some of my best friends are . . .
   Friend 1
Some people have all the luck!
   People
Swings and roundabouts **Swing**
That's life! **Life 6**
The grass is always greener on the
   other side **Grass**
There's no accounting for tastes
   Taste
There's one born every minute
   Born 4
Two's company, three's a crowd
   Company 2
We aim to please **Aim**
We're just good friends! **Friend 3**
We've got a right one 'ere
   Mother 3
You can't keep a good man down
   Man 10
You pays your money and you
   takes your choice **Money**

Non-committal replies
I have and I haven't **Have 3**
I'm easy **Easy 3**
No comment **Comment**
Not in so many words **Word 10**
So what? **What 6**
What about it? **What 6**
What of it? **What 6**
Yes and no **Yes**

Oneself, talking about
I'm all right, Jack **Jack 2**
Muggins here **Muggins**
Number one **Number**
Yours truly **Yours 3**

Opinions, asking
How about . . .? **About 1b**
How is it for . . .? **How 11**
How's that? **How 15a**
What about . . .? **About 1b**
What do you say? **Say 37a**

Opinions, one's own
As far as I can see **See 1**
As I see it **See 2**
. . . for one **One 2**
If you ask me **Ask 5**
Mind you **Mind 12**
Something tells me
   Something 3
To tell you the truth **Truth b**

**Opinions, stating or
   introducing**
As far as I'm concerned **Concern**
By and large **Whole**
I wouldn't say **Say 15**
If you ask me **Ask 5**
Let's face it **Face 1**
Let's say **Say 22**
On the whole **Whole**
Something tells me
   Something 3
The point is . . . **Point 6**

The thing is . . . **Thing 13**
This is it **This 2b**
You see **See 15**

Other people, talking about
Ladies and gentlemen **Lady 1**
Mine host **Host**
My better half **Half 4**
My dear **Dear 1**
My good man **Man 6**
My good woman **Woman**
My love **Love 4**
My son **Son 1**
Old boy **Boy 2**
Old girl **Girl**
Old man **Boy 2**
Old thing **Thing 10**
Son of a gun **Son 2**
Take someone's name in vain
    Name 4
The missis **Missis**
The wife **Missis**
Who's she? The cat's mother?
    Cat 3
Your good lady **Lady 3**

Patient, requests to be
All in good time! **Time 1**
Hold your horses! **Horse**

Pause markers
I mean **Mean 4**
Let me see **See 9**
Let me think **See 9**
Let's see **See 9**
Now I come to think of it
    Come 12
You know **Know 25a**
You see **See 15**

Permission, asking
Can I . . .? **Can 1**
Could I . . .? **Could 1**
Do you mind . . .? **Mind 1**
May I . . .? **May**
Might I . . .? **Might**

Would you mind . . .? **Mind 1**

Permission, refusing
Don't you dare! **Dare 3**
It's no go **Go 14**
Just you dare! **Dare 3**
No dice **Dice**
No way **Way 3**

Photographers
Hold it! **Hold 1b**
Say cheese! **Cheese 2**
Watch the birdie! **Cheese 2**

Pleasure and happiness
Bless me! **Bless 2**
Bless my soul! **Bless 2**
Far out! **Far 3**
Full of the joys of spring **Joy 1**
Gee whiz! **Gee 2**
Glory be! **Glory**
God bless my soul! **Bless 2**
Good egg! **Egg**
Good riddance! **Riddance**
Holy smoke! **Holy**
I can't tell you . . . **Tell 5**
I'll be blessed! **Bless 2**
I'm blest! **Bless 2**
It's a good thing **Thing 6**
Jolly hockey sticks! **Stick 1**
Man alive! **Man 4**
My, my! **My 1**
Oh boy! **Boy 1**
On top of the world **World 2**
Over the moon **Moon**
That's great! **Great**
That's more like it! **Like 4**
That's my boy! **Boy 3**
There's my boy! **Boy 3**
This is the life! **Life 7**
Those were the days! **Day 9**
To be sure **Sure 10b**
Too much! **Much 3**
Top hole! **Hole**
Upon my soul! **Bless 2**
Well I'm blest! **Bless 2**

Words fail me **Word 13**
You should be so lucky! **Lucky 2**
You're laughing! **Laugh 3**
You've not lived **Live 3**

Politeness

Age before beauty! **Age 2**
At your service **Service 1**
Could I . . .? **Could 1**
Do you mind . . .? **Mind 1**
Forgive me, but . . . **Forgive 1**
I don't suppose **Suppose 1**
I suppose **Suppose 2a**
I thank you . . . **Thank 1**
I wonder if . . . **Wonder 2**
I wouldn't mind **Mind 6**
I wouldn't say no **Say 16**
I wouldn't say that **Say 17**
If I may say so **Say 18**
If you could **If 4**
If you please **Please 1a**
If you would **If 4**
I'm afraid **Afraid**
I'm much obliged to you **Oblige**
I'm not saying that **Say 17**
I'm sorry! **Sorry b**
Ladies first **Lady 2**
May I . . .? **May**
Might I . . .? **Might**
Much obliged **Oblige**
Present company excepted
    Company 1
Shall we . . .? **Shall**
With all due respect **Respect**
Would you be good enough to
    . . .? **Good 15**
Would you be so good as to . . .?
    Good 15
Would you mind . . .? **Mind 1**
You could . . . **Could 5**
You're not as young as you used
    to be **Young**

Praise *see* **Approval and
praise.**

Promises

Cross my heart **Heart 2**
Cross my heart and hope to die
    Cross 2
God's honour! **Honour 2**
I promise you **Promise 1**
On my honour **Honour 3**
Promises, promises! **Promise 2**
So help me **Help 4**

Public, phrases in

Action stations! **Action**
Attention, please **Attention**
Going, going, gone **Go 10a**
Ladies and gentlemen **Lady 1**
Order! Order! **Order**
Shame, shame! **Shame 2**
Speech, speech! **Speech**
Testing, testing **Test 2**
The customer is always right
    Customer
Unaccustomed as I am to public
    speaking . . . **Unaccustomed**
Your attention, please
    Attention

Public transport, phrases on

All aboard! **Aboard**
All change! **Change 2**
Attention, please **Attention**
Thank you **Thank 4c**
Your attention, please
    Attention

Punishment

Are you looking for a fight?
    Look 1
Are you looking for trouble?
    Look 1
. . . for my sins! **Sin**
Here's something to remember
    me by **Remember**
It serves you right! **Serve 2**
Judgement on you **Judgement**
Just you wait **Wait 3**
Step outside **Step 3**

Take that! **Take 10**
There'll be the devil to pay
   Devil 7
Woe betide **Woe 1**
You're asking for it! **Ask 2**
You're asking for trouble! **Ask 2**

Quiet, requests to be
Belt up! **Belt**
Dry up! **Dry**
Enough said **Say 25**
Give it a rest! **Rest 2**
Give over! **Give 6**
Go to hell! **Hell 1**
Not another word **Word 9**
One more word out of . . .·
   Word 11
Pipe down! **Pipe 1**
Put a sock in it! **Sock 3**
Say no more **Say 25**
Shut up! **Shut**
Shut your face! **Shut**
Shut your mouth! **Shut**
Wrap up! **Wrap**
You've made your point **Point 8**

Races *see* **Games and races.**

Reassurance
Don't get me wrong **Get 1**
Don't worry **Worry 1**
Never fear! **Fear 1**
Never mind **Mind 17**
Not to worry **Worry 2**
Take it easy! **Take 7a**
There, there! **There 5**
You should worry! **Worry 3**

Refusing
I wouldn't have it if you gave it to
   me! **Have 5**
It's no go **Go 14**
No go **Go 14**
No way **Way 3**
Nothing doing **Do 14b**
Thank you **Thank 4b**

Up yours! **Up 3**
You can keep . . . **Keep 5**
see also **Information, refusal
   to give.**

Regret
Dear, dear **Dear 2**
Dear me! **Dear 2**
Dear, oh dear! **Dear 2**
Deary me! **Dear 2**
If only . . .! **If 3**
I'm afraid **Afraid**
It's too bad **Bad 1**
More's the pity **Pity 2**
Not have an earthly **Earthly**
Oh dear! **Dear 2**
Oh mother! **Mother 2**
Oh no! **No 2**
That will teach you **Teach**
That's that **That 19a**
Too bad **Bad 1**

Relaxation, inviting
Be my guest! **Guest**
Feel free **Feel 1**
Let it all hang out! **Hang 5**
Let your hair down! **Hair 2**
Make yourself at home! **Home 3**
Please yourself **Please 3**
Suit yourself! **Suit**
Take it easy! **Take 7b**

Reminders
After all **All 1b**
First things first **Thing 2**
How about . . .? **About 1d**
Of course **Course b**
What about . . .? **About 1d**
You know **Know 25e**

Repeat, requests to
All together now! **All 9**
Beg pardon **Pardon a**
Come again? **Come 2**
How's that? **How 15d**
I beg your pardon **Pardon a**

Once again! **Once 2**
Pardon (me)? **Pardon a**
Say again? **Come 2**
You what? **What 25a**

Repetition of the same word
Boy, oh boy! **Boy 1**
But me no buts **But 1**
Come, come! **Come 5**
Dear, dear **Dear 2**
Going, going, gone **Go 10a**
Groan, groan! **Groan**
Hear! hear! **Hear 1**
Hello, hello, hello! **Hello 1**
Hint, hint! **Hint**
Hip, hip, hurrah! **Hip**
I say, I say! **Say 14**
Knock, knock **Knock 2**
My, my! **My 1**
Naughty, naughty! **Naughty**
Night, night **Night 2**
No, repeat, no **Repeat**
Now, now! **Now 2**
On, on! **On 2**
Order! Order! **Order**
Pip, pip! **Pip**
Promises, promises! **Promise 2**
Rhubarb, rhubarb **Rhubarb**
Shame, shame! **Shame 2**
Speech, speech! **Speech**
Stir, stir! **Stir**
Temper, temper **Temper**
Testing, testing **Test 2**
There, there! **There 5**
Tut, tut! **Tut**
Well, well **Well 9**
Well, well, well **Well 9**

Requests, agreeing with or obeying
As you say **Say 2**
Aye, aye **Aye a**
By all means **Means 1**
Not a bit **Bit**
Right you are! **Right 6**

Sure thing! **Thing 11**
Three bags full, sir! **Bag 2**
Very good **Good 14**
Very well **Well 5**
Will do! **Do 25**
With pleasure **Pleasure 3**

Requests, making
After you with . . . **After 2**
Can I . . .? **Can 1**
Could I . . .? **Could 1**
Do you mind . . .? **Mind 1**
Get it? **Get 6**
I could do with . . . **Do 13**
I don't suppose **Suppose 1**
I thank you . . . **Thank 1**
I wouldn't mind . . . **Mind 6**
If you could **If 4**
If you don't mind **Mind 8**
If you please **Please 1a**
If you won't mind **Mind 8**
If you would **If 4**
May I . . .? **May**
Might I . . .? **Might**
Off with . . . **Off 2**
Shall we . . .? **Shall**
Why don't . . .? **Do 24**
Would you be good enough to
. . .? **Good 15**
Would you be so good as to . . .?
Good 15
Would you mind . . .? **Mind 1**
You could . . . **Could 5**

Resignation *see*
Disappointment and resignation.

Responsibilities, giving other people
It's your baby **Baby**
It's your funeral **Funeral**
It's your look-out **Look 2**
The ball is in your court **Ball**

Robberies
Hands up! **Hand 4b**
Put 'em up! **Hand 4b**
Stand and deliver! **Stand 2**
Stick 'em up! **Hand 4b**
Stop, thief! **Thief**

Rudeness, responses to
Don't mind me **Mind 3b**
He's got a nerve! **Nerve**
How dare you! **Dare 1**
I hope you feel proud of yourself!
    Hope 1
Shame on you! **Shame 1**
Shame, shame! **Shame 2**
Some nerve! **Nerve**
Take that grin off your face
    Grin 2
Thank you for nothing
    Nothing 5
The nerve of it! **Nerve**
What a liberty! **Liberty**
What a nerve! **Nerve**
What next? **What 18**
What's the big idea! **Idea 6**

Sarcasm see **Irony and**
    sarcasm.

Sayings see **Mottoes and**
    sayings.

Secrets, telling
Between you and me **Between**
Let the cat out of the bag **Cat 2**
Mum's the word **Mum**
My lips are sealed **Lip**
Not a word **Word 8**
To tell you the truth **Truth b**
You can't tell him anything
    Tell 20a

Self-effacement
For what it's worth **Worth**
It was nothing **Nothing 1**

Seriousness
And no kidding! **Kid 1**
It's no joke **Joke 1**
Joking apart **Joke 2**

Shops
Can I help you? **Help 1**
Here you are **Here 3a**
It's all part of the service!
    Service 2
It's what we're here for!
    Service 2
The customer is always right
    Customer
What can I do for you? **Help 1**

Statements, agreement with
And a good job too **Good 2**
And a good thing too **Good 2**
And how! **How 1**
And so say all of us **Say 1**
As you say **Say 2**
Don't I know it **Know 3b**
I see what you mean **See 5b**
I suppose so **Suppose 3**
Isn't it just! **Just 1**
It is that **That 5**
Just so **Just 4**
No fear! **Fear 2**
Not half **Half 5c**
Quite so **Just 4**
Right on! **Right 4**
Same here **Same 3**
So I see **See 13**
That it is **That 5**
That's it **That 17g**
That's right! **Right 8**
That's the thing **This 2c**
This is it **This 2c**
Too right! **Right 9**
Too true! **Right 9**
You can say that again! **Say 38**
You could say that **Say 39**
You said it! **Say 38**
You've got a point there **Point 7**

Statements, alleged
Arise, Sir . . . **Arise**
Evening all! **All 14**
Let's be having you **Have 6**
Open sesame! **Open**

Statements, contrast with previous
All the same **Same 1b**
Anything but **Anything 1**
At any rate **Rate**
But that's quite another story **Story 2a**
Curiously enough **Enough 5**
Far from it **Far 2**
From the sublime to the ridiculous **Sublime**
Funnily enough **Enough 5**
Hey presto! **Hey b**
I wouldn't say **Say 15**
Mind you **Mind 12**
Oddly enough **Enough 5**
On the one hand . . . and on the other **Hand 6**
Strangely enough **Enough 5**
That's a different kettle of fish **Story 2a**

Statements, disagreement with
And how! **How 1**
Come, come! **Come 5**
Hang about **Hang 3b**
Hang on **Hang 3b**
Hear! hear! **Hear 1**
I beg your pardon **Pardon c**
I don't know about that **Know 11**
I don't know that **Know 13**
I wouldn't say that **Say 17**
If you think that, you've got another think coming **Think 8**
I'm not saying that **Say 17**
I'm not so sure **Sure 4**
I'm sorry! **Sorry b**
. . . I'm sure **Sure 5b**

Isn't it just! **Just 1**
It's a free country! **Country**
Just a moment **Just 2b**
Like hell **Hell 3b**
My eye! **Eye 3**
My foot! **Foot**
Not if I can help it **Help 3**
Not if I know it **Help 3**
Not my idea of . . . **Idea 2**
Not on your life! **Life 4**
Or something **Something 1a**
Over my dead body **Body**
Pardon me **Pardon c**
Present company excepted **Company 1**
Same here **Same 3**
Say what you like **Say 27**
Says who? **Say 29**
Says you! **Say 29**
Sez you! **Say 29**
Speak for yourself! **Speak 2**
Stuff and nonsense! **Stuff 2**
That's not the point **Point 4**
That's what you say! **Say 31**
The devil you do! **Devil 6**
The hell you will **Hell 3b**
Up yours! **Up 3**
Wait a minute **Wait 4b**
Wait a moment **Wait 4b**
What a load of cobblers! **Load 2**
With all due respect **Respect**
You can't be serious! **Serious**

Statements, end of
Follow that! **Follow**
. . . full stop **Stop 1**
. . . in your old age **Age 3**
Last but not least **Last**
Put that in your pipe and smoke it! **Pipe 2**
That's all **That 12a**
That's all there is to it **That 12a**
That's how it is **That 16**
That's that **That 19a**
There you are **There 6d**

Statements, support of earlier

Have the last laugh **Laugh 2**
I thought as much **Think 6**
I told you so **Tell 8**
Right enough **Sure 8**
Sure enough **Sure 8**
Surprise, surprise! **Surprise b**
There you are **There 6b**
Trust you to . . . **Trust**
What did I say! **Say 36**
What did I tell you! **Say 36**

Stop, requests to

Act your age! **Age 1**
Be your age! **Age 1**
Break it up! **Break 1**
Chuck it (in)! **Chuck**
Cut it out! **Cut 1**
Do you mind! **Mind 2**
Enough is enough! **Enough 1**
Enough of . . . **Enough 2**
Give it a rest! **Rest 2**
Give over! **Give 6**
Grow up! **Grow**
Hold everything! **Hold 1a**
Hold it! **Hold 1a**
Knock it off! **Knock 1**
Lay off! **Lay 2**
Leave it at that **Leave 1**
Leave off! **Leave 2**
Less of . . . **Less**
Not so fast **Fast**
Pack it in! **Pack**
Pack it up! **Pack**
Put a sock in it! **Sock 3**
Stand and deliver! **Stand 2**
Thank you **Thank 4d**
That will teach you **Teach**
That's enough! **Enough 8**
Time, gentlemen, please! **Time 5**
Time's up! **Time 6**
Wait for me! **Wait 6**
We'll soon see about that! **See 14**
When you're quite ready!
　Quite 3

When you've quite finished!
　Quite 3

Success

And Bob's your uncle **Bob**
Do you see what I mean? **See 3b**
Have the last laugh **Laugh 2**
It's all happening **Happen**
Well done! **Do 19**
What did I say! **Say 36**
What did I tell you! **Say 36**

Suggestions, agreement with

All right **All 6b**
And so say all of us **Say 1**
As you say **Say 2**
Be my guest! **Guest**
Fair enough! **Enough 4**
Good thinking! **Think 1**
Hands up! **Hand 4a**
I don't mind if I do **Mind 5**
I guess **Guess 2**
I suppose so **Suppose 3**
If you like **Like 3a**
I'll say! **Say 19**
It's a bargain! **Bargain**
Just so **Just 4**
Not half **Half 5c**
Now you're talking **Talk 1**
Put it there! **Put 2**
Quite so **Just 4**
Right on! **Right 4**
Right you are! **Right 6**
Same here **Same 3**
Stick it there! **Put 2**
Suppose we **Suppose 4**
Sure do **Do 15**
That's a bargain! **Bargain**
That's an idea **Idea 3**
Very well **Well 5**
You do that **Do 26**
You've got a point there **Point 7**

Suggestions, disagreement with

Hang about **Hang 3b**

By Jiminy! **Jiminy**
By jingo! **Jingo**
By Jove! **Jove**
Can you beat that! **Beat 2**
Christopher Columbus!
   Columbus
Damn me! **Damn 3**
Did you ever? **Do 3**
Do you mean to say? **Say 4**
Don't say . . . **Say 5**
Don't tell me! **Tell 3**
Fancy that! **Fancy**
For God's sake! **Goodness 1**
For goodness' sake! **Goodness 1**
For heaven's sake! **Goodness 1**
For mercy's sake! **Goodness 1**
For Pete's sake! **Goodness 1**
For pity's sake! **Goodness 1**
Gee whiz! **Gee 2**
Glory be! **Glory**
God almighty! **God 17**
God bless my soul! **Bless 2**
God preserve us! **Preserve**
Golly gumdrops! **Gumdrop**
Good God! **Good 7**
Good gracious! **Good 7**
Good grief! **Grief**
Good heavens! **Good 7**
Good Lord! **Good 7**
Goodness gracious me! **Good 7**
Goodness me! **Good 7**
Gordon Bennett! **Bennett**
Great Scott! **Scott**
He's been and . . . **Be 5**
He's been and gone and . . . **Be 5**
He's gone and . . . **Be 5**
Heaven preserve us! **Preserve**
Heavens above! **Heaven 8**
Heavens to Murgatroyd!
   Heaven 8
Holy smoke! **Holy**
How about that, then! **About 2**
How do you do it? **Do 12**
I ask you! **Ask 4**
I don't know **Know 10a**

I mean to say **Say 11a**
I say **Say 13a**
I should have thought . . .
   Think 3
I'd like to see . . . **Like 2**
I'll be blessed! **Bless 2**
I'll be damned! **Damn 3**
I'll be darned **Darn 2**
I'll be hanged **Hang 4**
I'm blest! **Bless 2**
I'm damned! **Damn 3**
I'm hanged **Hang 4**
I'm jiggered! **Jigger**
Imagine that! **Imagine**
In all my born days **Day 3**
Is that so? **So 3**
It's a wonder that **Wonder 3**
Jeepers creepers! **Jeeper**
Just a moment **Just 2c**
Just fancy! **Fancy**
Just imagine! **Imagine**
Lo and behold! **Lo**
Man alive! **Man 4**
My eye! **Eye 3**
My foot! **Foot**
My giddy aunt! **Aunt**
My God! **God 17**
My goodness! **Good 7**
My hat! **Hat 2b**
My, my! **My 1**
My sainted aunt! **Aunt**
My word! **Word 7**
No kidding? **Kid 2**
Now that's what I call . . . **Call 3**
Of all the . . . **All 21**
Oh brother! **Brother**
Oh God! **God 17**
Oh Lord! **God 17**
Oh mother! **Mother 2**
Oh my! **My 2**
Oh really **Really 2**
Saints preserve us! **Preserve**
Shiver me timbers! **Timber**
Stone me! **Stone**
Stone the crows! **Stone**

Strike a light! **Strike**
Strike me dead! **Strike**
Strike me pink! **Strike**
Surprise, surprise! **Surprise a**
That'll be the day! **Day 8**
That's a turn-up for the book!
  Turn 1
That's big of you **Big**
The mind boggles **Mind 19**
The wonder is **Wonder 5**
To be sure **Sure 10b**
Upon my life! **Life 9**
Upon my soul! **Bless 2**
Wait a minute **Wait 4c**
Wait a moment **Wait 4c**
Well I do declare! **Declare**
Well I never! **Do 20a**
Well I never did! **Do 20b**
Well if . . . **If 5**
Well I'll be! **Blow 3**
Well I'll be blowed! **Blow 3**
Well I'm blest! **Bless 2**
Well, well **Well 9**
Well, well, well **Well 9**
Well, what do you know
  Know 23
What about that! **About 2**
What do you think? **Think 14**
What on earth? **Earth 2**
What the blazes? **Blaze 3**
What the deuce? **Deuce**
What the devil? **Devil 9**
What the dickens? **Dickens**
What the heck? **Hell 5**
What the hell? **Hell 5**
Who should . . .? **Should 2**
Wonders will never cease
  Wonder 6
Words fail me **Word 13**
Ye gods! **God 20**
You don't say? **Say 40**
You what? **What 25b**

Sympathy *see* **Comfort or**
  sympathy.

Sympathy, mock
Hard cheese! **Cheese 1**
My heart bleeds for you **Heart 4**
You're breaking my heart
  Heart 4

Thanking
Bless you **Bless 4**
Bless your heart **Bless 4**
God bless you **Bless 4**
I'm much obliged to you **Oblige**
Many thanks **Thank 4a**
Much obliged **Oblige**
Praise be **Praise 1**
Praise be to God! **Praise 1a**
Praise the Lord! **Praise 1a**
Thank God! **Thank 3**
Thank goodness! **Thank 3b**
Thank heavens! **Thank 3**
Thanks for having me **Thank 7**
Thank you **Thank 4a**
Thank your lucky stars! **Star**
You shouldn't have **Have 9**

Thanks, acknowledging
A pleasure! **Pleasure 1**
Any time! **Time 3**
Don't mention it! **Mention 1**
Forget it! **Forget**
It was nothing **Nothing 1**
It's a pleasure! **Pleasure 1**
It's all part of the service!
  Service 2
It's all right **All 23**
It's what we're here for!
  Service 2
My pleasure! **Pleasure 1**
Not at all! **Not 1**
Skip it! **Skip**
That's all right **All 23**
Think nothing of it! **Nothing 9**
You're welcome! **Welcome**

Threats
I Promise you **Promise 1**

Just you wait **Wait 3**
Mark my words! **Word 5**
One more word out of . . .
   Word 11
Or else! **Else**
Step outside **Step 3**
Two can play at that game
   Game 4
Woe betide **Woe 1**

Toasts
All the best! **Best 1**
Bottoms up! **Bottom**
Down the hatch! **Hatch**
Good health! **Health**
Good luck! **Luck 4b**
Happy landings! **Landing**
Here's how! **Here 4**
Here's mud in your eye! **Mud 1**
Here's to . . . **Here 5**
To absent friends! **Friend 2**
Your health! **Health**

Truth, drawing out the
But me no buts **But 1**
Tell it like it is **Tell 13**

Truth, emphasising
Believe it or not **Believe 1**
Cross my heart **Heart 2**
Cross my heart and hope to die
   Cross 2
God's honour! **Honour 2**
Honest to God **God 15**
Make no bones about it! **Make 5**
Make no mistake about it!
   Make 5
On my honour **Honour 3**
So help me God **Help 5a**
There are no buts about it **But 2**

Uncertainty
Expect me when you see me
   Expect
I don't know **Know 10b**
It all depends **Depend 1**

Or something **Something 1b**
So far, so good **Far 4**
That's as may be! **That 13**
You never can tell **Know 28**
You never know **Know 28**

Understanding
I get it **Get 14**
I see **See 4**
I see what you mean **See 5a**
That's what it is **That 20**
The penny dropped **Penny 2**

Understatement
For what it's worth **Worth**
Not half bad **Bad 3**
You're telling me! **Tell 24**

Vagueness
A kind of . . . **Kind 1**
A sort of . . . **Kind 1**
Kind of thing **Thing 9**
Or anything **Anything 8**
Or something **Something 1b**
Sort of thing **Thing 9**

Wait, requests to
Half a mo **Just 2a**
Half a moment **Just 2a**
Half a tick **Just 2a**
Hang on **Hang 3a**
Hold on **Hold 2**
Just a jiffy **Just 2a**
Just a minute **Just 2a**
Just a moment **Just 2a**
Just a second **Just 2a**
Just a tick **Just 2a**
Wait a minute **Wait 4a**
Wait a moment **Wait 4a**

Warnings
I promise you **Promise 1**
Look here! **Look 4**
Look out! **Look 6**
Mark my words! **Word 5**
Mind your step! **Step 1**

Now, now! **Now 2b**
One more word out of . . .
  Word 11
Or else! **Else**
See here! **Look 4**
There'll be the devil to pay
  Devil 7
Two can play at that game
  Game 4
Watch it! **Watch 1**
Watch out! **Watch 2**
Watch your step! **Step 1**
You ought to . . . **Want 2b**
You should . . . **Want 2b**
You want to . . . **Want 2b**

Well-wishing
All the best! **Best 1**
Better luck next time **Luck 2**
Bless you **Bless 4**
Bless your heart **Bless 4**

God bless **Bless 3**
God bless you Bless 3, 4
Good luck! **Luck 4a**
Keep one's fingers crossed for
  Finger 2
May the best man win! **Man 5**
The best of British! **Best 2**
You never know your luck
  Luck 11
You'll be lucky! **Lucky 2**

Wishes *see* **Hopes or wishes.**

Worry
God almighty! **God 17**
It's a dog's life **Life 3**
My God! **God 17**
Oh God! **God 17**
Oh Lord! **God 17**
What's biting you? **Bite**
What's eating you? **Eat 2**

Reference and information

☐	**A Guide to Insurance**	Margaret Allen	£1.95p
☐	**North-South**	Brandt Commission	£2.50p
☐	**Save It! The Energy Consumer's Handbook**	Gary Hammond, Kevin Newport and Carol Russell	£1.25p
☐	**The Multilingual Business Handbook**	P. Hartley *et al.*	£3.95p
☐	**Militant Islam**	Godfrey Jansen	£1.50p
☐	**Dictionary of British History**	John Kenyon	£3.95p
☐	**How to Study**	H. Maddox	£1.75p
☐	**A Guide to Saving and Investment**	James Rowlatt	£2.50p
☐	**Career Choice**	Audrey Segal	£2.95p
☐	**Logic and its Limits**	Patrick Shaw	£2.95p
☐	**A Guide to Letter Writing**	Thomson and Bland	£1.95p
☐	**Straight and Crooked Thinking**	R. H. Thouless	£1.95p
☐	**The New Fascists**	Paul Wilkinson	£2.50p
☐	**Dictionary of Astronomy**		£2.95p
☐	**Dictionary of Economics and Commerce**		£1.50p
☐	**Dictionary of Life Sciences**		£2.95p
☐	**Dictionary of Physical Sciences**		£2.95p
☐	**Dictionary of Political Thought**		£3.95p
☐	**Harrap's New Pocket French/English Dictionary**		£2.50p
☐	**Pan Dictionary of Synonyms and Antonyms**		£1.95p

All these books are available at your local bookshop or newsagent, or can be ordered direct from the publisher. Indicate the number of copies required and fill in the form below

9

....

Name_____
(Block letters please)

Address_____

_____

Send to Pan Books (CS Department), Cavaye Place, London SW10 9PG
Please enclose remittance to the value of the cover price plus:
35p for the first book plus 15p per copy for each additional book ordered
to a maximum charge of £1.25 to cover postage and packing
Applicable only in the UK

While every effort is made to keep prices low, it is sometimes
necessary to increase prices at short notice. Pan Books reserve
the right to show on covers and charge new retail prices which
may differ from those advertised in the text or elsewhere

A Dictionary of Contemporary Idioms